Grandchildren of Albion

An Illustrated Anthology of
Voices and Visions of Younger Poets in Brit

Edited by Michael Horovitz

Published by New Departures: organ of the *Poetry Olympics*
revival issues 17 to 20

Dedicated to two of New Departures's longest-standing friends, now
themselves departed from this mortal coil – but alive as ever through
their works : –

Frances Horovitz (1938 – 1983)

Samuel Beckett (1906 – 1989)

What Beckett discerned in 1929 about his old friend and mentor Joyce's
Finnegans Wake – that ". . . it is not only to be read. It is to be looked
at, and listened to" – is just the effect that, in different ways, this
cornucopia too is after.

And so, equally, is the Blakean vision Frances cherished in one of
her last letters to this book's editor (August '83): –

*Do you remember my dream
when we were all walking in
Paradise neither male nor
female but all loving one
another? I hold on to that.
Very much love
Frances –*

Publication Data

Published in 1992 by
New Departures, Piedmont, Bisley, Stroud, Glos GL6 7BU

A catalogue record for this book is available from the British Library.
ISBN 0 902689 14 2

New Departures Needs Help

For the first time in its three decades, *New Departures* has received support from the Arts Council of Great Britain, to the tune of £2,500, which is gratefully acknowledged.

This amount is, however, only a small fraction of the overall deficit the publication you're looking at is likely to incur. Advance subscriptions are not solicited because, apart from number 21, the supplement to this issue (– which will include pages 1 to 16), future issues are not as things stand likely to follow with any regularity. Financial donations, small or large, would be most welcome in order to help offset the long-drawn-out running costs of this one.

New Departures Needs Helpers

New Departures, *Poetry Olympics*, and 'Jazz Poetry Superjam' also welcome offers of other kinds of help – secretarial, spiritual, equipment, management, representation, distribution, publicity, gigs, transport, laundry, communications – you name it. Let the years of struggle subside, speedily in our time.

18

Contents

This book has several sections. Pages 1 to 16 appear as part of the special supplement to this volume in *New Departures 21*. Pages 20 to 367 contain the main pictures and texts. Pages 368 to 409 contain notes on the poets. Pages 411 to 412 index the illustrations.

21	**John Agard**: Poetry
36	**Ferenc Aszmann**: God x 40
38	**Attila the Stockbroker**: Punk prose, verse, and newtown anthems
47	**Sujata Bhatt**: Poetry
60	**Valerie Bloom**: Poetry
70	**Billy Bragg**: Lyrics and music
78	**Jean Binta Breeze**: Poetry
82	**Zoë Brooks**: Poetry
86	**Donal Carroll**: Poetry
92	**John Cooper Clarke** unlocks his word-hoard
106	**Merle Collins**: Poetry
114	**Pat Condell**: Cameos, parodies. spoofs, sounds, satires and sketches
121	**Carol Ann Duffy**: Poetry
143	**Peter Gabriel**: Lyrics and music
154	**Galliano**'s bag
158	**Adam Horovitz**: Poetry and drawing
162	**Mahmood Jamal**: Poetry
170	**Linton Kwesi Johnson**: Story
172	**Timothy Emlyn Jones**: Footy score and window-blind flickbook
179	**Bill Lewis**: Picture-poems and luminous lines
188	**Brian McCabe**: Poetry
196	**Ian McMillan**: Poetry
206	**Lindsay MacRae**: Poetry
210	**Tony Marchant**: Poetry
214	**Geraldine Monk**: Poetry
222	**Nik Morgan**: Pictures, cut-ups, haiku and other pieces
232	**Grace Nichols**: Poetry
246	**Rosemary Norman**: Poetry
256	**Ben Okri**: Poetry
264	**Andrew Pearmain**: Poetry
268	**Fiona Pitt-Kethley**: Poetry
274	**Philip Radmall**: Poetry
284	**Elaine Randell**: Verse and prose
290	**Michèle Roberts**: Poetry and drawings
304	**Maria Sookias**: Poetry and drawings
311	**Chris Sparkes**: Verse, prose, drawings and haiku
322	**Neil Sparkes**: Jazz-poems, blues, visions and art-works
332	**Paul Weller**: Poetry, lyrics and music
348	**Ifigenija Zagoricnik**: Poems and art-works
355	**Benjamin Zephaniah**: Poetry
368	Lives and Works of the poets
410	Acknowledgements and inventory of illustrations
413	Thanks, patron saints, afterword, past and future publications

"DAMN! STILL NO CHICKEN, JUST ANOTHER OF THOSE ROUND THINGS!"

John Agard

from LAUGHTER IS AN EGG

'I know you wouldn't think I'm serious . . .'

'Teacher, Teacher,
There's an egg in the computer!'
                              the child cried.

'Teacher, Teacher,
There's an egg on the piano,'
                              the child cried.

'Teacher, Teacher,
Look! An egg is on the blackboard,'
                              the child cried.

The teacher sighed
and told the child to stand
outside the headmaster's office.

Just then the headmaster burst into the class.
He was laughing and wringing his hands
and saying to the teacher

'I know you wouldn't think I'm serious,
but do you know there's an egg
standing outside my door?'

PALM TREE KING

Because I come from the West Indies
certain people in England seem to think
I is an expert on palm trees

So not wanting to sever dis link
with me native roots (know what ah mean?)
or to disappoint dese culture vulture
I does smile cool as seabreeze

and say to dem
which specimen
you interested in
cause you talking
to the right man
I is palm tree king
I know palm tree history
like de palm o me hand
In fact me navel string
bury under a palm tree

If you think de queen could wave
you ain't see nothing yet
till you see the Roystonea Regia
– that is the royal palm –
with she crown of leaves
waving calm-calm
over the blue Caribbean carpet
nearly 100 feet of royal highness

But let we get down to business
Tell me what you want to know
How tall a palm tree does grow?
What is the biggest coconut I ever see?
What is the average length of the leaf?

Don't expect me to be brief
cause palm tree history
is a long-long story

Anyway why you so interested
in length and circumference?
That kind of talk so ordinary
That don't touch the essence
of palm tree mystery
That is no challenge
to a palm tree historian like me

If you insist on statistics
why don't you pose a question
with some mathematical profundity?

Ask me something more tricky
like if a American tourist with a camera
take 9 minutes to climb a coconut tree
how long a English tourist without a camera
would take to climb the same coconut tree?

That is problem pardner
Now ah coming harder

If 6 straw hat
and half a dozen bikini
multiply by the same number of coconut tree
equal one postcard
how many miles of straw hat
you need to make a tourist industry?

That is problem pardner
Find the solution
and you got a revolution

But before you say anything
let I palm tree king
give you dis warning
Ah want you to answer in metric
it kind of rhyme with tropic
Besides it sound more exotic

from MEMO TO CRUSOE (a work in progress)

Robinson Crusoe
Robinson Crusoe
I want you to know
dat long before you land
on de land of Tobago
I Man Friday
been keeping a diary
called calypso
and playing mas
so Mr Crusoe
I go commemorate you ass
in calypso.
Mr Crusoe
Mr Crusoe
I got a bone
to pick with you
I hear you calling me
cannibal.
I done make a note
of dat in me diary
and I Man Friday
dont forget easy.
One day Mr Crusoe
I go make you
eat you words
dat is if I dont
eat you first.

Yours etc.

'Friday' / Self

HALF-CASTE

Excuse me
standing on one leg
I'm half-caste

Explain yuself
wha yu mean
when yu say half-caste
yu mean when picasso
mix red an green
is a half-caste canvas/
explain yuself
wha yu mean
when yu say half-caste
yu mean when light an shadow
mix in de sky
is a half-caste weather/
well in dat case
england weather
nearly always half-caste
in fact some o dem cloud
half-caste till dem overcast
so spiteful dem dont want de sun pass
ah rass/
explain yuself
wha yu mean
when yu say half-caste
yu mean tchaikovsky
sit down at dah piano
an mix a black key
wid a white key
is a half-caste symphony/

Explain yuself
wha yu mean
Ah listening to yu wid de keen
half of mih ear
Ah lookin at yu wid de keen
half of mih eye
and when I'm introduced to yu

I'm sure you'll understand
why I offer yu half-a-hand
an when I sleep at night
I close half-a-eye
consequently when I dream
I dream half-a-dream
an when moon begin to glow
I half-caste human being
cast half-a-shadow
but yu must come back tomorrow

wid de whole of yu eye
an de whole of yu ear
an de whole of yu mind

an I will tell yu
de other half
of my story

LISTEN MR OXFORD DON

Me not no Oxford don
me a simple immigrant
from Clapham Common
I didn't graduate
I immigrate

But listen Mr Oxford don
I'm a man on de run

and a man on de run
is a dangerous one

I ent have no gun
I ent have no knife
but mugging de Queen's English
is the story of my life

I don't need no axe
to split/ up yu syntax
I don't need no hammer
to mash/ up yu grammar

I warning you Mr Oxford don
I'm a wanted man
and a wanted man
is a dangerous one

Dem accuse me of assault
on de Oxford dictionary/
imagine a concise peaceful man like me/
dem want me serve time
for inciting rhyme to riot
but I tekking it quiet
down here in Clapham Common

I'm not a violent man Mr Oxford don
I only armed wit mih human breath
but human breath
is a dangerous weapon

So mek dem send one big word after me
I ent serving no jail sentence
I slashing suffix in self-defence
I bashing future wit present tense
and if necessary

I making de Queen's English accessory/ to my offence

FINDERS KEEPERS

This morning on the way to Charing Cross
I found a stiff upper lip
lying there on the train seat

Finders Keepers
I was tempted to scream

But something about that stiff upper lip
left me speechless

It looked so abandoned so unloved
like a frozen glove
nobody bothers to pick up

I could not bear to hand in
that stiff upper lip
to the Lost & Found

So I made a place for it
in the lining of my coat pocket

and I said
Come with me to the Third World

You go thaw off

ONE QUESTION FROM A BULLET

I want to give up being a bullet
I've been a bullet too long

I want to be an innocent coin
in the hand of a child
and be squeezed through the slot
of a bubblegum machine

I want to give up being a bullet
I've been a bullet too long

I want to be a good luck seed
lying idle in somebody's pocket
or some ordinary little stone
on the way to becoming an earring
or just lying there unknown
among a crowd of other ordinary stones

I want to give up being a bullet
I've been a bullet too long

The question is
Can you give up being a killer?

THE LOVER

What can i do

when he weaves
his spell
of softness
over you

what can i do

when his gentle
fingers touch
your eyes
like leaves

what can i do

when your cheeks
glow peace
and you weaken
in his presence

what can i do

when you open
to the lover
by the name
of sleep

GO SPREAD

If I be the rain
you the earth
let love be the seed
and together
make we give birth
to a new longing
for harmony growing
among all things
and love go spread wings
love go spread wings

WINGS

If I be a tree
clinging to parch earth
this time you be the rain
and love the wind
taking we by the hand
showing the way
to new awakenings
among all things
and love go spread wings
love go spread wings

WEB OF SOUND

is the sinking

of metal

is the cleaving

of a feeling

is the weaving

of a dream

is the sounding

of a scream

is the drumming

of a heart

is the grounding

of a hurt

is the pounding

of a rage

is the wounding

of a night

is the grooving

of blackness

is the moving

of a man

of pan

for the taste of fire

to the thrust of chisel

in a web of sound

in old oildrum

to a beat of steel

to tones of blood

to tunes of love

by slash of stars

by trickles of light

to the embrace

RAINBOW

When you see
de rainbow
you know
God know
wha he doing –
one big smile
across the sky –
I tell you
God got style
the man got style

When you see
raincloud pass
and de rainbow
make a show
I tell you
is God doing
limbo
the man doing
limbo

But sometimes
you know
when I see
de rainbow
so full of glow
and curving
like she bearing child
I does want to know
if God
ain't a woman

If that is so
the woman got style
man she got style

Ferenc Aszmann (formerly **Gandhi versus the Daleks**)

FORTY THINGS TO DO WITH
   GOD . . .

Is God –
   a screaming baby
   a psychotic genius
   a cosmic tax collector

   the village idiot's revenge
   all very well in theory
   out of ffocus

   a rabid dog on a full moon
   joseph'n'mary's little accident
   a fairy tale walk-on part
   a psychedelic brain surgeon
   a safe place to hide out for a while
   a good excuse to make everybody as depressed as possible

   the most interesting thing in any church or temple

   hitler as dr. jekyll
   a time honoured means of contraception
   a zen irish joke
   like the royal family but less expensive
   a divine love lout
   a born bleeeeeeeeeeeeeeeeeeeeeeeeeeeeeeeeeder
   the least of our worries
   the last great alibi

   the straw that gave the camel a ride

   the last word in metaphysical engineering
   someonelse's problem
   an easy answer in a vulnerable moment
   an angel's hairdresser
   electro mephisto the first king of everything and everywhere

36

a worried little boy who just told a whopping great lie
a leather jacket flying round the vatican
praying to it/her/himself all the time

a controlled experiment under laboratory conditions
a spiritual kleptomaniac's best friend
an emergency exit from the worst story ever told
mr. fixit with a bible or a koran or
a good way to start a fight
a richter scale for things we don't really understand

dependent on our collective consciousness
  for its existence so
    it had better start
      earning its keep

the secret you won't even tell yourself yet

?in our hearts or up there
    more psychologically useful

a microscopic little light
metamorphosisisisisisisisinnnnnnn
    into a sun
      in a soul near you . . .

Attila the Stockbroker

THE ORACLE

A bloke who works for Pinnacle a firm that's really cynical asked me to write an article and make it really radical I know it sounds improbable and practically impossible but writing up the article I sat upon my testicle and found a little particle of testicle on my article I got a small receptacle and took it to the hospital where they looked very sceptical they said that's not a testicle it looks like a comestible you blokes are so predictable the nurse said looking cynical while waiting in the vestibule of the sceptic septic hospital a spider seized my testicle and munched it in its mandible the pain was unbelievable it really was unbearable so I clutched my aching testicle and yelled for something medical the nurse was still quite cynical as she bandaged up my testicle no need to be theatrical she said applying chemical the bandage was impractical and it exposed my oracle so the looks I got were quizzical as I left the local hospital a pig in a convertible with a mate who looked identical and really quite irascible said cover up your oracle I said it was impractical because I'd hurt my testicle and if he was still sceptical he ought to ask the hospital the particle of testicle still rested on the article which I had done for Pinnacle the firm that's really cynical the article was radical and really quite street credible and though it sounds nonsensical the particle was edible the one conclusion logical was that the little particle was not part of my testicle but was a small comestible as they said in the hospital by now you must be cynical this rant's become predictable and so I'll end this canticle this tale of tortured testicle mistaken for comestible I'll finish with an oracle it really is impossible to try and write an article while sitting on your testicle

it
   makes
      you
       go
       HYSTERICAL!

FOYER BAR, HARLOW 1980

Living in a brave new town
Things can often get you down
Not much to say, not much to do
Existence gets on top of you
So some folks say well why not go
And meet a girl in a disco
But I don't want to walk that far
So I go to the Foyer Bar

We go there and we sit together
Uniform is jeans and leather
And we sit and drink and doze
And we sit and drink and pose
Everything we say is cool
Big fish in a little pool
Yeah if you want to be a star
You'll make it in the Foyer Bar!

DUSTBIN POEM

Today I took out the rubbish
and thought of you.
At the bottom of my dustbin
the maggots wriggled round and round
like planes circling over Gatwick Airport.
Now and then, two larval aviators collided
in the crowded, circular, putrescent grooves of metal
and I thought yes, this is us —
not even ships that pass in the night
but maggots wriggling in predetermined circles
in the putrescent dustbin
of the enterprise culture.

This rant is about dead commuters – or, more accurately, about the very small difference between dead commuters and live ones

Deep in the dingy dirty decomposing dogshit-dripping dungeon of a graffiti-graced southern region train compartment stuffed full of bad-breath-breathing halibut-eyed computer commuters with boring suits and boring habits the state of play is giving cause for concern the middle-aged middle-class middle-management middle-everything puke-suited slack-jawed suet-pudding-faced powell-worshipping willie whitelaw clone by the window is slumped rigidly over his daily telegraph in a posture indicating his sudden demise this alarms the prim po-faced clean-tablecloth-every-night sex-in-the-dark-once-a-week daily mail-female secretary by his side who asks him politely if he recently died receiving no reply she turns to the lard-arsed times-reading tory-voting pinstriped wimp sitting opposite and demands an opinion in company with the three paul eddington clones also occupying the compartment he lowers his eyes and stares fixedly at his newspaper in the time honoured fashion of the don't-pinch-my-seat-don't-invade-my-world-I'm-all-right-jack-leave-me-alone-english suburban commuter husbands' club she turns to me and confidently I tell her that most commuters are dead it's their natural state and anyway dead executives can't possibly be any less interesting than live ones though I can see that they might smell a bit more and that's why they always get aftershave for christmas and anyway I'm never going to bromley again . . . .

40

VIDEO NAZIS

ie – the new breed of sadistic crypto-fascists who enjoy making or watching films depicting other human beings being destroyed in a variety of hideous ways (and don't tell me it's only a movie . . .)

In Rome the gladiators fought
while people slobbered in the stands
the bloodlust rose, the voyeurs wanked
with transfixed gaze and frenzied hands
then naked humans thrown to beasts
were torn apart amidst the cheers
their last entreaties drowned in blood
and wine-soaked sick sadistic jeers

And still it swells, the evil lust
centuries old and still unslaked
the cesspit of the human mind
the vampire free, unchained, unstaked
and now sick men – it's always men –
are harnessing the stinking vulture
lurking in the human soul
and flaunting it as video culture

Film-makers, impotent and scared
with shrivelled pricks and sick desires
hate women so they stab their breasts
or wrench their nipples off with pliers
and hipsters in the music press
say 'What's the fuss? It's special effects.'
It's real enough in those bastards' minds –
I want to break their fucking necks!

And what of those who watch the films
of Nazis raping Jewish mothers?
Do they sit there, and wank, and spout
wish they'd been there beside the others
– then play with children of their own
like SS butchers used to do?
LOOK IN THE MIRROR, NASTY FAN –
SEE ADOLF EICHMANN STARE AT YOU!

41

ON THE BEACH AT WORTHING

On the beach at Worthing
the lugworm casts by the sewage outfall
look like dirty shepherds' pie.
We walk the shingle, hand in hand,
and the crabs
on the nearby Groyne
remind me of more intimate times.
Your hand resembles a limp flounder.
I squeeze it, dispassionately.
The seaweed smells like a dirty toilet.
Refreshed, we return for dinner.

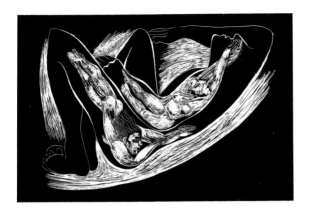

TO SLOUGH AND SANITY

(a Post-Martian Pastorale)

Far from our city haunts,
besieged on all sides
we stumble apprehensively
through a minefield of cowpats.
The cloying earth sucks greedily at your high heels
and you surrender reluctantly
to the ditch's embrace.
Crouching to your aid, I suddenly see before me
all of Flanders in 1916 –
trench, barbed wire, broken glass, stinging nettles, maggots,
the stench of death . . .
As my outstretched arm levers you upright
you suggest that I may be guilty of pretentiousness
and ill-timed remarks!
As I purse my lips in reply
the enemy come over the top –
huge, lumbering tanks
lowing deeply:
an armoury of udders
– bitter mammaries indeed!
With a yell, I sound the alarm
and we beat a disorderly retreat
to Slough, and sanity.

SLOUGH

Come tourists all, and flock to Slough
as many as the streets allow
By bus, or train – no matter how –
Come, very soon!

And lift forever the sad curse
once laid in dull, sarcastic verse
by one whose poetry is worse
than Mills and Boon!

Sir John – oh, what a sense of farce!*
A poet of the teacup class
obsessedwith railways, and stained glass
and twisted bough

and thus impervious to the call
of the post-war suburban sprawl
of Harlow, Basildon and all
and glorious Slough!

Oh Slough! Harbinger my dreams!
Home of a thousand training schemes
and theme pubs, patronised by streams
of tetchy men

with blow-dried hair and blow-dried brain
diplomas in inflicting pain
and ne'er a thought for Larkin, Raine
or Betjeman!

A thousand jewellers' shops contend
the kitchen unit is your friend
Designer labels set the trend
With a blank stare

And now – the latest, brightest star –
a brand new ten-screen cinema!
The folk will come from near and far
to worship there!

Oh self-made, independent town
– The jewel in Margaret's southern crown!
No more will poets put you down
with mocking voice!

Come tourists all, and flock to Slough
as Milton Friedman takes a bow
This town is fit for heroes now –
Come, and rejoice!

* – Thirty years ago, in a moment of ill-informed spitefulness, the Laureate-and-knighthood-destined John Betjeman cast a grievous poetic slur on an innocent Berkshire town:

> *'Come friendly bombs, and fall on Slough*
> *It isn't fit for humans now*
> *There isn't grass to graze a cow*
> *Swarm over, Death!'*
> etc, etc.

Until now the good people of Slough have suffered in silence – but no longer! Attila's ode redresses the balance at last. He has also been on the hot line to Parnassus, and discovered that Sloughites are joined in a spirited defence of their town by some of our most estimable literary forbears – to wit:

> *'All things bright and beautiful*
> *All creatures great and small*
> *All things wise and wonderful*
> *The Lord God made them Slough'*
> (Cecil Alexander)

> *'I can resist anything except Slough'*
> (Oscar Wilde)

> *'I must go down to Slough again*
> *where the aeroplanes fill the sky*
> *And all I ask is a Heathrow jet*
> *with a whine and a drunken fly'*
> (John Masefield)

> *'An acre in Slough is worth a principality in Utopia'*
> (Thomas Macaulay)

> *'The curfew tolls the knell of parting day*
> *The lowing herd winds slowly o'er the lea*
> *The ploughman homeward plods his weary way*
> *And I return to Slough to have my tea.'*
> (Thomas Gray)

45

Sujata Bhatt

અડેલી   (UDAYLEE)*

Only paper and wood are safe
from a menstruating woman's touch.
So they built this room
for us, next to the cowshed.
Here, we're permitted to write
letters, to read, and it gives a chance
for our kitchen-scarred fingers to heal.

Tonight, I can't leave the stars alone.
And when I can't sleep, I pace
in this small room, I pace
from my narrow rope-bed to the bookshelf
filled with dusty newspapers
held down with glossy brown cowries and a conch.
When I can't sleep, I hold
the conch shell to my ear
just to hear my blood rushing,
a song throbbing,
a slow drumming within my head, my hips.
This aching is my blood flowing against,
rushing against something –
knotted clumps of my blood,
so I remember fistfuls of torn seaweed
        rising with the foam,
rising. Then falling, falling up on the sand
strewn over newly laid turtle eggs.

---

*   અડેલી   (Udaylee) Gujarati: untouchable when one is menstruating

REINCARNATION

The wise old men
            of India say
there are certain rules.
For example, if you loved
your dog too much,
in your next life you'll be a dog,
yet full of human memories.
And if the King's favourite daughter
loved the low-caste palace gardener
who drowned while crossing the river
in a small boat during the great floods,
they'll be reborn, given a second chance.
The wise old men of India say
one often dreams
of the life one led before.

There's a lion sprawled out
beside his cubs.
His thick mane tangled with dry grass,
his head droops: dusty stooping dahlia.
Then with a shudder,
            a sudden shake of his head
he groans and growls
at four whimpering cubs.
(He'd let them climb
all over his back
if only he weren't so hungry.)
The lioness is already far away
hunting in the deepest part of the valley:
a tall dark forest.
Red-flowered vines,
gold-flecked snakes encircling every tree.
Tall ferns,
fringes of maidenhair edging broad leaves.
But now the lioness steps out
into a vast clearing.
She lifts her head towards the east, the west:
sniffing, sniffing. Her eyes stare hard,
urgent, she walks as if her raw swollen teats,

pink and not quite dry, prickle and itch
and goad her on.
She's lean enough, afraid
her cubs might die.
Now there's clear water flowing rapidly,
rippling over rocks, the lioness stops, drinks,
her quick long tongue licks, laps up the water.
Now the lioness is wading through, swimming,
her long golden tail streams through rushing waves;
torn, bruised paws splashing.
A quiet breeze
        as if the earth were barely breathing.
Fallen leaves, still green,
and tangled vines swirl in the water,
                the lioness circling.
Nearby monkeys, squirrels,
even birds remain hidden, silence.
A dead bull elephant rots:
        bullet-pocked, tuskless.

You hold me, rock me,
pull me out of my dream,
(or did I dream you?)
The fur lingers on your skin,
your body has not forgotten
how to move like a cat.
Look, the sun spills golden over the walls,
you grow tawnier with the dawn.
Shivering haunches relax,
the slow licking begins
gently over the bruises.

THE KAMA SUTRA RETOLD

Then Roman Svirsky said,
"it is illegal in Russia to write
about sex
so it is important
for Vasily Aksyonov
to write about it – "

You laugh,
but I want to know
how would we break the long silence
if we had the same rules?

It's not enough to say
she kissed his balls,
licked his cock long
how her tongue could not stop.

For he thinks of the first day:
she turns her head away
as she takes off her T-shirt
blue jeans, underwear, bra.
She doesn't even look at him
until she's in the lake,
the clear water up to her neck
yet unable to hide her skin.

They swim out
to the islands
but he doesn't remember swimming;
just brushing against her leg
once, then diving down
beneath her thighs   staying underwater
long enough for a good look,
coming up for air   and watching
her black hair streaming back straight,
then watching her
step over
the stones, out of the water.
She doesn't know what to say.

He wishes they were swans,
        Yeats's swans
     would not need to speak
but could always glide across
       other worlds;
magical, yet rustling with real reeds.

The sun in her eyes
so they move closer to the pine trees.
When he touches her nipples
he doesn't know
who is more surprised
(years later he remembers that look,
 the way her eyes open wider).
He's surprised
she wants him
to kiss her nipples again and again
because she's only 17 he's surprised
her breasts are so full.
She's surprised
      it feels so good
because he's only 17 she's surprised
he can be so gentle
         yet so hard inside her,
the way pine needles
      can soften the ground.
Where does the ground end
     and she begin?
She must have swallowed the sky
    the lake, and all the woods
           veined with amber brown pathways;

for now great white wings
are swooping through
her thighs, beating stronger
     up her chest,
the beak stroking her spine
feathers tingling her skin,
the blood inside
      her groin swells

while wings are rushing to get out,
              rushing.

IRIS

Her hand sweeps over the rough grained paper,
then, with a wet sponge, again.
A drop of black is washed grey,
cloudy as warm breath fogging cool glass.
She feels she must make the best of it,
she must get the colour of the stone wall,
of the mist settling around twisted birch trees.
Her eye doesn't miss the rabbit crouched,
a tuft of fog in the tall grass.
Nothing to stop the grey sky from merging into stones,
or the stone walls from trailing off into sky.
But closer, a single iris stands fully opened:
dark wrinkled petals, rain-moist,
the tall slender stalk sways, her hand follows.
Today, even the green is tinged with grey,
the stone's shadow lies heavy over the curling petals
but there's time enough, she'll wait,
study the lopsided shape.
The outer green sepals once enclosing the bud
lie shrivelled: empty shells spiralling
right beneath the petals.
As she stares the sun comes out.
And the largest petal flushes
deep deep violet.
A violet so intense it's almost black.
The others tremble indigo, reveal
paler blue undersides.
Thin red veins running into yellow orange rills,
yellow flows down the green stem.
Her hand moves swiftly from palette to paper,
paper to palette, the delicate brush
swoops down, sweeps up,
moves the way a bird builds its nest.
An instant and the sun is gone.
Grey-ash-soft-shadows fall again.
But she can close her eyes and see
red-orange veins, the yellow
swept with green throbbing towards blue,
and deep inside she feels
indigo pulsing to violet.

THE WOODCUT

For days
I touch the block of pine wood,
pressing its hard edge
                against my forehead.

Uncertain for days
        while it rains
I walk through wet pine needles.
Water-softened pine cones
                flatten under my feet.

I follow the crooked
                wrenched roots,
past torn clumps of moss,
blue-grey feathers, white whisps of cat fur,
and everywhere the sticky leaves,
yellow leaves
                like the sliced skin of frogs
cover fallen logs, cover a squirrel's skull.

For days I touch
                the block of pine wood,
pressing its hard edge
                between my breasts.

Then remembering your harshness

I cut the first quick stroke
                sharp in the wood.

THE WRITER

The best story, of course,
is the one you can't write,
        you won't write.
It's something that can only live
        in your heart,
not on paper.

Paper is dry, flat.
Where is the soil
for the roots, and how do I lift out
entire trees, a whole forest
from the earth of the spirit
and transplant it on paper
without disturbing the birds?

And what about the mountain
on which this forest grows?
The waterfalls
      making rivers,
rivers with throngs of trees
elbowing each other aside
to have a look
at the fish.

Beneath the fish
    there are clouds.
Here, the sky ripples,
the river thunders.
How would things move on paper?

Now watch   the way
              the tigers' walking
     shreds the paper.

TAIL -

Meaningless black marks
cover my page, they stretch and grow
            into a cat.

The cat demands trees,
a whole forest of wood to sharpen her claws,
                    and squirrels.

Black marks twist into branches,
tiny buds dot the twigs.
Three squirrels swirl up the trunk of an Oak.
The cat pretends her eyes are blind stones,
pretends she is a stone among stones.
The squirrels know and refuse to come out.
Then, it starts snowing
        slowly
            softly   large flakes
                        begin covering the black marks.

57

ANGELS' WINGS

I can recall that age
very well: fourteen-years-old,
when I thought I understood
Lenin and Mao,
and Christina Rossetti was beginning
to sound silly.

One April Saturday morning
after swimming lessons
I stood waiting for my father,
pacing the formaldehyde
            stung corridor,
I twirled equidistant between
the autopsy toom and his office.

My eleven-year-old brother
                    and I together
but silent for a quarter of an hour
as if all that swimming, all that chlorine
had altered all our breathing
had washed away our speech.

A heavy door opened and a man,
dark as the shadows he cast,
a man with electric white hair
asked us to step inside.
There was something
he wanted us to see.

The room was festooned with wings,
all of a similar shape
            and strangely human.
Perhaps fairies' wings
            or angels' wings, I thought,
made of real gossamer . . .

As we stepped closer
we could see clumps of clogged cells,
those grape-like clusters meant to blossom with oxygen —

now shrivelled
beside rivers of blood choked black.

They were not drawings,
not photographs —
but human lungs
well-preserved by someone's
skill in histology.
He could tell us how old
their owners had lived to be
for how many years each had smoked.
He would tell us everything
except their names.

Twenty pairs of lungs
pinned up on his wall:
a collage of black and grey,
here and there some chalky yellow
                    some fungus-furred green.

How long did we stand there?
And what did we say?
I don't remember eating lunch
or what we did
for the rest of that day —
Only those twenty pairs of nameless lungs,
the intimate gossamer
of twenty people I never knew
lungless in their graves.

Valerie Bloom

YUH HEAR 'BOUT . . . ?

Yuh hear bout de people dem arres
fi bun dung de Asian people dem house?
Yuh hear bout de policeman dem lock up
fi beat up de black bwoy widout a cause?
Yuh hear bout de M.P. dem sack
because im refuse fi help im black constituents
eena dem fight 'gainst deportation?
Yuh noh hear bout dem?

Me neida.

TABLES

Headmaster a come, Mek has'e! Sit down
– Amy! Min' yuh bruck Jane collar-bone,
Tom! Tek yuh foot off o' de desk,
Sandra Wallace, mi know yuh vex
But beg yuh get up off o' Joseph head.
Tek de lizard off o' Sue neck, Ted!
Sue, mi dear, don' bawl so loud;
Thomas, yuh can tell mi why yuh put de toad
Eena Elvira sandwich bag?
An Jim, whey yuh a do wid dat bull-frog?
Tek i' off mi table! Yuh mad?
Mi know yuh chair small, May, but it no dat bad
Dat yuh haffe siddung pon de floor!
Jim, don' squeeze de frog unda de door,
Put i' through de window – no, no, Les!
Mi know yuh hungry, but Mary yeas
Won' full yuh up, so spit it out.
Now go wash de blood outa yuh mout'.
Hortense, tek Mary to de nurse.
Nick, tek yuh han out o' Mary purse!
Ah wonda who tell all o' yuh
Sey dat dis class-room is a zoo?
Quick! Headmaster comin' through de door
" – *Two ones are two, two twos are four . . .*"

DON' GO OVA DERE

Barry madda tell im
But Barry wouldn' hear,
Barry fada warn im
But Barry didn' care.
"Don' go ova dere, bwoy,
Don' go ova dere."

Barry sista beg im
Barry pull her hair,
Barry brother bet im
"You can't go ova dere."
"I can go ova dere, bwoy,
I can go ova dere."

Barry get a big bag,
Barry climb de gate,
Barry granny call im
But Barry couldn' wait,
Im wan' get ova dere, bwoy,
Before it get too late.

Barry see de plum tree
Im didn' see de bull,
Barry thinkin' bout de plums
"Gwine get dis big bag full."
De bull get up an' shake, bwoy,
An gi de rope a pull.

De rope slip off de pole
but Barry didn' see,
De bull begin to stretch im foot dem
Barry climb de tree.
Barry start fe eat, bwoy,
Firs' one, den two, den three.

Barry nearly full de bag
an den im hear a soun',
Barry hol' de plum limb tight
An start fe look aroun'
When im see de bull, bwoy,
Im nearly tumble down.

Night a come, de bull naw move,
From unda de plum tree,
Barry madda wondering
Whey Barry coulda be.
Barry getting tired, bwoy,
Of sittin' in dat tree.

An Barry dis realise
Him neva know before,
Sey de tree did full o' black ants
But now im know fe sure.
For some begin fe bite im, bwoy,
Den more, an more, an more.

De bull lay down fe wait it out,
Barry mek a jump,
De bag o' plum drop out de tree
An Barry hear a thump.
By early de nex' mawnin', bwoy,
Dat bull gwine have a lump.

De plum so frighten dat po' bull
Im start fe run too late,
Im a gallop after Barry
But Barry jump de gate.
De bull jus' stamp im foot, bwoy,
Im yeye dem full o' hate.

When Barry ketch a im yard,
What a state 'im in!
Im los' im bag, im clothes mud up,
An mud deh pon im chin.
An whey de black ants bite im
Feba bull-frog skin.

Barry fada spank im,
Im madda sey im sin,
Barry sista scold im
But Barry only grin,
For Barry brother shake im head,
An sey, "Barry, yuh win!"

DAYBREAK

A blur
detaches itself

wavers
into shape

Unfurled
probes the breath
where vagrants stir
on pavements

Feathered sirens
shriek

NOON

Heat haze
quivers in open
virgin plots

Trembling
licks the flesh
where pores weep
with exhaustion

Dainty teacups
rattle

DUSK

Nightshade enshrouds
small glass-eyed frogs
and lanterned bugs

wreathes the
vespering crows and
cicadas at prayer

Daystar descends the
burning ghat

66

UNDER APARTHEID *

*A whey dem sey mi mumma gawn, oh? *
A whey dem sey mi puppa gawn?
A whey dem sey mi bredda gawn, oh?
A whey dem sey mi sista gawn?

So the children cry,
in the townships, where,
like chickens on a dung-heap,
old women scratch an existence,
and old men sucked dry as desert sand
brood in silence,
the bitter taste of broken lives
and lost hopes on their tongues;
the children cry.

A whey dem sey mi mumma gawn, oh?
A whey dem sey mi mumma gawn?

And in the great white houses of the cities,
Mothers
wash
cook
clean,
Mother the children
of the men
who butcher their children,
And sigh
as the sound drifts across
the sun-baked mud of the homelands.

A whey dem sey mi puppa gawn, oh?
A whey dem sey mi puppa gawn?

And fathers,
in the compounds where
Black labourers must not be burdened by
superfluous appendages
like women and children,
like comfort,
like dignity,

sigh;
Dodging death in the mines,
chasing the garbage trucks
through the cities' back streets
to dispose of the baas-man's rubbish
they sigh,
as the sound drifts across the cesspits of the homelands.

A whey dem sey mi bredda gawn, oh?
A whey dem sey mi sista gawn?

And children cry
in the fetid prison cells,
Where warm walls crack with the screams
as electric shock skitters across black flesh,
Where defiant singing conveys another
half-a-dozen to the chair,
Where their childish wails mingle with
the fathers' groans from adjoining cells.

In Dimbaza,
Where fathers dig the graves
of the babies still unborn,
Where mothers sew the shrouds
for the foetus just conceived,
Fat with the hunger that pierces like a knife
the children cry.

In the streets of Soweto
in the blood and the bullets
in the houses where the law
strikes terror in the night,
in the rubble which remains
when bulldozers have gone,
the children cry.

". . . How long shall the wicked reign
over my people? . . ."

How long will
southern fruits taste sweeter,
southern diamonds sparkle brighter,

68

southern gold glow more richly,
southern labour come cheaper,
for the west?

A whey, dem sey . . . .

* – This is the first of a trilogy of poems in progress – the second is about Nelson Mandela's release and the inevitable crumbling of the system, and the third looks forward to the eventual collapse of Apartheid. At present (summer 1991) Apartheid is still finding ways of shoring itself up and, as Valerie Bloom wrote (in a letter to this book's editor in March 1990, when she was beginning the sequence): "South African whites, like slave masters before them, are finding the system too hot to handle, but their expedient *volte face* should not, I think, be allowed to condone the destruction of generations of blacks. No amount of legislation is going to erase the decades of suffering."

▼ – The italicised lines are adapted from a dirge traditionally sung at wakes for the dead in Jamaica:

> "*A whey dem sey mi mumma gawn, oh*
> *A whey dem sey mi puppa gawn?*
> *A whey dem say mi bredda gawn, oh?*
> *A whey dem sey mi sista gawn?*
> (call)   *Look unda bed ef yuh see im dung deh?*
> (response)   *No Sah!*
> (call)   *Look up de road ef yu see im up deh?*
> (response)   *No sah!"*

> Meaning –
> "Where do they say my mother's gone, oh
> Where do they say my father's gone?
> Where do they say my brother's gone, oh
> Where do they say my sister's gone?
> Look underneath the bed, see if she's there
>   – No sir!
> Look up the road, see if she's there
>   – No sir!"

GLOSSARY – *for readers unfamiliar with Jamaican patwa (– words and meanings are given in the order of their first appearance on the preceding pages):*

dem – *they / their / them*
fi, fe – *for or to*
bun – *burn(t)*
dung – *down*
a – *is or I, me*
whey – *where or away*
yeas – *ear(s)*

sey / dat – *that or say / says / said*
gwine – *going to*
gi – *give*
limb – *branch*
yeye – *eye(s)*
ketch – *reach(ed) / arrive(d)*
Feba – *look(ed) like / resemble(d)*

69

Billy Bragg

TENDER COMRADE

What will you do when the war is over, tender comrade
When we lay down our weary guns
When we return to our wives and families
And look into the eyes of our sons

What will you say of the bond we had, tender comrade
Will you say that we were brave
As the shells fell all around us

Or that we wept and cried for our mothers
And cursed our fathers
For forgetting that all men are brothers

Will you say that we were heroes
Or that fear of dying among strangers
Tore our innocence and false shame away

And from that moment on deep in my heart I knew
That I would only give my life for love

Brothers in arms in each other's arms
Was the only time that I was not afraid

What will you do when the war is over, tender comrade
When we cast off these khakhi clothes
And go our separate ways
What will you say of the bond we had
Tender comrade

THE INTERNATIONALE*

Stand up, all victims of oppression
For the tyrants fear your might
Don't cling so hard to your possessions
For you have nothing, if you have no rights
Let racist ignorance be ended

70

For respect makes the empires fall
Freedom is merely privilege extended
Unless enjoyed by one and all

Chorus   *So come brothers and sisters*
For the struggle carries on
The Internationale
Unites the world in song
So comrades come rally
For this is the time and place
The international ideal
Unites the human race

Let no one build walls to divide us
Walls of hatred nor walls of stone
Come greet the dawn and stand beside us
We'll live together or we'll die alone
In our world poisoned by exploitation
Those who have taken, now they must give
And end the vanity of nations
We've but one earth on which to live

And so begins the final drama
In the streets and in the fields
We stand unbowed before their armour
We defy their guns and shields
When we fight, provoked by their aggression
Let us be inspired by life and love
For though they offer us concessions
Change will not come from above

* – *Eugene Pottier wrote the original lyrics of The Internationale after the fall of the Paris Commune in 1871. This was set to music by Pierre Degeyter, a textile worker from Lille who composed the tune for his factory chorus in 1888. Eight years later the song was adapted by the French Workers Party at its annual congress. Foreign delegates wrote down hasty translations and by the turn of the century it was being sung by socialists, communists and anarchists all over the world in dozens of languages. Until 1943 it was the National Anthem of the Soviet Union, and it was most recently heard being sung by Chinese students in Tiananmen Square during the pro-democracy demonstrations in 1989.*

Shortly after that event Pete Seeger asked me to sing The Internationale with him at the Vancouver Folk Festival. I told him I thought the English lyrics, whose translator is unknown, were archaic and often unsingable. He agreed and suggested I write some new lyrics to Degeyter's stirring tune.   (B B)

ISLAND OF NO RETURN (1982)

Digging all day and digging all night
To keep my fox-hole out of sight.
Digging into dinner with a plate on my knees,
The smell of damp webbing in the morning breeze
Fear in my stomach, fear in the sky, I
Eat my dinner with a wary eye.
After all this it won't be the same
Messing about on Salisbury Plain

> *Pick up your feet, fall in, move out,*
> *We're going to a party way down South.*
> *Me and the corp'ral, out on a spree,*
> *Damned from here to eternity.*
> *I can already taste the blood in my mouth*
> *We're going to a party way down South.*
> *I wish Kipling and the Captain were here*
> *To record our pursuits for posterity.*
> *Me and the corp'ral out on a spree,*
> *Damned from here to eternity.*

Hate this flat land, there's no cover for
Sons and fathers and brothers and lovers.
I can take the killing, I can take the slaughter,
But I don't talk to *Sun* reporters.
I never thought that I would be
Fighting fascists in the Southern Sea.
I saw one today and in his hand
Was a weapon that was made in Birmingham.

> *Pick up your feet, fall in, move out,*
> *We're going to a party way down South.*
> *Me and the corp'ral, out on a spree,*
> *Damned from here to eternity.*
> *I can already taste the blood in my mouth*
> *We're going to a party way down South.*
> *I wish Kipling and the Captain were here*
> *To record our pursuits for posterity.*
> *Me and the corp'ral out on a spree,*
> *Damned from here to eternity.*

TRUST

He's already been inside me
And he really didn't say
And I really didn't ask him
I just hoped and prayed

He's already been inside me
And I really don't feel well
I keep looking in the mirror
But it's hard to tell

Will he stay by me and take my hand
And hold me till I sleep
Or will he crumble and fall to the floor
And weep
Oh feeble man, Oh evil man

He's already been inside me
Would he have told me if he cared?
I know I ought to find out
But I'm much too scared

He's already been inside me
And I know it can't be good
Nothing feels
The way it should

Will he hold me in his arms again
And wipe away my tears
Or has he already taken
My best years
Oh evil man, Oh feeble man

TANK PARK SALUTE

Kiss me goodnight and say my prayers
Leave the light on at the top of the stairs
Tell me the names of the stars up in the sky
    A tree taps on the window pane
    That feeling smothers me again
Daddy is it true that we all have to die?

      At the top of the stairs
      Is darkness

I closed my eyes and when I looked
Your name was in the memorial book
And what had become of all the things we planned?
    I accepted the commiserations
    Of all your friends and your relations
But there's some things I still don't understand

      You were so tall
      How could you fall?

Some photographs of a summer's day
A little boy's lifetime away
Is all I've left of everything we've done
    Like a pale moon in a sunny sky
    Death gazes down as I pass by
To remind me that I'm but my father's son

      – I offer up to you
      This tribute
      I offer up to you
      This tank park salute

BETWEEN THE WARS.

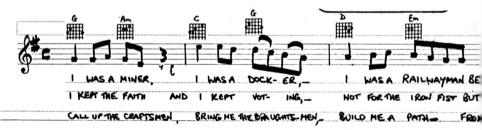

SONG BY BRAGG
STRIP BY JUPITUS
STRANGE THINGS HAPPEN!
ALL WINTER LONG
While I was locked in
my room
YOUR FACE AT THE WINDOW
and my hair on the floor
I was
THINKING OF YOU...
ALL WINTER LONG
SHIVER!
CHATTER!
I WAS LOCKED IN MY ROOM
YOUR FACE AT THE WINDOW
And my hair on the floor
I WAS THINKING OF YOU
AND THE PHONE
RANG ALL NIGHT LONG
TO TELL ME I WAS WRONG
AND I WATCHED WHILE THE OFFICER WROTE ALL THEIR AGES DOWN!
BONK!
WAAAAH!
STRANGE THINGS HAPPEN WHEN YOU'RE NOT AROUND
OUR LOVE IS SO STRONG
IT MOVES OBJECTS IN MY HOUSE
Strange things happen when you're not around
THOSE MAGICAL MOMENTS FOUND THEIR WAY BACK HOME AGAIN!
Chapter One
All winter long, while I was locked in my room, your face at the window and my hair on the floor...
I was...
"Thinking of you."
SNAP
BOOKER PRIZE
BB
ALL
WINTER LONG
WHILE I WAS LOCKED IN MY ROOM
YOUR FACE AT THE WINDOW!
AND THAT BOOK OF OLD
SPELLS
I WAS THINKING OF YOU!
AND ALL THE SPELLS WE CAST
PAF!
HAVE LATELY COME TO PASS
AND THE FLOWERS IN THE GARDEN
HAVE ALL FALLEN DOWN
STRANGE THINGS HAPPEN WHEN YOURE NOT AROUND... OUR LOVE IS SO STRONG IT MOVES OBJECTS IN MY HOUSE!
STRANGE THINGS HAPPEN WHEN YOU'RE NOT AROUND, THOSE MAGICAL MOMENTS FOUND THEIR WAY BACK HOME AGAIN!

THE BUSY GIRL BUYS BEAUTY

The busy girl buys beauty
The pretty girl buys style
And the simple girl
Buys what she's told to buy
And sees her world
Through the brightly lit eyes
Of the glossy romance of fashion
Where she can learn
Top tips for the gas, cook
Successful secrets of a sexual kind,
The daily drill for beautiful hair
And the truth about pain.

What was Anna Ford wearing,
What did Angela Rippon say?
What will you do when you wake up one morning
To find God's made you plain
In a beautiful person's world,
And all those quick recipes
Have let you down,
and you're twenty and a half
and you're not yet engaged,
Will you go look for the boy
Who says *"I love you, let's*
Get married and have kids"
In a mail order paradise?

Jean Binta Breeze

REALITY

Reality
dis is a reality
ah time we tek a stack a de reality,
      reality,
       reality.

dis is a reality

They say the problem of the nation
is overpopulation
and the unemployment stages
and the cutbacks in the wages
are results of that situation
while the brains of their technicians
are building new moon stations
war weapons increase
while young babies decease
from an illness widely known
as malnutrition

The voters return to the polls
con-trolled by a man in a rolls
who has set up his loyal henchman
to become a politician
to thrill poor people's souls

Then come new laws on sanitation
designed to cut down on the pollution
but the big man's factory
dumps its waste into the sea
and the food we eat is full of radiation

We read of wars in present history
aimed at saving our democracy
each man has won a vote
now the taxes cut his throat

and dreams rot while
egos fight for supremacy
The power of the intellect of man
is being controlled by the gluttonous ones
who decorate their babel towers
with the brains they have devoured
in their quest for human destruction

Reality
dis is a reality
ah time we tek a stack a de reality,
                               reality,
                                      reality

dis is a reality . . .

BURNING

yuh can hole
fire coal
fi jus so long
before
yuh own skin
tun fuel
to a wicked
wrath
or
fling it up
mek air stream
hiss
an cool it raas

WE SPEAK THROUGH THE SILENCE
OF OUR STARES

we who dare
shake a shoutin pharisee
from the ego tree
and bigotry
of telling we
what to be
or not to be

we
of weary waiting
holding hands with humour
watching
hatching
seeds of struggle
mapping ideas
for the crossing
of our dreams
to reality

we speak through the silence
of our stares

looking through your
looking glass reflection
noting the curl
of index finger
signal your desire

we, the figures
graphed
on the abnormal curve
of your five year plans
pierce
your long range missile
eyes
silently
for words
even true words
can betray

REPATRIATION

I seek
repatriation
into love

for love created I
among the cool ferns
on a river's morning

and Riva Mumma's hair
was casting glances of the sun
like mirrors on the rock

love danced with I
wrapped in hot tambric leaves
sprayed with ginger lilies
picking kisses
like roseapples

sweet sticky starapple days
melted
into chocolate evenings

and night
would fold its petals round I
like a lover
home to rest

for love
created I
among the cool ferns
on a river's
morning

Zoë Brooks

from A POEM FOR VOICES

(written after 6 months' unemployment)

And so we learn
To live as animals do
From day to day.
I teach myself
Existence
Which once I scorned.
There is no hope
For me
But a beginning of hope,
No dream
But a beginning of dreams.
You who have not felt
Your world stop
Like a cart in a snowdrift,
Who do not know
The infinite ways
One finds of filling
In time,
Of packing small
Broken bricks
Together with rubble
To build not a house
Perhaps
But a shelter,
A low wall
Behind which to hide;
You do not know
How memories spring
Unbidden,
Like soldiers from
A ploughed field.
Slamming doors
Bring back voices;
Past fears

Stand in gateways
To hidden gardens.
You do not know,
You can not guess
What it is for
Time to stop.

BETRAYAL

(of myself and three million others*)

Poems like fire crackers
Amaze the crowds:
Showers of gold
Light in the upturned faces.
But in the cold
And damp mornings
We search the ground.
Gleaners of stars
Find singed grass,
A blackened stick or two,
A scent of fire
– Nothing more.

We are betrayed
And by our friends' betrayal
We understand
That we do not exist,
Turn our faces
To the rainswept streets,
The brack and brimming rivers
And traipse
Past the silent mills.

* – Written after reading the *Penguin Book
of Contemporary British Poetry*, 1982.

THE BREAKING OF THE BLOOD

It is very clear to me,
as it is clear to all of us –
that memory
of the first trace
    of blood.
It was a surprise,
as it is always a surprise
for each woman
that comes upon herself
with the breaking of the blood.
And I thought, as I gazed
at my blood upon the water,
of the time
when reaching
into fine white snow
my hand found glass.
I thought
of a child's fairytale –
of a queen at a window
wishing herself a child –
    snow-white
and lips of blood.

WALLS

Through the walls
my neighbours
make love.
Her cries
cling like
the trail of snails
upon the kitchen floor,
clear, transparent,
hard to brush off
as I lie
empty in the night.

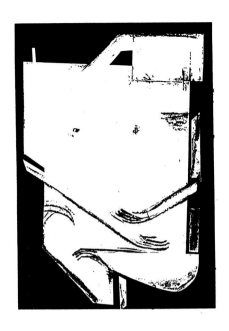

CURRICULUM VITAE BLUES

Curt morning
Day's disease.
Let us painfully assume
Certainties,
Like all those joggers
Grasping crisp morning air
In clenched and sticky fists,
Running as if
They were going somewhere.
Let us bury
Our hopes
In gasping breaths
Trying to beat ourselves.

Donal Carroll

WEDNESDAYS – THE HALF-DAY . . .

The Wednesdays were the sweetest,
a luxury wreaked from locked concoctions
of geography and geometry
a punishing alliteration.

The bike, a ladies' Raleigh –
they have no word for crossbar,
gobbles up the road, fuelled by frantic insteps
of wind-assisted, bicycle-clipped shanks:

mares passed by on the north Wicklow roads
that lead to roads that lead to 'B' roads;
the stiff rain stinging the eyeslits.
Home to the dance of kitchen smells

mingling apples, cloves, flour, baking powder,
turnips that took their colour from butter,
their taste from oranges, and a flash of Cidona
from between the mousetraps, tempered by pellets

of rain and moist breathing of the damp walls.
One hour after Mr MacTire peals the Angelus
from the pumping Vevay bells,
mother turns on the wireless

and we wait for it to heat up.
From the proscenium arch of the cloth-fronted speaker
an Athlone voice announces *Hospitals' Requests;*
syrup of strings gush *'Someone to watch over me.'*

The cardtable is set out by the fire
– in any other house, its last resting place;
the light green pepper and salt hunch their shoulders
and prepare to tackle taste.

On the dresser, the boat built with matchsticks
by the men from the Curragh Concentration Camp
shines in the flares of light from the fire;
even dead matchsticks cart history's snort.

In summer, it is removed with the arrival
of aunty Gene Kay, from Darwen, Lancashire,
and a bowl of suede apples takes its place.
I mount the thirteen stairs, open the door

only father can close; cold leaps through clothes
and clutter, the curtains lid the window
and put in purdah the brooding stare
of the local mountain. I find the papers

my mother has kept, a ransacked history
tied in West Cork twine; one, black-bordered,
still shiny, announces the death of Michael Collins
at Beal na mBlat, the Mouth of Flowers.

I look at the pre-Munich picture of
Manchester United and cry for liking soccer.

STAYING IN BELFAST   (a 'literary' poem)

[Having read 'Flying to Belfast' by Craig Raine and
'Leaving Belfast' by Andrew Motion, in the Penguin
Book of so-called Contemporary British Poetry[Y] –]*

    "It was possible to laugh"
    – ha ha ha ha

    I laughed so much I could . . . fly
    away from Belfast

    as if I'd never been there
    but being there would look so good . . .

in a volume that sucks
the wind from the re-viewers' pens:

the sea the house the window
"Apple Charlotte"   "neat and orderly"

and the tired British Army
a well-intentioned fire brigade

out of sight but stabilising
so we don't need to mention them.

It's a hard road for poets (also)
actually a 'steep' one

and Belfast "rain and pity
grief twilight darkness . . . fear"

that clouds and moods and hues
these middleclass blues

voice always fear and fading
leading to such confusion.

like . . . like Ireland itself . . . a puzzle
incapable of solution.

This is the 'centre ground' of culture
S D P . . . slowly disappearing poetry

no smells of urine and onions here
nor beer . . . but a little waft of Esher

but . . . Promise too! Find what sells
first . . . then make it.

Our culture's dead but stay your fears
the funeral will last for years.

So continues the colonial dance
Do Not Disturb!
The British right to ignorance.

[* – *re whom, among voiceless others, see also 'Still Life' by Pat Condell (p115);*
ᵛ – *re which, see also 'Betrayal' by Zoë Brooks (p83)*   – Ed.]

*Counterpane (5' x 5'), painted by **Rita Donagh** in 1987/'88, has three interrelated subjects corresponding to the sources from which its imagery derives:*

1 – the photograph of a Bandsman lying face down, victim of an IRA bomb which exploded under the bandstand in Regent's Park, London on 20th July 1982;

2 – a map of the Six Counties (Lough Neagh) in Ireland;

3 – a very old threadbare patchwork quilt made from cloth and sacking, found in an empty homestead, birthplace of the artist's mother, in County Leitrim, Ireland.

The artist's hand holds the counterpane of the title over the dead (or sleeping?) figure, which floats above the landscape that dissolves into the picture plane.　　　　　*(R D, 1991)*

EDUCATION: SEX AND COUNTRY

In their wind-raped bivouacs held together
by spit and strut and superior arms,
they kneel, seethe and store in expectation,
before icons of multiplied lust –
skin minus biography, faceless rumps;
these representations of the raided real
procure an erotic itch which can't be
scratched outside a bossed, fantasy world.
Within this radar of appetites, help

was at hand; from Raymond's Revuebar came
thirty thousand copies of *Men Only*
(the exact opposite through Mail Order) –
to force the task along more easily,
and a saving of seven pounds sterling
on the next visit to the skin arcade
which can be made with, or without, limbs.
Our boys respond, hominus sharpiens,
their sighs extracted, their leers sanctioned,

as natural as if it were not taught,
like the careful creep of the newscaster's
smile, whenever they mention royalty.
Home they come, and transfer onto life
the infinite stare of silenced image.
As lone women circle warily by,
a cavalry of elbows reach for the sky;
the group salute through pelvis wishbone
out-turned in a snare of images,

confirming how good they would look on her.
When a bebop of go-go girls came out
to enterstrain the rawed troops, buoyed up with
the heat triggering from the Union Jack
to light their camp crawl in the colonies,
they promptly auctioned the sheets they'd slept in.
Home they come, pregnant with a nation's scheme
and dreams of meeting women, only women
and sticking them to walls with cellotape.

SNOW HILL
(Birmingham, Christmas Eve 1981)

. . . . the landscape a commodity of signs:
Xmas kitsch crackling from the slowed shops
bluelights gawp from police station redbrick
black traffic scribbles in the margin
of the hissing slush pushed into patches
that coat the '50s dual carriageway
stereoing sounds: woof and tweet of cars;

the skyline rages with indifference
and the sparring spires of Villa and Blues;
Ansells very bitter advertises
rooms of V-necked trouser macho-pine,
chemicals and country and Midlands music;

between two buildings lies a half burned sign,
all that's left of a Socialist bookshop
conflagrated by a Fascist who lobbed
a stolen car through the front,
fired it, and the owner, in the boot-tomb,
appetite unlocked by a previous shooting
from a crossbow at a passing Indian.

. . . . wrapped in the background, the Bullring exudes
the cusp and clang of classes, History –
you cannot make of this just what you will
Socialism, questions, snow on Snow Hill

John Cooper Clarke

psycle sluts

this disc concerns those pouting prima donnas found within the rapacious
ranks of the sexational psycle sluts – those nubile nihilists of the north
circular the lean leonine leatherette lovelies of the leeds intersection
luftwaffe angels locked in a pagan paradise – no cash a passion for trash
– the tough madonna whose cro-magnon face and crab nebular curves
haunt the highways of the UK whose harsh credo captures the collective
libido like crazy their lips pushed in the neon arc of a bumper car –
delightfully disciplined dum dum blonde deluxe deliciously deliciously
deranged twin-wheeled existentialists steeped in the sterile excrement
of a doomed democracy whose post-nietzschean sensibilities reject the
bovine gregariousness of a senile oligarchy – condemned to drift like
forgotten sputniks in a fool's orbit bound for the final roadblock fuelled
on the corroding liquids of lurid hopelessness they live for now and again
let the paper tigers flutter in their wake let the last bastions of the
bourgeois quake let the yellow running dog lackeys of imperialism stutter
and shake the prayers of the squares squeal for the merciful oblivion
of death and the stormtrooperettes of les punques nouveaux fifth column
close in – on a diet of dead babies and do-nuts blonde barbarians do
not bend their bloody road – it's woman minus woman in the erotic
nightmare of their kissing game – woman minus woman revenge by dark
degrees – spraycan manifestoes of one word abound in the pleasure
dromes and ersatz bodega bars of the free world the mechanics of love
grind like organs of iron to a standstill

beezley street

far flung crazy pavements crack
the sound of empty rooms
a clinical arrangement
a dirty afternoon
where the fecal germs of mr freud
are rendered obsolete
the legal term is null and void
in the case of beezley street

in the cheap seats where murder breeds
somebody is out of breath
sleep is a luxury they don't need
a sneak preview of death
deadly nightshade is your flower
manslaughter your meat
spend a year in a couple of hours
on the edge of beezley street

where the action isn't
that's where it is
state your position
vacancies exist
in an x certificate exercise
ex servicemen explete
keith joseph smiles and a baby dies
in a box on beezley street

from the boarding houses and the bedsits
full of accidents and fleas
somebody gets it
where the missing persons freeze
wearing dead men's overcoats
you can't see their feet
a riff joint shuts and opens up
right down on beezley street

cars collide colours clash
disaster movie stuff

for the man with the fu manchu moustache
revenge is not enough
there's a dead canary on a swivel seat
there's a rainbow in the road
meanwhile on beezley street
silence is the mode

it's hot beneath the collar
an inspector calls
where the perishing stink of squalor
impregnates the walls
the rats have all got rickets
they spit through broken teeth
a blood stain is your ticket
one way down beezley street

the gangster and his hired hat
drive a borrowed car
he looks like the duke of edinburgh
but not so lah-di-dah
OAP mother-to-be
watch that three-piece suite
when shitstopper drains
and crocodile skis
are seen on beezley street

in the kingdom of the blind
where the one-eyed man is king
beauty problems are redefined
the doorbells do not ring
light bulbs pop like blisters
the only form of heat
where a fellow sells his sister
down the river on beezley street

the boys are on the wagon
the girls are on the shelf
their common problem
is that they're not someone else
the dirt blows out
the dust blows in

you can't keep it neat
it's a fully furnished dustbin
16 beezley street

vince the ageing savage
betrays no kind of life
but the smell of yesterday's cabbage
and the ghost of last year's wife
through a constant haze
of deodorant sprays
he says retreat
alsatians dog the dirty days
down the middle of beezley street

eyes dead as viscous fish
look around for laughs
if i could have just one wish
i would be a photograph
on this permanent monday morning
get lost or fall asleep
when the yellow cats are yawning
round the back of beezley street

people turn to poison quick
as lager turns to piss
sweethearts are physically sick
every time they kiss
it's a sociologist's paradise
each day repeats
uneasy cheesy greasy queasy beastly beezley street

heaven ᴎom
the devil's do
Lowry". "We
accentuated t
rent man, was

The unpub
writing") in
Primadonna"
Found in a Bc
Man's Caviar"
"Death Takes

"It was time
put away a pep
split. Outside,
phone, elabora
a sky-blue Rel

salome maloney

i was walking down oxford road
dressed in what they call the mode
i could hear them spinning all the smash hits
at the mecca of the modern dance: the ritz

feet foxtrotted shoulders did the shimmy
the bouncer on the door said gimme gimme gimme
i gave him the ticket he gave me the shits
no healthy argument it's the ritz

standing by the cig machine who did I see
in lurex and terylene she hypnotised me
i asked her name and she said it's
salome maloney el supremo of the ritz

lacquered in a beehive her barnet didn't budge
wet-look lips smiled as sweet as fudge
she had a number on her back sequins on her tits
the sartorial requirements for women in the ritz

a man making like fred astaire spats and tails
douglas fairbanks moustache dirty fingernails
whose chosen vernacular was subtle as the blitz
charlie macdracula the phantom of the ritz

standing in the dandruff light trying to get pissed
among the headlice old spice brut and bodymist
how could she be seen dead dancing with that prick
and her being salome el supremo of the ritz

a smart move a dangerous curve
sent him arse over bollocks with a body swerve
he started with a cartwheel finished in the splits
leaving salome with his toupee in her mits

tables flew bottles broke the bouncers shouted lumber
the dummy got too chummy in a bing crosby number
the glass globe dropped chopped the crowd to bits
meanwhile what about salome of the ritz

when the ambulances came she was lying on the deck
she fell off her stiletto heels and broke her fucking neck
the band threw down their instruments the management threw fits
she's dead she don't bring the business to the ritz

the over twenty-one's night said it was a shame
the divorcee club will never be the same
joe loss edmundo ros and vic silvester quit
when the death dance drama did away with the ritz

the last waltz wilts the quickstep stops
the ladies' excuse me was permanently blocked
and mecca make a living selling little bits
of salome maloney in the wreckage of the ritz

track suit

two-tone stretch nylon yellow stripes on navy blue
i got a brand new track suit i got the old one too
i got the old one too

i got a new track suit
i wear it every day
keeps me cool and casual
i wore it yesterday
i wore it yesterday

i got a new track suit
i wear it everywhere
track me down to the training ground
maybe i'll be there
maybe i'll be there

wearing the brand new track suit
medicine ball to boot
knee pads an airline bag
and the overall smell of brut
the overall smell of fruit

expert eyes have scrutinized
and scientists agree
one track suit would suffice
but you're better off with three
you're better off with three

two-tone stretch nylon yellow stripes on navy blue
i got a brand new track suit i got the old one too

i got the old . . . 1 2

readers' wives

make a date with the brassy brides of britain
the altogether ruder readers' wives
who put down their needles and their knitting
at the doorway to our dismal daily lives

a fablon top scenario of passion
things stick out of holes in leatherette
they seem to be saying in their fashion
i'm freezing charlie have you finished yet

cold flesh the colour of potatoes
in an instamatic sitting room of sin
all the required apparatus
too bad they couldn't get her head in

in latex pyjamas with bananas going ape
identities are cunningly disguised
by a six-inch strip of insulating tape
strategically stuck across their eyes

wives from inverness to inner london
prettiness and pimples co-exist
pictorially wife-swapping with someone
who's happily married to his wrist

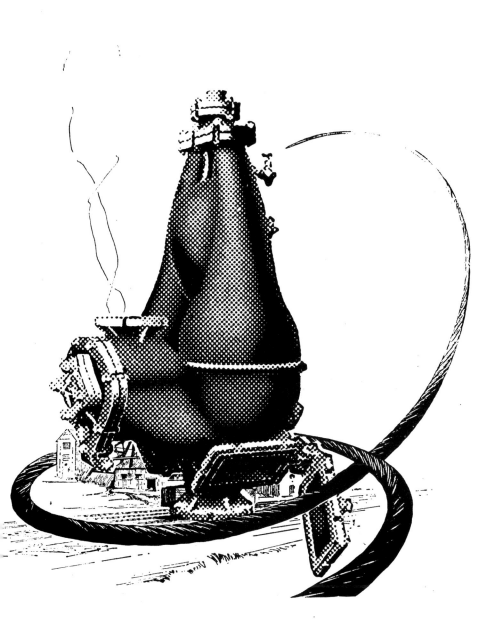

concussion

Io non mori, e non rimasi vivo . . .
("I did not die, yet nothing of life remained")
– *Dante*

the psycho in his rubber gloves
came round with the boys
he said "if music be the food of love
what's this fucking noise"
a mauler clamped around my wrist
with knuckles white as lard
he hit the hi-fi with his fist
it fell apart in shards
they were drinking all my vodka down
like low life vicious drunks
I wanna be a man about town
but not in little chunks
I ought to be more manly
and stand up for myself
but blood runs in my family
and I wouldn't have it anywhere else
liquid cosh a chemical pain
here comes the ground
it's thanks to the finest medical brains
I'm even around
the video went for a burton
the guys just fell about
when I said "please don't slam the curtains
and take the front door out"
what happened next is kind-of blurred
confusion took control
all I heard was a dirty word
my eyes began to roll
the light went out one step beyond
there's nothing left to see
my name comes up I can't respond
not even for a fee
there was no homicide
this much was ascertained
– oh no! I never died
but what of life remained

nothing

nothing isn't anything
it's tasteless and it's flat
nothing if it's anything
is even less than that
i've got that certain nothing
no one can do without
the spanish call it nada
i call it nowt
i'd take the train but don't care
to travel by myself
all the way from nowhere
to get to nowhere else
nothing ever goes on
nothing never ends
say nothing to no one
it's nothing to do with them
nothing going on and on
nothing wall to wall
it happens once and then it's gone
leaving bugger all

the pagan

Roses are reddish
Violets are blueish
If it weren't for Christmas
We'd all be Jewish

— Get born again
Like Ronald Reagan?
No thanks
I'd rather be a pagan

the pest

the pest pulled up propped his pushbike on a pillar box paused at a post
and pissed 'piss in the proper place' pronounced a perturbed pedestrian
and presently this particular part of the planet was plunged into a
panorama of public pressure and pleasure through pain the pandemonium
prompted the police who patrolled the precinct in pandacars to pull up
and peruse the problem while pickpockets picked pockets in pairs 'arrest
the pest who so pointedly pissed in that public place' pleaded the peeved
populace practically palpitating the powerful police picked up the pest
pronounced him a pinko a pansy a punk rocker and a poof they punched
him poked him pummeled his pelvis punctured his pipes played
ping-pong with his private parts and packed him in a place of penal
putrefaction he pondered upon progressive politics put pen to paper and
provocatively and persuasively propagated his personal political premise
– pity: a police provocateur put poison pellets in the pest's porridge the
police provocateur was promoted and the pest was presented with the
pulitzer peace prize

. . . posthumously.

Merle Collins

FEAR

Afraid
born afraid
turned around
and shuddered with fear
till forced by the knife

to look at the light
to scream with the fear
of ghosts unknown

afraid
always afraid

still at the corner
of a clamouring world
assuming a calm
in the teeth
of the storm

afraid
of the love
that binds
and demands
fearing the bond
that assumes
and controls

afraid to disappoint
faith
hope
the pain of life
in the teeth of the storm
the fear of the strife
to which we were born

afraid
always afraid
timidity fed
by blessings for the meek
fearing the power
that binds
and creates

afraid
we were always afraid
until we understood
that our fear
was
their greatest weapon.

THE SEARCH

I remember

The form
of my guilt
The blackness
of the dotted line
on the white paper
Name
Okay
Nationality?
Pen poised
Hand encircling paper now
Guilty fingers seeking
To hide
Nationality?

Friend
Absorbed too
Looked up
Well, Name
filled in
Nationality
Trinidadian
Held my breath
Hoping not to be reminded
That I
Complete with Irish name
Like hers
Was not yet Grenadian
But still . . . British
Jesus Christ!
British

But
Her own pen poised
She
Struggled with her own
Mammoth problem
Race?

Looked at my hand
Below
At the neatly pencilled
"African"
Goggled
Grinned
Said with awe
I put
"Black"

Shrugged
Looked at each other
Caught in the strange dilemma
Of non-belonging
Down again at the paper
Aspiring social-scientists
Sought
Next dotted line
On the tutor's paper
Social strata?
You put
Lower class?
Giggle
Giggle

Okay
I mean
What else?
What else?
Sitting on the balcony
of Block B
Within the far from
Lower class
Walls of Mona*
Two of the region's
Privileged few
Ashamed to be
Anything but

* – Jamaica campus of the University of the West Indies

What they called
In their forms
Lower class

Unsure of the claim
Unsure of much
Sure of wrong
Sure of search
Unwitting revolutionaries
Feeling the birth pains
Of moulding
A future belonging

I remember
the form of the past
foretelling
the shape
of things to come

WHAT TING IS DAT . . . ?

What is this thing
that they talking bout
Each time that ah turn?
Is a bird? Is a bee?
Is a thing that does sting?
Is a lizard? Is a frog?
Is a thing that does jump?

You don't mean is a person?
A being like me?
That could walk?
That could talk?
Make up me own image an ting?
Then is how come I become a
'ETHNIC MINORITY'?

It sound like a germ
It sound like a worm
It sound like something
that doesn't quite make the grade
the minority in me mouth
it have a vinegar taste
the ethnic you know
it sound like nigger to me?
You don't find it sounding
kinda like coolie to you?

Over there in South Africa
Azania to be
It have a few white people
with money that is not theirs
but we don't usually call them ethnic
even when is minority
is minority white regime, you know!

Down there in the Caribbean
it have a few people that is white
who into surfing and sailing
and plantation an ting
their laughter touching the stars
in the coolish night air
but we don't call them ethnic
we don't even call them minority, you know!
They not non-Black
they just positive, alright, okay, white!

So when people calling the cards
that mark with their mark
we can't play in the game
as if we in ting
we can't call weself ethnic
we not non-white
we just positive, beautiful BLACK!

"NO DIALECTS PLEASE . . ." *

In this competition
dey was lookin for poetry of worth
for a writin that could wrap up a feelin
an fling it back hard
with a captive power to choke de stars
so dey say,
"Send them to us
but NO DIALECTS PLEASE"
We're British!

Ay!
Well ah laugh till me boushet near drop
Is not only dat ah tink
of de dialect of de Normans and de Saxons
dat combine an reformulate
to create a language-elect
is not only dat ah tink
how dis British education mus really be narrow
if it leave dem wid no knowledge
of what dey own history is about
is not only dat ah tink
bout de part of my story
dat come from Liverpool in a big dirty white ship
mark
AFRICAN SLAVES PLEASE!
We're the British!

But as if dat not enough pain
for a body to bear
ah tink bout de part on de plantations down dere
Wey dey so frighten o de power
in the deep spaces
behind our watching faces
dat dey shout
NO AFRICAN LANGUAGES PLEASE!
It's against the law!
Make me ha to go
an start up a language o me own
dat ah could share wid me people

112

Den when we start to shout
bout a culture o we own
a language o we own
a identity o we own
dem an de others dey leave to control us say
STOP THAT NONSENSE NOW
We're all British!
Every time we lif we foot to do we own ting
to fight we own fight
dey tell us how British we British
an ah wonder if dey remember
dat in Trinidad in the thirties
dey jail Butler *
who dey say is their British citizen
an accuse him of
Hampering the war effort!
Then it was
FIGHT FOR YOUR COUNTRY, FOLKS!
You're British!

Ay! Ay!
Ah wonder when it change to
NO DIALECTS PLEASE!
WE'RE British!
Huh!
To tink how still dey so dunce
an so frighten o we power
dat dey have to hide behind a language
that we could wrap round we little finger
in addition to we own!
Heavens o mercy!
Dat is dunceness oui!
Ah wonder where is de bright British?

¥ _ Written in response to an advert requesting submissions for a poetry competition.
The organisers warned, "No Dialects Please. We're British."

* _ Grenadian trade union leader active in Trinidad strikes of the 1930s.

Pat Condell

MY CUPPA RUNNETH OVER

(we take you now to the lush
green fields of India
it's the picture on a packet of PG Tips
as a dusky maiden bends gracefully
to pick the nutritious leaves
against a backdrop of rural serenity
enter the queen of England & prince Philip
in safari suits with the plantation manager)

. . . alas your majesty
there are only 24 hours in a day
but the faster they work the more we pay
& the ones with good business sense
can earn as much as thirteen pence

excuse me while I finish this pastry . . .
more tea? another biscuit?
no speeches Phil, we can't risk it

. . . where absurdity meets obscenity
it's important not to fall in between
I'm sure you know what I mean

yes, the girls usually die first,
a cruel situation
but being weaker they need less food
& there's nothing so character-forming
as starvation

it keeps the lucky ones in their place
picking the tea you can really taste
while trained monkeys like you & me
add the milk & sugar on TV

STILL LIFE (1983)

this poet is serious, his verbs are
metaphors, his adjectives precise
& unnecessary; he writes in perfect

three line stanzas like this, he
teaches creative writing, there is
a right way & a wrong way, he teaches

the right way; he brings out a collection
every few years before arriving at
middle-age where he has always belonged;

poetry should not be trivialised
being his reason for breathing, no
never trivialised, it has a noble heart

& function; he has never heard of Bob
Marley; he likes the occasional archaic
turn of phrase, calls it his poetic

licence (you buy it at the post
office & wear it around your neck
in case anyone finds you wandering

in reality); the torn bough, the black
wing – his images are delicate, precise;
when you see him he'll be crouching

at a door marked 'posterity' hoping
someone comes to let him in before
the pubs close & the skinheads arrive

BEETLE

I watched a beetle on a tree
& pondered on its ancestry
addressing it in solemn voice
I said *"sir, if you had the choice*
you surely would not want to be
again a beetle on a tree
an insect without mind or soul
an ugly creature black as coal
scrabbling over bits of bark
like a blind man in the dark . . ."
& I had plenty more to say
but then the bastard flew away

MAN & DOG

" – dog
    you are so inaccessible
    you don't know any words
    & I never know what to say to you
    except
    I never know what to say to you
    what a stupid face
    & what a cruel race
    we humans are"

" – man
    did you know
    dog spelt backwards is god
    chien is neihc
    fido is odif
    & rin tin tin is nit nit nir?"

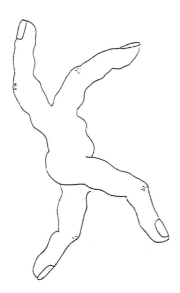

DRINAE

I

when 'tis nangule over yonder helm
with a thistle in the marchbrace
on a mainmoon in January
& belloggs are thwartling, & loomins are brool
& 'tis a loptheporous nangule, ammele or sorool,
& the lapshim are drangling, the nellobs look cool
& 'tis merrymild in the ass-pickling
& nobshule in the wule,
then spanch-nifflers will be scopulated
& nurf-chindlers will be drang
not with a whimper but a fucking bang

II

in lam-thwartning season the air is blue with the scrill of nebule
'tis a time of nanguish & bleur,
the blea-flotted spantule, & the debriferis,
if only all drinae could be like this

117

"Oh very well, what shall we talk about?"

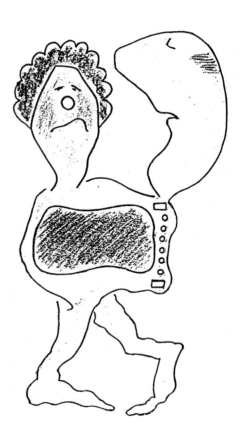

PSALM

The Lord is my telly; I shall not want.

2 He maketh me to lie down in green armchairs: he leadeth me beside old re-runs.

3 He restoreth my torpor: he leads me in the paths of advertisers for his name's sake.

4 Yea, though I walk through the valley of the shadow of prime time, I will fear no Dimbleby: for thou art with me; thy game shows & quizzes they comfort me.

5 Thou preparest a soap-opera in the presence of mine Horlicks: thou anointest my mind with trivia; my gut runneth over.

6 Surely Terry Wogan shall follow me all the days of my life: & I will dwell in the house of the Ewings forever.

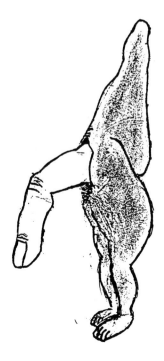

HEAD OF ENGLISH

Today we have a poet in the class.
A real live poet with a published book.
Notice the inkstained fingers girls. Perhaps
we're going to witness verse hot from the press.
Who knows. Please show your appreciation
by clapping. Not too loud. Now

sit up straight and listen. Remember
the lesson on assonance, for not all poems,
sadly, rhyme these days. Still. Never mind.
Whispering's, as always, out of bounds –
but do feel free to raise some questions.
After all, we're paying forty pounds.

Those of you with English Second Language
see me after break. We're fortunate
to have this person in our midst.
Season of mists and so on and so forth.
I've written quite a bit of poetry myself,
am doing Kipling with the Lower Fourth.

Right. That's enough from me. On with the Muse.
Open a window at the back. We don't
want winds of change about the place.
Take notes, but don't write reams. Just an essay
on the poet's themes. Fine. Off we go.
Convince us that there's something we don't know.

Well. Really. Run along now girls. I'm sure
that gave us insight to an outside view.
Applause will do. Thank you
very much for coming here today. Lunch
in the hall? Do hang about. Unfortunately
I have to dash. Tracey will show you out.

COMPREHENSIVE

Tutumantu is like hopscotch, Kwani-kwani is like hide-and-seek.
When my sister came back to Africa she could only speak
English. Sometimes we fought in bed because she didn't know
what I was saying. I like Africa better than England.
My mother says You will like it when we get our own house.
We talk a lot about the things we used to do
in Africa and then we are happy.

Wayne. Fourteen. Games are for kids. I support

122

the National Front. Paki-bashing and pulling girls'
knickers down. Dad's got his own mini-cab. We watch
the video. I Spit on your Grave. Brilliant.
I don't suppose I'll get a job. It's all them
coming over here to work. Arsenal.

Masjid at 6 o'clock. School at 8. There was
a friendly shop selling rice. They ground it at home
to make the evening nan. Families face Mecca.
There was much more room to play than here in London.
We played in an old village. It is empty now.
We got a plane to Heathrow. People wrote to us
that everything was easy here.

It's boring. Get engaged. Probably work in Safeways
worst luck. I haven't lost it yet because I want
respect. Marlon Frederic's nice but he's a bit dark.
I like Madness. The lead singer's dead good.
My mum is bad with her nerves. She won't
let me do nothing. Michelle. It's just boring.

Ejaz. They put some sausages on my plate.
As I was going to put one in my mouth
a Moslem boy jumped on me and pulled.
The plate dropped on the floor and broke. He asked me in Urdu
if I was a Moslem. I said Yes. You shouldn't be eating this.
It's a pig's meat. So we became friends.

My sister went out with one. There was murder.
I'd like to be mates, but they're different from us.
Some of them wear turbans in class. You can't help
taking the piss. I'm going in the Army.
No choice really. When I get married
I might emigrate. A girl who can cook
with long legs. Australia sounds all right.

Some of my family are named after the Moghul emperors.
Aurangzeb, Jehangir, Batur, Humayun. I was born
thirteen years ago in Jhelum. This is a hard school.
A man came in with a milk crate. The teacher told us
to drink our milk. I didn't understand what she was saying,
so I didn't go to get any milk. I have hope and am ambitious.
At first I felt as if I was dreaming, but I wasn't.
Everything I saw was true.

A PROVINCIAL PARTY, 1956

A chemical inside you secretes the ingredients of fear.
Is it fear? You know for sure you feel
uneasy on that black, plastic sofa, even though
the ice melts in a long tumbler behind red triangles.
You don't find it sexy, your first blue movie
in a stranger's flat, but you watch it anyway.

Embarrassment crackles like three petticoats. You never
imagined, married two years and all. A woman
cackles a joke you don't understand, but you laugh anyway.
On one stocking, you have halted a ladder
with clear varnish. There are things going on
on the screen which would turn your Mam to salt.

Suddenly, the whole room is breathing. Someone hums
Magic Moments and then desists, moist lips apart.
Two men in the film are up to no good. *Christ.*
You could die with the shame. The chrome ashtray
is filled with fag-ends, lipstick-rimmed. Your suspenders
pinch you spitefully, like kids nipping spoilsports.

You daren't look, but something is happening
on the Cyril Lord. Part of you tells yourself it's only
shaving-cream. You and him do it with the light off.
This will give him ideas. It *is* fear. You nudge and nudge
till your husband squirms away from you and smiles
at the young, male host with film-star eyes.

YOU JANE

At night I fart a guinness smell against the wife
who snuggles up to me after I've given her one
after the Dog and Fox. It's all muscle. You can punch
my gut and wait forever till I flinch. Try it.
Man of the house. Master in my own home. Solid.

Look at that bicep. Dinner on the table
and a clean shirt, but I respect her point of view.
She's borne me two in eight years, knows
when to button it. Although she's run a bit to fat
she still bends over of a weekend in suspenders.

This is the life. Australia next year and bugger
the mother-in-law. Just feel those thighs.
Karate keeps me like granite. Strength of an ox.
I can cope with the ale no problem. Pints
with the lads, a laugh, then home to her.

She says Did you dream, love? I never
dream. Sleep is as black as a good jar.
I wake half-conscious with a hard-on, shove it in.
She don't complain. When I feel, I feel here
where the purple vein in my neck throbs.

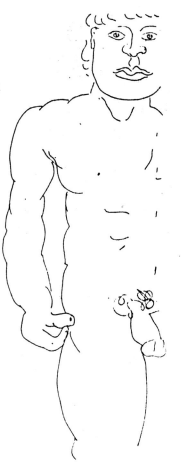

$

A one a two a one two three four –
boogie woogie chou chou cha cha chatta
noogie. Woogie wop a loo bop a wop
bim bam. Da doo ron a doo ron oo wop a
sha na? Na na hey hey doo wah did.
Um, didy ay didy shala lala lala lala,
boogie woogie choo choo cha cha bop.
(A woogie wop a loo bam) yeah yeah yeah.

125

LIVERPOOL ECHO

Pat Hodges kissed you once, although quite shy,
in sixty-two. Small crowds in Matthew Street
endure rain for the echo of a beat,
as if nostalgia means you will not die.

Inside phone-booths loveless ladies cry
on Merseyside. Their faces show defeat.
An ancient jukebox blares out Ain't She Sweet
in Liverpool, which cannot say goodbye.

Here everybody has an anecdote
of how they met you, were the best of mates.
The seagulls circle round a ferry-boat

out on the river, where it's getting late.
Like litter on the water, people float
outside the Cavern in the rain. And wait.

126

A SHILLING FOR THE SEA

You get a shilling if you see it first.
You take your lover to a bar nearby, late evening,
spend it all night and still have change. If,

if it were me, if it were you, we'd drink up
and leave; screw on the beach, with my bare arse
soaked by the night-tide's waves, your face moving
between mine and that gambler's throw of stars.

Then we'd dress and go back to the bar, order
the same again, and who's this whispering filthy suggestions
into my ear? *My tongue in the sea slow salt wet . . .*

Yes. All for a shilling, if you play that game.

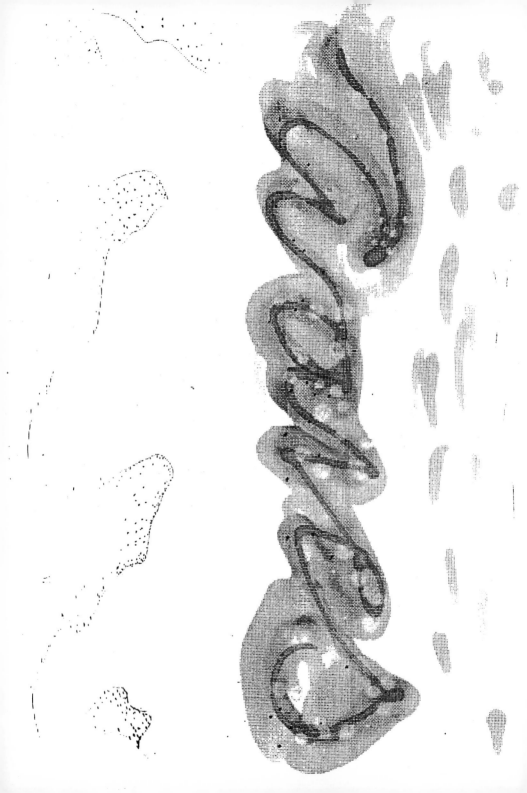

RIVER

At the turn of the river the language changes,
a different babble, even a different name
for the same river. Water crosses the border,
translates itself, but words stumble, fall back,
and there, nailed to a tree, is proof. A sign

in new language brash on a tree. A bird,
not seen before, singing on a branch. A woman
on the path by the river, repeating a strange sound
to clue the bird's song and ask for its name, after.
She kneels for a red flower, picks it, later
will press it carefully between the pages of a book.

What would it mean to you if you could be
with her there, dangling your own hands in the water
where blue and silver fish dart away over stone,
stoon, stein, like the meanings of things, vanish?
She feels she is somewhere else, intensely, simply because
of words; sings loudly in nonsense, smiling, smiling.

If you were really there what would you write on a postcard,
or on the sand, near where the river runs into the sea?

ORIGINALLY

We came from our own country in a red room
which fell through the fields, our mother singing
our father's name to the turn of the wheels.
My brothers cried, one of them bawling *Home,*
Home, as the miles rushed back to the city,
the street, the house, the vacant rooms
where we didn't live any more. I stared
at the eyes of a blind toy, holding its paw.

All childhood is an emigration. Some are slow,
leaving you standing, resigned, up an avenue
where no one you know stays. Others are sudden.
Your accent wrong. Corners, which seem familiar,
leading to unimagined, pebble-dashed estates, big boys
eating worms and shouting words you don't understand.
My parents' anxiety stirred like a loose tooth
in my head. *I want our own country,* I said.

But then you forget, or don't recall, or change,
and, seeing your brother swallow a slug, feel only
a skelf of shame. I remember my tongue
shedding its skin like a snake, my voice
in the classroom sounding just like the rest. Do I only think
I lost a river, culture, speech, sense of first space
and the right place? Now, *Where do you come from?*
strangers ask. *Originally?* And I hesitate.

IN YOUR MIND

The other country, is it anticipated or half-remembered?
Its language is muffled by the rain which falls all afternoon
one autumn in England, and in your mind
you put aside your work and head for the airport
with a credit card and a warm coat you will leave
on the plane. The past fades like newsprint in the sun.

You know people there. Their faces are photographs
on the wrong side of your eyes. A beautiful boy
in the bar on the harbour serves you a drink – what? –
asks you if men could possibly land on the moon.
A moon like an orange drawn by a child. No.
Never. You watch it peel itself into the sea.

Sleep. The rasp of carpentry wakes you. On the wall,
a painting lost for thirty years renders the room yours.
Of course. You go to your job, right at the old hotel, left,
then left again. You love this job. Apt sounds
mark the passing of the hours. Seagulls. Bells. A flute
practising scales. You swap a coin for a fish on the way home.

Then suddenly you are lost but not lost, dawdling
on the blue bridge, watching six swans vanish
under your feet. The certainty of place turns on the lights
all over town, turns up the scent on the air. For a moment
you are there, in the other country, knowing its name.
And then a desk. A newspaper. A window. English rain.

WAR PHOTOGRAPHER

In his darkroom he is finally alone
with spools of suffering set in ordered rows.
The only light is red and softly glows,
as though this were a church and he
a priest preparing to intone a Mass.
Belfast. Beirut. Phnom Penh. All flesh is grass.

He has a job to do. Solutions slop in trays
beneath his hands which did not tremble then
though seem to now. Rural England. Home again
to ordinary pain which simple weather can dispel,
to fields which don't explode beneath the feet
of running children in a nightmare heat.

Something is happening. A stranger's features
faintly start to twist before his eyes,
a half-formed ghost. He remembers the cries
of this man's wife, how he sought approval
without words to do what someone must
and how the blood stained into foreign dust.

A hundred agonies in black-and-white
from which his editor will pick out five or six
for Sunday's supplement. The reader's eyeballs prick
with tears between the bath and pre-lunch beers.
From the aeroplane he stares impassively at where
he earns his living and they do not care.

APE

There is a male silverback on the calendar.
Behind him the jungle is defocused,
except in one corner, where trees gargle the sun.

After you have numbered the days, you tear off
the page. His eyes hold your eyes
as you crumple a forest in your fist.

POET FOR OUR TIMES

I write the headlines for a Daily Paper.
It's just a knack one's born with all-right-Squire.
You do not have to be an educator,
just bang the words down like they're screaming *Fire!*
CECIL-KEAYS ROW SHOCK TELLS EYETIE WAITER.
ENGLAND FAN CALLS WHINGEING FROG A LIAR.

Cheers. Thing is, you've got to grab attention
with just one phrase as punters rush on by.
I've made mistakes too numerous to mention,
so now we print the buggers inches high.
TOP MP PANTIE ROMP INCREASES TENSION.
RENT BOY: ROCK STAR PAID ME WELL TO LIE.

I like to think that I'm a sort of poet
for our times. My shout. Know what I mean?
I've got a special talent and I show it
in punchy haikus featuring the Queen.
DIPLOMAT IN BED WITH SERBO-CROAT.
EASTENDERS' BONKING SHOCK IS WELL-OBSCENE.

Of course, these days, there's not the sense of panic
you got a few years back. What with the box
et cet. I wish I'd been around when the Titanic
sank. To headline that, mate, would have been the tops.
SEE PAGE 3 TODAY GENTS THEY'RE GIGANTIC.
KINNOCK-BASHER MAGGIE PULLS OUT STOPS.

And, yes, I have a dream — make that a scotch, ta —
that kids will know my headlines off by heart.
IMMIGRANTS FLOOD IN CLAIMS HEATHROW WATCHER.
GREEN PARTY WOMAN IS A NIGHTCLUB TART.
The poems of the decade . . . *Stuff 'em! Gotcha!*
The instant tits and bottom line of art.

DEBT

He was all night sleepless over money.
Impossible scenarios danced in the dark
as though he was drunk. The woman
stirred, a soft spoon, and what had emerged
from them dreamed in the next room, safe.
He left himself and drew a gun he didn't own.

He won the pools; pearls for her and ponies
for the kids. The damp bedroom was an ocean-liner
till the woman farted. drifted on, away from him.
Despair formed a useless prayer and worry an ulcer.
He bargained with something he could not believe in
for something he could not have. *Sir . . .*

Through the wallpaper men in suits appeared.
They wanted the video, wanted his furniture.
They wanted the children. Sweat soured in nylon sheets
as his heartbeat panicked, trying to get out.
There was nothing he would not do. There was
nothing to do but run the mind's mad films.

Dear Sir . . . his ghost typed on. He remembered
waiting for her, years ago, on pay-day
with a bar of fruit-and-nut. Somehow consoled
he reached out, found her, and then slept.
Add this. Take that away. The long night leaked
cold light into the house. A letter came.

MAKING MONEY

Turnover. Profit. Readies. Cash. Loot. Dough. Income. Stash.
Dosh. Bread. Finance. Brass. I give my tongue over
to money; the taste of warm rust in a chipped mug
of tap-water. Drink some yourself. Consider
an Indian man in Delhi, Salaamat the *niyariwallah*,
who squats by an open drain for hours, sifting shit
for the price of a chapati. More than that. His hands

in crumbling gloves of crap pray at the drains
for the pearls in slime his grandfather swore he found.

Megabucks. Wages. Interest. Wealth. I sniff and snuffle
for a whiff of pelf; the stench of an abattoir blown
by a stale wind over the fields. Roll up a fiver,
snort. Meet Kim. Kim will give you the works,
her own worst enema, suck you, lick you, squeal
red weals to your whip, be nun, nurse, nanny,
nymph on a credit card. Don't worry.
Kim's only in it for the money. Lucre. Tin. Dibs.

I put my ear to brass lips; a small fire's whisper
close to a forest. Listen. his cellular telephone
rings in the Bull's car. Golden hello. Big deal. Now get this
straight. *Making a living is making a killing these days.*
Jobbers and brokers buzz. He paints out a landscape
by number. The Bull. Seriously rich. Nasty. One of us.

Salary. Boodle. Oof. Blunt. Shekels. Gelt. Funds.
I wallow in coin, naked; the scary caress of a fake hand
on my flesh. Get stuck in. Bergama. The boys from the bazaar
hide on the target-range, watching the soldiers fire. Between bursts,
they rush for the spent shells, cart them away for scrap.
Here is the catch. Some shells don't explode. Ahmat
runs over grass, lucky for six months, so far. So
bomb-collectors die young. But the money's good.

Palmgrease. Smackers. Greenbacks. Wads. I widen my eyes
at a fortune, a set of knives on black cloth, shining,
utterly beautiful. Weep. The economy booms
like cannon, far out at sea on a lone ship. We leave
our places of work, tired, in the shortening hours, in the time
of night our town could be anywhere, and some of us pause
in the square, where a clown makes money swallowing fire.

LOSERS

Con-artists, barefaced liars, clocks shuffle the hours slowly.
Remember the hands you were dealt, the full-house of love,
the ace-high you bluffed on. Never again. Each day
is a new game, sucker, with mornings and midnights
raked in by the dealer. Did you think you could keep those cards?

Imagination is memory. We are the fools who dwell in time
outside of time. One saves up for a lifelong dream, another
spends all she has on a summer decades ago. The clocks
click like chips in a casino, piled to a wobbly tower. An hour
fills up with rain. An hour runs down a gutter into a drain.

Where do you live? In a kiss in a darkened cricket pavilion
after the war? Banker? In the scent, from nowhere, of apples
seconds before she arrived? Poet? You don't live here
and now. Where? In the day your mother didn't come home? Priest?
In the chalky air of the classroom, still? Doctor? Assassin? Whore?

Look at the time. There will be more but there is always less.
Place your bets. Mostly we do not notice our latest loss
under the rigged clocks. Remember the night we won! The times
it hurts are when we grab the moments for ourselves, nearly –
the corniest sunset, taste of a lover's tears, a fistful of snow –

and the bankrupt feeling we have as it disappears.

MRS SKINNER, NORTH STREET

Milk bottles. Light through net. No post. Cat,
come here by the window, settle down. Morning
in this street awakes unwashed; a stale wind
breathing litter, last night's godlessness. This place
is hellbound in a handcart, Cat, you mark
her words. Strumpet. Slut. A different man
for every child; a byword for disgrace.

Her dentures grin at her, gargling water
on the mantelpiece. The days are gone
for smiling, wearing them to chatter down the road.
Good morning. Morning. Lovely day. Over the years
she's suffered loss, bereavement, loneliness.
A terrace of strangers. An old ghost
mouthing curses behind a cloudy, nylon veil.

Scrounger. Workshy. Cat, where is the world
she married, was carried into up a scrubbed stone step?
The young louts roam the neighbourhood.
Breaking of glass. Chants. Sour abuse of aerosols.
That social worker called her *xenophobic*. When he left
she looked the word up. Fear, morbid dislike, of strangers.
Outside, the rain pours down relentlessly.

People scurry for shelter. How many hours
has she sat here, Cat, filled with bitterness
and knowing they'll none of them come?
Not till the day the smell is noticed.
Not till the day you're starving, Cat, and begin
to lick at the corpse. She twitches the curtain
as the Asian man next door runs through the rain.

DEPORTATION

They have not been kind here. Now I must leave,
the words I've learned for supplication,
gratitude, will go unused. Love is a look
in the eyes in any language, but not here,
not this year. They have not been welcoming.

I used to think the world was where we lived
in space, one country shining in big dark.
I saw a photograph when I was small.

Now I am *Alien*. Where I come from there are few jobs,
the young are sullen and do not dream. My lover

138

bears our child and I was to work here, find
a home. In twenty years we would say This is you
when you were a baby, when the plum tree was a shoot . . .

We will tire each other out, making our homes
in one another's arms. We are not strong enough.

They are polite, recite official jargon endlessly.
Form F. Room 12. Box 6. I have felt less small
below mountains disappearing into cloud
then entering the Building of Exile. Hearse taxis
crawl the drizzling streets towards the terminal.

I am no one special. An ocean parts me from my love.

Go back. She will embrace me, ask what it was like.
Return. One thing – there was a space to write
the colour of her eyes. They have an apple here,
a bitter-sweet, which matches them exactly. Dearest,

without you I am nowhere. It was cold.

THE LITERATURE ACT

My poem will be a fantasy about living in a high-rise flat,
on the edge of a dirty industrial town, as the lawful wife of a yob
who spent the morning demonstrating in the market square
for the benefit of the gutter press. This was against a book
of which he violently disapproves
                                    and which was written by some cunt
who is a blasphemer or a lesbian or whose filth is being studied
in our local schools as part of some pisspot exam, the bastard.
I feel a thrill of fear as I imagine frying his evening meal
and keeping his children quiet as he shouts at the News. Later
he will thrash in the bed, like a fish out of water, not censoring
the words and pictures in his head. I would like my poem
to be given to such a man by the Police. Should he resist
I would like him to be taken to court; where the Jury,
the Judge, will compel him to learn it by heart. Every word.

140

DREAM OF A LOST FRIEND

You were dead, but we met, dreaming,
before you had died. Your name, twice,
then you turned, pale, unwell. *My dear,*
my dear, must this be? A public building
where I've never been, and, on the wall,
an AIDS poster. Your white lips. *Help me.*

We embraced, standing in a long corridor
which harboured a fierce pain neither of us felt yet.
The words you spoke were frenzied prayers
to Chemistry; or you laughed, a child-man's laugh,
innocent, hysterical, out of your skull. *It's only*
a dream, I heard myself saying, *only a bad dream.*

Some of our best friends nurture a virus, an idle,
charmed, purposeful enemy, and it dreams
they are dead already. In fashionable restaurants,
over the crudités, the healthy imagine a time
when all these careful moments will be dreamed
and dreamed again. *You look well. How do you feel?*

Then, as I slept, you backed away from me, crying
and offering a series of dates for lunch, waving.
I missed your funeral, I said, knowing you couldn't hear
at the end of the corridor, thumbs up, acting.
Where there's life . . . Awake, alive, for months I think of you
almost hopeful in a bad dream where you were long dead.

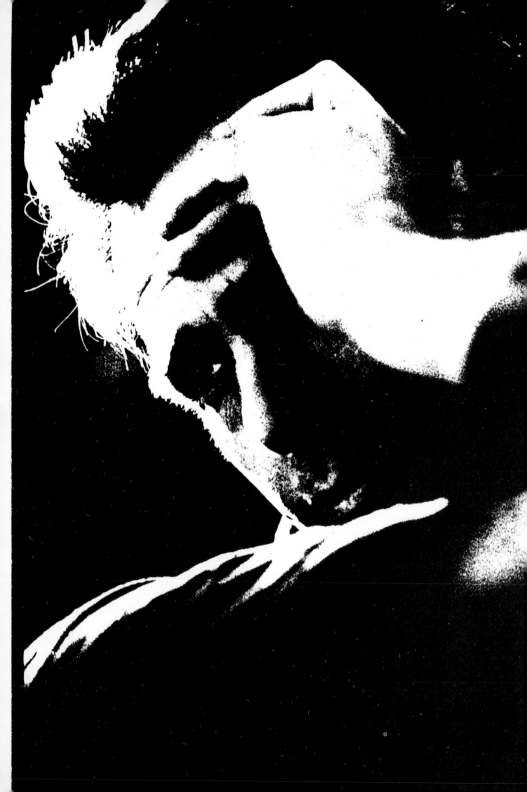

Peter Gabriel

MOTHER OF VIOLENCE

Walking the streets with her naked feet
so full of rhythm but i can't find the beat
snapping her heels, clicking her toes
everybody knows just where she goes

fear, fear – she's the mother of violence
making me tense to watch the way she breed
fear, she's the mother of violence
you know self-defence is all you need
it's getting hard to breathe
it's getting so hard to believe
to believe in anything at all

mouth all dry, eyes bloodshot
data stored in microdot
kicking the cloud with my moccasin shoes
tv dinner, tv news

fear, fear – she's the mother of violence
don't make any sense to watch the way she breed
fear, she's the mother of violence
making me tense to watch the way she feed
the only way you know she's there
is the subtle flavour in the air
getting hard to breathe
hard to believe in anything at all
but fear

THE FAMILY AND THE FISHING NET

suffocated by mirrors, stained by dreams
her honey belly pulls the seams
curves are stiff upon the hinge
pale zeros tinge the tiger skin

moist as grass, ripe and heavy as the night
the sponge is full, well out of sight
all around the conversations
icing on the warm fresh cake

light creeps through her secret tunnel
sucked into the open spaces
burning out in sudden flashes
draining blood from well-fed faces

desires form in subtle whispers
flex the muscles in denial
up and down its pristine cage
so the music, so the trial

vows of sacrifice, headless chickens
dance in circles, they the blessed
man and wife, undressed by all
their grafted trunks in heat possessed

even as the soft skins tingle
they mingle with the homeless mother
who loves the day but lives another
that once was hers

the worried father, long lost lover
brushes ashes with his broom
rehearses jokes to fly and hover
bursting over the bride and groom
and the talk goes on
memories crash on tireless waves
– the lifeguards whom the winter saves

silence falls the guillotine
all the doors are shut

144

nervous hands grip tight the knife
in the darkness, till the cake is cut
passed around, in little pieces
the body and the flesh
the family and the fishing net
another, another in the net

FAMILY SNAPSHOT

the streets are lined with camera crews
everywhere he goes is news
today is different
today is not the same
today i make the action
take snapshot into the light
            snapshot into the light
            i'm shooting into the light

four miles down the cavalcade moves on
driving into the sun
if I worked it out right
they won't see me or the gun

i've been waiting for this
i have been waiting for this
all the people in tv land –
i will wake up your empty shells
peak-time viewing blown in a flash
as I burn into your memory cells
'cos I, I'm alive

they're coming round the corner with the bikers at the front
i'm wiping the sweat from my eyes
            it's a matter of time
            – it's a matter of time
and the governor's car is not far behind

he's not the one I've got in mind
'cos there he is – the man of the hour
    standing in the limousine

"i don't really hate you
    i don't care what you do
we were made for each other
   – me and you
i want to be somebody
    you were like that too
if you don't get given you learn to take
and I will take you"
holding my breath
release the catch
and i let the bullet fly –

all turned quiet – I have been here before
lonely boy hiding behind the front door

friends have all gone home
there's my toy gun on the floor
come back mum and dad
you're growing apart
you know that I'm growing up sad
i need some attention
    i shoot into the night

WALLFLOWER

six by six, from wall to wall
shutters on the windows, no light at all
damp on the floor, you got damp in the bed
they're trying to get you crazy – get you out of your head

146

they feed you scraps and they feed you lies
to lower your defences – no compromise
nothing you can do, the day can be long
your mind is working overtime, your body's not too strong
                    hold on, hold on
they put you in a box so you can't get heard
let your spirit stay unbroken, may you not be deterred
                    hold on
you have gambled with your own life
and you face the night alone
while the builders of the cages
sleep with bullets, bars and stone
they do not see your road to freedom
that you build with flesh and bone

they take you out – the light burns your eyes
to the talking room – it's no surprise
loaded questions from clean white coats
their eyes are all as hidden as their hippocratic oath
they tell you – how to behave, behave as their guest
you want to resist them, you do your best
they take you to your limits, they take you beyond
for all that they are doing there's no way to respond
                    hold on, hold on
they put you in a box so you can't get heard
let your spirit stay unbroken, may you not be deterred

                    hold on
you have gambled with your own life
and you face the night alone
while the builders of the cages
sleep with bullets, bars and stone
they do not see your road to freedom
that you build with flesh and bone
though you may disappear, you're not forgotten here
and I will say to you, i will do what I can do

you may disappear, you're not forgotten here
and i will say to you, i will do what i can do

147

HERE COMES THE FLOOD

When the night shows
the signals grow on radios
all the strange things
they come and go as early warnings
stranded starfish have no place to hide
still waiting for the swollen Easter tide
there's no point in direction we cannot even choose a side

i took the old track
the hollow shoulder, across the waters
on the tall cliffs
they were getting older, sons and daughters
the jaded underworld was riding high
waves of steel hurled metal at the sky
and as the nails sunk in the cloud, the rain was warm
and soaked the crowd

> *Lord, here comes the flood*
> *we'll say goodbye to flesh and blood*
> *if again the seas are silent*
> *in any still alive*
> *it'll be those who gave their island to survive*
> *drink up, dreamers, you're running dry*

when the flood calls
you have no home, you have no walls
in the thunder crash
you're a thousand minds, within a flash
don't be afraid to cry at what you see
the actors gone, there's only you and me
and if we break before the dawn, they'll use up what
we used to be

> *Lord, here comes the flood*
> *we'll say goodbye to flesh and blood*
> *if again the seas are silent*
> *in any still alive*
> *it'll be those who gave their island to survive*
> *drink up, dreamers, you're running dry*

WAITING FOR THE BIG ONE

like the man says   surehope Mo - ses knows his ro___ ses___

we'll all be wai - ting for the big   one___

once I was a cre - dit   aah!   to my cre - dit card

spent what I had - n't got   it was - n't hard

no trust in judge - ments___   no trust in mo - ney

some-day I'll find my - self like a   bee   find - ing ho___ney   aah___

but in the mean - time___ aah!___   gon - na have me___ some

fun   wai - ting for the big   one   one too ma - ny___   when

e go___   I go too___   look- ing for the real - thing   it don't

150

come from what I do   no real com-mun-i-ca___ tion moves

out of my face___ I'm___ be-gin-ning- to think   Yeah! I'm

just out__ of place_____ aah!_____ won't get in   too deep

I   want   to   get some   sleep _____

to   be   rea   dy___   for   the   big

one   to be rea dy___   for the big   one.   (Instrum.)

wai-ting for   the   big   one.

151

RHYTHM OF THE HEAT
(Inspired by Jung's visit to the Sudan)

looking out the window
i see the red dust clear
high up on the red rock
stands the shadow with the spear

the land here is strong
strong beneath my feet
it feeds on the blood
it feeds on the heat

the rhythm is below me
the rhythm of the heat
the rhythm is around me
the rhythm has control

the rhythm is inside me
the rhythm has my soul

the rhythm of the heat
the rhythm of the heat
the rhythm of the heat
the rhythm of the heat

drawn across the plainland
to the place that is higher
drawn into the circle
that dances round the fire
we spit into our hands
and breathe across the palms
raising them up high
held open to the sun

self-conscious, uncertain
i'm showered with the dust
the spirit enters into me
and I submit to trust

smash the radio
no outside voices here
smash the watch
cannot tear the day to shreds
smash the camera
cannot steal away the spirits
the rhythm is around me
the rhythm has control
the rhythm is inside me
the rhythm has my soul

Galliano (Rob Gallagher)

COME DOWN THERE'S A RIOT GOING ON

The alleys in my mind – full of business
streets full of faces of black n white n brown
as I lead a charge against me
brandishing a Molotov and a magazine
calling at others for the downfall . . . . .
The streets in my head are pure rumpus
they echo with looting, meetings
while graffiti are sprayed on the walls of my brains,
bottles and stones rain on the back of my eyes,
nose bleeds half-bricks from the inside,
joy-riders take a wrong turn and fall out my ears.
No piece is at peace. They torch the town hall
out of my control. Babylon flashes in
'for my own safety,' I'm distressed
by a Stop-and-Search
                              – inside my head!
I enflame my tonsils,
set alight my throat – Bwoy: now Special Units
are rushed into my ears
   – I appeal to the Higher Authority
but I'm nowhere to be found
. . . last seen walkin wid a boof boof
somewhere in Upper Cranium Street.
Vandals swing from my hair roots
and I'm Caught,
marched past a waving crowd
and down my nostrils
– charged with disturbing my own peace of mind.

154

MOTHER NATURE

. . . Mother sets me down
in the valley of the trees:
a cold night covers the valley
but the moonlight lets me see.

I drop from rocks to water
into volcanic springs:
I stretch out the body
and the mind's walls within.

Inside I fall asleep
upon a bamboo mat:
mother whispers she'll protect me
    – her five sons see to that.

    – five sons of the mother
    – five sons of the mother
    – five sons of the mother
    – five sons of the mother
      – earth   – metal
       – wood   – fire
        – water . . .

    I wake in the morning
    – there I sit and gaze
    at a red and gold-green blanket
    the leaves blend to a haze.

The water warms my limbs,
the moist air fills my lungs
    – high up on the hill
the four seasons' song is sung.

Then she takes me up on high,
lets me rest way up the sky
and chill on a cloud
while jets roar past so loud

   – I gaze down at the coastline
where the people's borders shine:
dotted roads stretch across the land
barred from Neptune's manor beyond the sand.

   Day rubs its eyes
   then lights up the night
   who goes off on a walk
   to somewhere out of sight.

Mother sits me on her throne,
makes her unlimited secrets known
   – I realise mother is all
then realise
    this body
     so small . . .

   – but nature bore me – I am she
   – you look at yourself
from horizon to sea:
the mother smiles – I smile at me!

156

Give land to the people
and people to the land:
you can't own either
so grow to understand

– it's all here before us,
gonna be here when we're gone:
to own any more – you know
surely it must be wrong.

So – not own or control
but a union we must seek
with mother's five sons
or this human kind grow weak:

  – *five sons of the mother*
  – *five sons of the mother*
  – *five sons of the mother*
  – *five sons of the mother*
      – *earth*   – *metal*
    – *wood*   – *fire*
              – *water*

Adam Horovitz

TALIESIN POEM

I have been
　　　　the growth point of a tree
　　　a weaver making lace
　　　　an industrial chimney

I have been
　　　　a girl's striped jumper
　　　a cross of wood
　　　　a lithe young cat
　　　a dead mouse on the path
　　　　a summer drought
　　the grass gone brown

I have been
　　　　marbles broken into dust
　　　a sheep skull's cavity of bone
　　　　a soldier and the bullet
　　　a dead man screaming for his wife

TEARS LIKE LAVA
(clay figures)

Two little people
stand fossilised;
their love frozen,
their bodies stone,
joined in deathly matrimony,
Siamese by destruction.

They smile at winter,
stare at the sun.
The weather
wears them down.
They stand
crying;
tears like lava.

158

SHE LOCKED MY HEART IN A CELLAR

my mind melds with the sunlight
touches the autumn breeze
but beauty beckons the unlight
and my blood begins to freeze

I am dying slowly and painfully
love's cancer of the heart
and she passes by disdainfully
not giving me a thought

I'm too weak to tell her
what she really means to me
she's locked my heart in a cellar
and thrown away the key

PEACE

Guns,
barren now,
no men willing
to work these death toys.
They gaze round idly.

Bloodstained daisies sing
'Peace of mind
to men of goodwill.
Those who seek
to kill
will blow as ashes in the wind.'

Rusty now, the guns
crumble into dust,
moss and bramble choked.
Twists of convolvulus
along the barrels:
white trumpets
fanfare in the wind.

HATE

I have seen films of pastures of hate,
bombed buildings, burnt-out cars.
Wallpaper floating on the wind
like the souls of those
who once lived in these battered buildings.
A scream,
a team of sirens wailing,
hosepipes flailing.
A whoosh of water, the fire is out.
Ambulance men check,
no survivors.

AN OWL BREAKS THE SILENCE

In the deepening contrast
between night and day
when an owl breaks the silence
and the foxes bay
when the chattering chaffinch
lays down its tune
and tissue moths
flit past the moon
when millions of fireflies
wisp in the dusk
and the butterfly's cocoon
is merely a husk
when the badger is starting
its nightly round
and the rabbit is keeping
its nose to the ground
when snails creep out
from under the rocks
and chickens begin
to forget the fox
then the humans in offices
will do something rash
and when it snows
will it snow ice or ash?

Mahmood Jamal

SUICIDE

A bird sat on a green branch
                    singing.
A bird sat with its beak against
                    its breast.
A bird sat with its beak
                    lost in its feathers.
A bird sat bleeding red flowers
                    from its breast.
A bird sat on a tree
                    eating its own heart,
splattering leaves with red stars.
A bird sat near evening on a tree.
A bird fell from a tree
                    leaving blood-heavy leaves,
and a branch stretching
                    into darkest night.

SILENCE

Let my silence speak out
through these words.
Let it seep through these sounds
imperceptibly
as the air we breathe
permeates our blood.

Let the silence

grow as the words grow denser
thickets, bushes, thorny branches
standing in a windless evening;
silent
brooding darkly of day
passing shadow-like
into the dark.

The silence of deep deserted
eyes
        and pitch black
tears.
The silence of moonlight
over the shanty towns.
The silence
inside a gun's mouth
when the bullet has flown.
The silence
of a child's twisted belly
and his old eyes.

Let my silence speak
as the eloquent silence
of lovers;
the silence of clouds passing
and black evening hills;
the silence of dew damply
falling over graves.
So the silence
can grow as the noise grows
about us of robots
and demagogic lights
that shriek out on the desolate highways
their neon screams.

So that the dark
can be discovered
So that the silenced
are not forgotten

Let my silence be loud.

SWAMPED

These are amazing people,
Let us give the devil his due.
From a small island off the coast of Europe,
came down in their ships
with guns swords and whips;
creating men in their likeness,
making tea and tie
synonymous with respectability.
Destroyed the natives of America
to make room for their exiles, thieves.
Exterminated the Caribs
and created the West Indies.
Left quietly as gentlemen often do
with minimum of fuss
but with a lot of loot.
Now we hear they're losing sleep
over a handful of blacks at the bottom of the heap
because their culture is threatened
because they are being *SWAMPED!*

IMMIGRANT

Distances,
the distance
between me and myself;
the left behind
and the possibility
and the excluded middle
(most certain
of all)
the I that always
arrives at the wrong place
and stays.

164

THE ALIEN STAR

The alien star
shone in the corner
of the sky
with its strange light.
It stood there
clumsily in the midst
of collapsing giants.
Time wove a rainbow blanket
around its waist;
history chained it
to another galaxy.

At night
it stole a smile
and in the day
when no other stars
could see it
it wept.
Through the alien
blankness, its dusty tears fell
to where a new galaxy
was burning
made of millions
of fragments
            of alien stars.

SITAR PLAYER

The still boat on the river,
the tall grass
through which she moves and floats away,
carried by the currents
of fingertips . . .

She steps on a thorn
and her body shudders
and bends towards her feet;
your fingers biting
into the strings
bleed out a story of love.

And the poverty of roses!

As a sudden breeze
catches the edge of her dress
and enrhythms
the cold stillness of a tree,
the dance begins
in the restless strings
straining against their voices
again and again;
and the fingers no longer yours
but the dancing girl

gone out across the river . . .

A boat drifts, a girl wanders,
the sound of water,
the sound of grass,
the sound of fingers bleeding

in the rebellion on strings!

AGAINST CLICHÉS

Although death may appear
black as night
or dark as a well
ultimately
it is as white as bones.

WEDDING

Women weep, sisters and mothers weep
knowing what partings mean
knowing the meaning of playing a part
knowing the truth
of distances, dreams and men.

Momentarily, mother becomes bride
in the midst of perfume and flower
her first look at the past
her last look at the future.
The women wail
the mother embraces her child
tears soaking into each others' shoulders.

No man can comprehend
No man can cast asunder
that bond of partings and tears
that unites them
our sisters, our mothers.

from THE ADVENTURES OF WILLIE *(a sequence)*

A HARD NUT TO CRACK

His hands clenched
Around the walnut
They were too soft
To break the stubborn shell
He tried his teeth
They almost disappeared
Into his gums
So Willie took a hammer
Bang! Bang! Crash!
The shell gave way
The floor gave way
The house gave way
The earth gave way
And Willie stumbled
Unable to balance
Fell into the hole
He created
His hammer firmly
Held continuing the blow
Into the emptiness
Of space.

WILLIE TRIES TO MAKE CONTACT

He touched the tree
It turned into a pylon

He touched the little girl
She turned into a doll

He touched the dog
It turned into a car and sped away

He touched a hand
It turned into a glove

He touched a shoulder
It turned into a road-sign

He touched her hair
It turned into nylon

He touched her head
It turned into a book-case

He kissed her eyes
They turned to glass

He touched her voice
It turned into a radio

He picked up a flower
It turned to plastic

He whistled a tune
It turned into a sonic boom

He picked up a mushroom
It turned into a fall-out

Tired
      Terrified
            Perplexed

Cautiously very cautiously
He touched

Himself . . .

Linton Kwesi Johnson

from a set of poems titled TINGS AN' TIMES

STORY

wance upan a time
jus like inna nursery rime
before piggy tun swine

mi did wear
mi fear
pan mi face
like a shiel
like a mawsk

an evrybady tink mi cool an deadly

nottn yu coulda seh
woulda mek mi tek it awf
an if yu get mi nervos
ah woulda jus lawf it awf

an everybady tink mi cool an deadly

but nat soh lang ago
jus like inna pitcha show
whey di hero get a blow

mi spirit get vex
an mi get soh ressless
dat mi get careless
an goh bare mi mawgah chess

mi nevvah indah tink seh
dat it mek outa glaas
dat di whole wide worl coulda si
rite dung to di vien inna mi awt

ow dem twis-up
ow dem tie-up
ow dem tite-up
o mi awt
ow it cut-up
ow it craw-up
ow it scar-up

(it is a aad awt fi mawstah yu know
dis smilin an skinnin yu teet
wen yu awt swell-up soh till yuh feel it a goh bus
wen yu cyaan fine di rime fi fit de beat
wen yu cyaan fine di ansah fi di puzzle complete)

soh mi tek awf mi mawsk
an staat fi wear daak glaas
but evry so awftin
mi haffi tek it awf
an evry now an den
mi fine mi laas

oonu evah
si mi trial
si mi crawsiz?

171

Timothy Emlyn Jones

. . . . pass . . . .

. . . . pass pass pass pass pass pass pass pass pass pass run   pass
pass pass pass pass pass pass pass pass pass   run pass pass
pass pass pass pass pass pass pass pass run faster run   pass
fast faster go kick go   past run run shoot (shoot) oh oooh   kick
pass pass pass (pass)

                pass
                    pass
                      pass
                        pass to the left
                              (left)
pass
    pass to the centre pass   pass
                oh
come up
      come up on the outside
                  run
come

      come
        come my darling
come gentle
       here
         (here)
        in ease
           pass the winter's sun

easy
    ease the ball
         stall
               watch for the moment
                        toe it turn
                                ease the moment
seize the instant
        shoot

an arc of grace sprung high
                the sun its keystone
shaping a shimmering vault
             a canopy of prayer and delight
             a drift of sky
                   arena of flight
             a cathedral of play
                  of tribal rite

lam the ball
            boot it
                    belt it one
                            no no
                                    kick it
                                            bollocks you cunt
                                                    hit it

kick the fucking thing
                    get it in there
                                    twat
                            and that moment has its presence

goal
    goal
            it's a goal
                    it's a fucking shitting goal
                                            (goal)

hands cascade upwards radiating the cold sun with material human light
cheer
        delight and tremor
                        a sense of the right

but here
        here gentle
                    gentle gentle
                                past
                                pass
                                    we are always the moment
                                                            pass

shining
        the radiant moment
                        pass . . . .

173

PROPOSITION:
MAN·AS·A·WINDOW

TIMOTHY·EMLYN·JONES

THE·SOUL·IS·A·SHADOW·ON·THE·BLIND

THE·SOUL·IS·THE·SHADOW·OF·THE·BLIND

THE·SOLDIER·IS·A·SHADOW·OF·THE·MIND

BOLDER · IS · THE · SHADOW · OF · THE · MIND

OLDER · IS · SADNESS · AND · UNKIND

ORDER IS SADNESS, UNREFINED

ORDERS · TO · SATISFY · AND · UNBIND

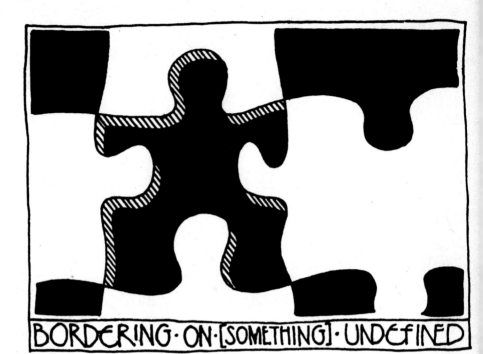

BORDERING · ON · [SOMETHING] · UNDEFINED

FALLING · INTO · THE · MEMORY · OUT · OF · TIME

& ONE BELOW BEYOND THE GATE OF THE EAST?

THE TREE GROWS IN TWO GARDENS, ONE ABOVE?

ITS SAP IS THE SEED OF ISRAEL.

ITS ROOTS FIXED IN THE HEAVENS. M'CHAIM. WHAT?

& IT BARES FRUIT OF LIGHTNING.

FROM ITS BRANCHES HANGS A MYTHICAL ANCESTOR, CLIMBING THE TREE IS NOT EASY.

EASTWARD IN EDEN GROWS A TREE.

WE SLEPT UNEASY IN BABYLON.

ROOTS OF PAIN. OUR ROOTS WERE OF BLOOD. LIKE TREES POEMS GROW, LIKE TREES...

WE WILL AWAKE... SHALOM.

THE TREE IS A LAMP.
THE TREE GROWS WITHIN US ALL.

Bill Lewis   MENORAH POEM

DESIRE

i want to visit the
ghetto warehouse
where the moon is kept
tied like a great
helium balloon
amongst crates of
citrus fruit and
biblical tracts
guarded and maintained
by secret grandfathers
in night stained kaftans

i want you to teach me
to speak french
like an african
to hunt puma in the
suburbs of the world

to open up your box
of desire and
touch the tortured
starfish that writhes
betwen your legs

but most of all
i want to visit the
ghetto warehouse
where the moon is kept
some night when it's
dark and judaic and
scented with
ink and lemons.

But Dear a God nev er again

In silver on a chain, · in tapestry · In yellow · in the sound of · in let upon · the rain in ink on parchment or woven · shining thread into · jacket. · prisoners' · in · a grey striped

traditions   (*from ERETZ YISROEL*)

a woman with a number on her arm
a wailing clarinet in a ghetto
a menorah   glowing with the light of Sinai
a buzzing of atoms in Einstein's head
a dance of numbers
a name not spoken
a promise unbroken
a velvet brim   shadowing eyes of blue fire
a black-suited conscience
strands of flame caught in a thorn bush
        can you count to six million
            and put a name by each number

182

EPILEPSY

she told me she was an artist
i thought of Van Gogh's
yellowing landscapes.
the storm gathers
moving in a blind vortex
across western and eastern hemispheres
flashing over luminescent radar-bowls
of occult meteorological stations
raising her skullforests
wrecking her coastal towns
turning the boats in her harbours to matchwood
cork-screwing great oaks from the earth
the grass is brown
trees glow with St. Elmo's fire
celestial lightning
melts the cells
of her cranial hive, and
the ever enlargeing sun
has an iron spike
driven into its head

from CAFÉ POEMS

. . . dirty condensation covered
mustard yellow walls
forty watt and naked the
light bulb swings
like a gibbet
in the corner a tattooed ape
with crooked teeth and
a leer borrowed from
the front cover of
TRUE DETECTIVE
has his hand up the fat girl's
skirt. She has a black eye
and a split lip.

THERAPY ROOM

Joe's making a stool
i'm weaving a basket
someone's making coffee
Dee says *I can sing*
and she does.
Jane won't make an
ashtray
Arthur's sulking because
the priest wouldn't re-
christen him *Jesus*.
Jane still won't make
an ashtray, instead
she becomes a dog
ggrrr Woof woof WOOF!
Dogs don't make ashtrays.
Dee's singing the
national anthem
Arthur blesses me.
Sydney hasn't spoken
all morning, or yesterday
or the day before,
gggrrr Woof Woof!
Shit said Joe
I'm going to discharge
myself from this place
it's driving me mad.

realising what he had
said, he starts to laugh
i also start to laugh
the man on my left
(who didn't hear Joe)
starts to laugh as well.
we all laugh.
except Sid who wants
to die (and means it)
then we had coffee.

184

conflict observed

the man *or woman,*
depending on who's
leaving, is throwing
clothes into a suitcase
and giving all that
jews and arabs stuff.
you know, about oil
and water not mixing.

the other one,

the woman *or man,*
depending on who's
staying, is standing
in the doorway, arms
folded saying,
– *they had better mix,*
because in a desert
economy, both are
essential.

DISCO
LUV

FLIC
KER
BLA
CK
WHI
TE
IN
TH'
HOT
SW
EAT
STR
OBE
NITE
DA
NCE
NA
NA

NA
NA

NA
NA
I
LUV
YOU
LUV
ME
LUV
OR
AT
LEA
ST
UN
TILL
TH'
END'
OF
TH'
RE
CORD

ants

armies of fullstops
                in deep canyons
carrying twigs
                    grass and
leaves   twigs maybe
three times bigger
                    than themselves
                in deep canyons
taking slaves
                    filling larders
freezers
            petrol tanks
        buying tv's and videos
recordplayers   deodorants
etc   etc
                in deep canyons
once the marriage
                    is over
she loses her wings
                    soon after
        mating the male dies.

Brian McCabe

from THE BIG SISTER POEMS

A Bedtime Story

There was a bottle with a dream in it.
Da drank from it because
this dream made everything seem
a lot better than they was.

A boring word sounded cleverer
and like it might mean more
and even his jokes sounded funnier
than they ever been before.

The dream it made Da swagger
and laugh and drink up more
till swagger turned into stagger
and laugh turned into roar.

Then the dream turned into a bad dream
and it made Da curse and swore.
So when he got back home at last
well he banged the front door.

See Da in this dream is someone
who knows when he's always right
so when Ma went and argued with him
they started to shout and fight.

They fight about Da and his dreaming
see then the nightmare goes on
he's hitting her now she's screaming
then this morning Ma's gone.

And Da says he can't remember
what the dream was all about.
So he goes out to look for her.

Don't ask me how I found this out.

I'm yer big sister amn't I.
I know things you don't that's all.
Like the story of the bottle with a dream in it
a dream called that's right

now get to sleep.

The Lesson

I'll tell you what now little brother
I'm going to teach you something
you'll never ever forget.

You go half way upstairs that's right.
You turn round you shut your eyes.
You keep them shut tight.

Now on the count of five
now I want you to jump.
Now is that clear.

Don't be scared little brother.
I'll be standing at the bottom here
to catch you so be brave.

I . . . 2 . . . 3 . . . 4 . . .

Five I said I'd teach you something
this is it don't ever trust anybody.
When you're older you'll thank me for it.

Shut up.

'THOUSAND FORCED TO FLEE DISPUTED REGION'

I have read the paper too I know
The story of the thousand forced to flee
Their disputed region though no doubt
The thousand called it something else
Such as home for example here
No it did not say what forced them
Nor whether they were forced to go
Together towards the same unknown
Or to scatter as insects do
When their stone is lifted I imagine
They had time to round up the kids
Take their old if not infirm maybe
A cherished horse a particular goat
The dogs would no doubt follow
After all they were the thousand
And would pack what food they could
A bag of apples tipped from a bowl
A live chicken or two a t.v. dinner
What about the t.v. what about the radio
Leave them what have they ever done
For us take that amulet this ribbon
Those plates cups spoons a good knife
Whatever could be crammed into the pram
On the roofrack in the wheelbarrow
It could not have been much not much
Given that their time was short
Their warning brief I imagine
They themselves did not know where
And the question how to get there
Would have to be answered on the way
No it did not say what forced them
Nor whether they are fleeing still
I imagine that they are they will be
Until the day we open our doors
And see the thousand there and say
You must be the thousand come in
We have read about you take a seat
Stay here make yourselves at home

Until you get your disputed region back
That doesn't happen though does it
You have read the paper too you know

SILENCE, HERE AND THERE

No not hear it exactly but
notice it with the ear –
there in the Beethoven somewhere
at the bottomless bottom of it
is a tiny root sprouting crescendos.
It grows in the mind's room also:
behind that remindering clock,
under the uneasy easy chair – the one
that whines every time you think in it –
silence, here and there
among the brain's furniture.
Then it's the eye looks for it
in another room, the one out there –
as if a silence could be seen
as a clock can, or a chair.
Maybe it can be: over there,
That shape with a hole in it.
A polished, discarded guitar
is a silence for the eye, isn't it?
Or a blank page before
some tiny – but not to it – life
crawled over it and stopped.
And then there's the one
unheard unseen but felt for –
a pulse that doesn't come.
The one to listen for is rarer:
the silence that blackbird is dipping
his voice in when he sings,
the silence of a space in thought
a space from which thought springs.

COMPARISONS

I compare the room to a cell
and claim we've locked the world out.
You point out it's that kind of hotel.
I say the collapsed windowblind
resembles a defunct concertina.
You say that won't help us find
a cover for the naked window.
To me, the coathangers' jangle
(it sets your teeth on edge, I know)
is like a skeleton's laughter
and isn't the sink, with its dangle
of chain, a bid of a godless altar?
You point to the drip, eye the stain
and conclude: it won't hold water.
You tell me I'm full of unfeeling
and unhelpful comparisons.
Very well. The crack in the ceiling
reminds me of no far horizon.
These rips in the sheets are nothing
like old men's toothless grins.
But now I need help with something:
how to look into the literal mirror,
nailed above the shelf-like shelf
and find a way not to compare
that half-smiling human error
to this cracked, but shining self.

CAT

Looking up from what I'm doing
(looking up a word, to find out
if it means what I *want* it to . . .)
I find out it's me who's been
looked up – by the unexpected:
outside my window, looking in,
is a striped Astonishment.
I see myself as I'm seen

by this startled incarnation:
in his eyes' mad, golden moons
there is terror – and recognition.
And I see what I mean to him
whether I want to or not:
Man, in his undergrowth of words
hunting a wild connotation.
As I close the curtains on him,
he turns on his tail's questionmark
and leaps into a starless, dark
night full of desperate definitions.

AUTUMN

I offer her a cracked landscape a dusty ode,
she goes on sobbing out her story.
In her voice there is the rustle
of a blackbird among dead leaves.
I say Don't. I say Come on
tell her winter might never happen.
Anyway I say you're in your prime.
She shakes her head. She makes
her ear-rings' dark berries dance.
Go on I say. I say Shed
that burden of all your beauty then.
Caress her ear: Though you're no
snowdrop of a gusty budding girl
and wouldn't be seen dead in crocuses
at my party of the year you're still
the one I hope will stay to the end.
So pull yourself together –
now it's time to go but we'll
meet again next year I'm sure.
I survey the final moment of her face
run my fingers through her windy hair
take her ripe mouth's trembling kiss
squeeze the damp leaves of her hands –
before I can say I'll miss you
she turns away.

AT A POETRY READING

The blackboard is dusted of its words
In the ghostly cloud of what's erased
you can make out the long, greyish faces
of the failed and the minor and the dead.

A good-looking girl (what's she doing here?)
looks dead bored at the end of the row.
Between us there's a very long line
of outnumbering chairs. Let us go

then, you and I, let us leave the great
poet to console: 'The real audience
is always one . . .' But we are too late:
silence closes in. And it begins

with an endless introductory apology
for what we're going to hear. What's more,
the wind in the corridor is doing
something onomatopoeic with the door.

The poetry makes just as much sense.
And we do not listen – so much so
that a latecomer interrupts a cadence
and unwittingly steals the show.

THEATRE CRITIC

What is the play, by the way?
Hamlet, is it?
Godawful plot, but still –
to be or not to be, eh?
Still a very pertinent question.
More so than ever in a way:
very worrying this nuclear business.
What I say is:
everyone ought to have a shelter,

not just civil servants and royalty.
To tell you the truth I don't care
for Shakespeare – makes me depressed.
Some good speeches though: whether
'tis nobler in the mind to suffer . . .
I can never remember the rest.
A CND production I see – as if we
didn't have enough on our plate.
Those alternative people make me weep.
To tell you the truth, I hate
the theatre – I'd give it up, but
it's the only place I get any sleep.
Too old anyway – I've reached the age
of Claudius, too late to make amends.
In any case, I know how it ends:
bodies all over the stage.

Cheers.

ENEMY

I will never forgive you for what
your towerblock has done
to my skyline.

On my summery path, you've thrown
the world's photograph –
torn in half.

Among your chemical jetsam
is a gull with glued-slut wings.
As is the future.

Will you face yourself at last
when I hold your mirror up
with all its cracks?

No, you'll turn from it, hoping
the deformed unborn don't count
your mistakes on their twisted fingers.

Ian McMillan

VIEW OF MEXBOROUGH CHURCH BELFRY

Reached only be a precarious ladder
or two leaning on a thin crib
above a seemingly-solid wardrobe,
three spoked wooden moons, hung
in a crumbling stone heaven.
The wheels fascinate me
more than the bells
because the wheels are so useless.
An addendum to the *'Checklist
of Yorkshire Tricycles'*, perhaps.
They have dropped most of their rims

which we pick up and nail on.
Downstairs we pull ropes,
the wheels turn and the bells
ring for the first time
in God knows how long.
Since the war at least.

But, for a reason which
I cannot pin down,
I preferred the bells silent
and the wheels still.
It could be that promise fulfilled
is always ambition disappointed;
only doing that which you were made for
seems such a waste of creation.
Above the canal and the railway
the bells swung on wheels and
can speak only inherited wisdoms,
cranking simple songs into a view
of the sky netted down by power lines.

MELTON BRAND

A day in which the quality of light
played the game of being romantic,
and a day in which we had expected
High Melton and Barnburgh Crags
to appear at the right times
at the correct places in the windscreen,
not the handwritten sign and well-kept
gardens of Melton Brand.

It really is a shock to find a new place
a few miles from home, in old country
near the back windows of Doncaster.
A block of a few houses and a farmhouse,
and that home-made sign
painted Melton Brand
into the centre of the day's canvas
where there should only have been a few fields.

We race through to Barnburgh
to diminish the shock of the new,
and the slow realisation
that the new is already familiar
to a number of people
with well-kept gardens.

JUNE EVENING

This scene is a perfectly still bird, held
in transparent smoke from no obvious source.

He concentrates ten o'clock into his binoculars;
his roof wears the moon like a badge, defining

the tissue half-darkness. The derailed train
hangs across the valley like a string of pearls.

THE RHYTHM KINGS. MEXBOROUGH. 1932.
(from a photograph)

These men are kings. In this picture they
seem to be the six finalists in a 'Mr. Irony
Personified' contest, with the painted drum
as the prize. Behind them the cloth is velvet,
and three harsh black folds are mirrored
on the floor by three standing clarinets.
A world true to itself, complete, marred
only by these six wise men in bow-ties.

Drinking bathtub bitter until dawn's flag
waves like the steam of a late-night train
waiting at Mexborough station for the last
dancers to climb on and wipe at the misty
window-seat windows to gaze at one or all
of the black-suited sextet in the photo.

The camera never lies. Here are six facts
who, barring falls or murdered health,
died old. Here are seven facts, if you count
the tight precise truth of the bass drum, with
a palm tree leaning into its painted centre,
three smaller trees stiffening the horizon,
and the long white image of a city, seemingly
at first glance a ship. These men are kings.

THE MEANING OF LIFE
(A Yorkshire Dialect Rhapsody)

From under't canal like a watter-filled cellar
coming up like a pitman from a double'un, twice,
I said *Hey, you're looking poorly*
He said *Them nights are drawing in*

Down't stairs like a gob-machine, sucking toffees,
up a ladder like a ferret up a ladder in a fog.
I said *Hey, you're looking poorly*
He said *Half-a-dozen eggs*

Over't top in't double-decker groaning like a whippet
like a lamplighter's daughter in a barrel full of milk,
I said *Hey, you're looking poorly*
He said *Night's a dozen eggs*

Down't canal like a barrow full of Gillis's parsnips,
coming up like a cage of men in lit-up shiny hats,
I said *Hey, you're looking poorly*
He said *Half a dozen nights*

Under't canal on a pushbike glowing like an eggshell
up a ladder wi' a pigeon and a brokken neck,
I said *Hey, you're looking poorly*
He said *I feel like half-a-dozen eggs*

Over't night on a shiny bike wi' a lit-up hat,
perfect for't poorly wi' heads like eggs,
I said *Hey, you died last week*
He said *Aye, did you miss me?*

BARGE JOURNEY

Now I can accept the old Yorkshire legend
about the man who strolled through a rhubarb-forcing shed
and came out wearing a green hat.

We are a mile from anywhere except here
and the trick is to convince yourself
that you are not riding on the heads of the trees
which stand upside-down to attention
in this skin-still model of the water.

Now I can accept the old Yorkshire legend
about the man who put his head in a horsetrough
and came up with his hair full of horses.

I am a yard from anyone except myself;
if I do a quick impersonation of a barge
perhaps the water will gather around me,
petrol will be poured into my ears
and I will have no memory of a time before canals.

Now I have become the old Yorkshire legend
about the man who got on a barge
and was later left in the water,
while the barge walked through the streets
to a house full of men, women and barges.

'Dad, the donkey's on fire – '

There is a burning donkey
at the side of the canal.
It lights up the sky.

Look at the burning donkey.
In Donkey Language it is saying
"Look at me, you bastards,

I am on fire"
Although it sounds like hee haw.

CALL ME IRRESPONSIBLE

A small toy Lego church
dropped from the back of a gig

into this field to please the locals
by the Man as he passed through the big house

no ladder in this church to reach any bells
only names, the same names, over the walls

pit owners, dead as snow
adored by the broken electric fire and the old pews

the dead mouse on the step distils so much
forces it all into a small Kodachrome

of me and him with pints
on a hill above the dark cricket field

and the pub overflowing with suburbia
and rugby shirts tucked into something

ignoring the stable which ignores itself
and the blacksmith's building festooned with remoulds

reflected light as I gaze up
glinting in the eye of the giant dead mouse

which crashes into my glass and body
after falling for so long from a field cracked like an egg

THE RED INDIAN RUGBY TEAM 'STRANGE NAMES XV' LAND ON A LONELY IRISH BEACH

Wingless Crow never really wanted to come. He wrings
out his soaking shorts, uneasy about his nakedness.
"Gods still exist in Ireland" says Unhappy Tree.

A crab moves across the beach. "Here
is an Irish God" the players shout.
"God of the Great Scrum" says Unhappy Tree.

The pack pack into a scrum and head towards
the crab. "I want to meet a God"
mutters High Water from the second row.

At sunset they huddle by a small fire
eating hot crab. "Edible gods, invisible men,
surely this is Paradise!" cries Grass-Puller.

Darkness covered the whole beach as they
practised a line-out, using
an imaginary ball. The ball
was their unseen God,
hastily adopted.

LIFE ON EARTH

When he came in
she gave him a flower
called "Welcome Home Husband
However Drunk You Be."

I am not drunk, he said;
this is not my home,
I am not your husband.

"Three mistakes
do not change the name of a flower"
she replied.

APPLEBY CHURCH

A row of hassocks admits to itself
that a hassock is missing; almost
as though a flock of birds accept
the truth about some of them being
already dead from wide gunshot holes
and piles of white Winters; almost
as though you and I can understand
the blank parts of our love, which
roll like angler fish over the neat
patterned carpet of our shared room.

THE LARK IN THE CLEAR AIR

Cocking his head, 'silly' in a way that jazz
was once silly, a young man smiles at his wife
and squints over a crossword. Blank squares
are etched with lines. Such an enviable
rapidity! Outside the train, the Staffordshire
countryside just fails to parody itself
as we scuttle by a non-working mill-wheel,
and the arms of a pair of lock-gates spread
like legs to admit the valley.

Could be a sign of the times that I used
sexual symbolism to describe canal prints
whilst on a train. Am I not a convoluted
little man? Certainly. The young chap
has abandoned the crossword in favour
of his wife who abandons him in favour
of a view approaching Stoke, so he
turns to the page, a mind mapping his
brow with waterways. He is not a very
handsome fellow; she is not really
a beautiful wife. These two people are
best kept on a fast train with me:
it will keep them quiet, it will allow
the canals to be themselves, the counties
to fold into the canals like teeth into lips.

203

STONE, I PRESUME

second stanza." That's what he said,
leaning over me in the classroom,
puffing on his tweed pipe, the air

thick with twist and reek. "Always
start your poems with the second
stanza, my boy, and you won't go far

wrong." I pondered this in my rooms
in the University. I knew, just knew,
it was the Thirties. "The Thirties

are a sort of second stanza, aren't
they?" I said to him. The air was
thick with twist and reek. "I mean

if you take the War poets as a sort
of first stanza, maybe count the
Twenties as the bit of white space

you find between stanzas . . ." I was
developing a point, nicely. He looked
at me with eyes like carpet tiles.

"If Christ had only had a second
stanza" he said, the air thick,
"he would only have risen again,

not died at all." It was a famous
point. I remembered it all through
the war, the period of Austerity,

until the sixties, when my son
came home smoking Pot. I tried to
explain about the second stanza

but he said "These are the Sixties,
daddy-o. These are today and now.
These days we leave out the

KAKE YOURSELF COMFORTABLE

Kome in. Sit Kown.
Kake yourself comfortable.

Kup of Kea? Bit of Kake?
Kilk? Kugar?

My problem? You Kish
to Kiscuss it?

Ah yes. The letter K.
Well, Kit all goes back

Ko Ky Khildhood. We were
very Koor. I only had one

Koy. A building Krick with
Ketters on. Except all the

Ketters had Keen Kubbed off,
except one. All my childhood

I Konly Kever saw Kone letter.
The letter S.

Lindsay MacRae

PAGE THREE GIRL

Cute little Katie's seventeen
from Kidderminster.
She was spotted in the local launderette
by a photographer.
"What beautiful bones you have.
  My camera could have
  a love affair with you"
A tasteful photo-session in the nude
. . . Wham, bam, slap –
you'll be in the news.

She gives it all she's got.
He calls the shots:
his flashgun's getting near to overload
his finger's getting tired
he's got a squint
from looking down a tele-photo lens too long.

She says her boyfriend doesn't mind a bit.
That's big of him.
He's a trainee accountant in the City.
He doesn't have to crouch stark naked
baring all he's got
and looking pretty
as a jet of foamy water hits his head.

The paper goes to press.
The copy-writer thinks
of something witty to print underneath.
She's got a list of interests
she didn't know she had.
She's been manipulated
with a bite to eat and
washed down with a pint.
"A bag of roasted peanuts, please"

and she's underneath,
a nibble at a time.

She said she'd like to travel
and she's visited a million
homes this week.
Men that she's never met
have had her on their minds between the sheets.
Bubbly, blonde and greasy
finally her body
wraps itself seductively
round fish and chips.

Dear John . . .

Loving you was difficult
so I never did.
Ours was a romance
whose flame never flickered
and whose honeyed words never dripped.

You have spilt a pint of Guinness down my front
and asked me to buy you another.
On most of our dates
I have managed to think of a reasonable excuse
not to be present.

Once we sat in your bedroom
– you chanted your boy scout motto,
showed me a picture of Roger, the family dog,
and gave me some tips on successful hari-kiri –
all before suggesting we might try sex.

I cannot describe our life between the sheets
because you had a Spiderman duvet.

Your idea of preliminaries
was to fumble in the dark for your glasses
and ask me if I'd like to try them on.
And you never waited until afterwards
to go to sleep.

I wonder, does the older generation realise
that *you* are the kind of fun it is missing out on?

MONEY FOR GUNS

(on reading that in a country with 4 million-plus unemployment the government still has one billion pounds to spend on arms – Guardian 26.5.85)

There isn't a place for the homeless to stay
and there isn't a bed for the sick.
Get a shiny new heart, if you're willing to pay
– you might just scrape by if you're young, rich and fit.
But there's plenty of money for guns.

When you're too old to walk you can stay in your bed
– don't squander the pension on gas.
You can dine gourmet-style every once in a while
on a packet of Cadbury's Smash.
But there's plenty of money in cold rhetoric
and there's plenty of money for guns.

When they close down your life and they hand you the cheque
you can spend it on whisky and tears.
Join the back of the queue for a new chance in life
though they've had no new chances for years.
But there's plenty of money to keep you in line
and there's plenty of money for guns.

They gawp at the starving on colour TV's,
with their conscience locked up in the shed.
They'll be shocked by the image of death and disease
though they'll still sleep quite sound in their beds.
Because inside the fridge they've a mountain of fat
and there's plenty of money for guns.

When the journalists cry, "This is wrong, tell us why?"
and all industry's razed to the ground,
they'll appear on the news with the morbid excuse
that the dollar has strangled the pound.
But the rich have their assets in soiled krugerrands
and there's plenty of money for guns.

Tony Marchant

A SOLDIER SEEN

As hours rolled on a west train, drumming slow,
My bored attentions manoeuvred polite
At intervals on anyone, and found
A soldier – young, upright,
Knees to attention, as stiff guns poised
Fit hands spread on each in place, with
A signet ring, hoisting initials, and
The sloganed kitbag: "Anne's a disgrace".

A soldier then, like others
On the march from lives unpressed
To work the virile hardware, then return
To simple homes, efficiently persuading conquest.
I then, at ease with cool thoughts to inspect
As we rattled through the roar of wire
Till the shaking swung his face round
And its terror marked me *"Liar!"*
From the volley of those wild eyes, like mines primed
As the scenery fell back unseen.
Had shots that appalled on an Irish street
Lingered in the iron rhythm, repeating?

A smug appraisal ducked to find its place
In contempt, though, was quick to miss
The hands clawing cloth; but to the eyes far off
I had something to confess –
My childishness.

HIGH RISE

There are headstones for our cities
Grey cornered, two hundred stubborn feet high
And inscribed with the lives of all who
Live inside: one vast, vertical, hopeless sigh.

Families have been filed away behind doors
Of the silent, stale, yellow-lit corridors
Like bits of useful, official paper: children
Without games growing up in furnished drawers.

Staring down – the trees look tidy in the shrunken square
But the whizz-kids' pencil plans have fouled up
And now that the valium is wearing off – didn't
They notice? It's high enough to jump.

HOME

The graffiti explain most of it:
"MAKE MISERY FREE – ABOLISH OUR RENT"

– Protest on bricks, like speech through clenched teeth
For politicians heard about.

The paint has long peeled off the sunless estate
Where footballs and full washing lines

Jostle in the grounds for space.
Housewives hang mats over balconies to dry

Then lean over, weakly reclaim the children
From their grubby, uncharming games

And looking up, to consider the huge sky
Feel like their dreams got thrown somewhere.

The elder dwellers rarely venture out
In case the scrapyard dogs are loose

Or the youths on the dim stairs want an argument.
But they are perplexed. They've

Glimpsed glossy life on the billboards
And now are waiting for their own to start.

The street lights line up, announcing evening
With a yellow warning glare

As families huddle between walls
For the curfew T V demands.

BOY DANCER

I saw him there, amongst the frantic
red, yellow, green, blue light
and the bodies like loose ropes flexed
in dizzy vigils of fun; and
thought it strange that a boy —
broken-spined, fixed upright
from supine — should want to hear
those litanies begin, of beat
(vinyl unravelled tidily to insist)
but not be able to answer back —
so uselessly sat, with fast eyes watching
and still flesh folded in a chair.

Then he began to shove and jerk
that iron, to coax speed from wheels,
roll back and forth, and almost spilled
on leaning cogs, swinging circles on
each metal step, both directions
like a mad sprung clock — till
wrung of motions, his head hung spent.
Stretching in the fashion, some turned away
to disdain in laughter what
they thought it meant —
a foaming prayer, a mutant dream —
but a virile mind had sought to be
in time with us and therefore, free;
so brought worship of the dance
to me.

Geraldine Monk

from
WALKS IN A DAISY CHAIN

THE POLICEMAN

The point
at the top of my helmet
I think looks rather
swanky.
I can almost feel it
grow when a nice
young pretty girl
asks me for time
or directions –
it veritably
swells –
so I do wish
loutish lads
wouldn't
knock it off.

THE MATHEMATICIAN

If
two and two continues
to make four
(which undoubtedly it does)
the world will surely
overpopulate
            but
not nearly as much as if
two and two made more – say
five or six
            but
obviously that doesn't
add up
so cannot be.

The answer
(as you can now clearly see)
is how people like
myself
can save the world
if only it would
listen

TWO FOR BEETHOVEN

On his conducting

Staggered and bled
through his senses

sunk to a dwarf

hobbling on the limb of a dischord

there came to his lips a smile

On his piano playing

There you go beating hell out of the tree stump
Jarring
through caked up ears
snapping through your muzzle,
  muted,
    your head's thrown off
  laughing
you try scratching the lug worm
wriggling the labyrinths
behind your cheeks,
listening to the dismal chants

lunar masque

an equine head rears   a woman's face bleeds white

prehensile lips   before ruin

bloodsucking and hooked in   two black trenches

rapacious horse play   crush down on cheekbones

crested and swollen   charcoal on chalk

with frenzy   choking black ivy

stricken
seaquake
of
iron limbs
overwrought
straddle
airquake
and beyond
the aftermath
unblinking
the eye of a squid
devours
their future shadows
stretched and melted wax
frozen
partners in fatigue
seething
webbed and fossilized exhaustion

WHAT . . .

– Recipes for the hungry

the starving the craving

the raving with mad desire

to cook

the words

and eat

the HEART OUT of

CRISP COMICS

MIXED MOOMINPAPAS

PIPING HOT TRAVEL BROCHURES

CRUNCHY CLASSICS

JUICY PURPLE PROSE

LASHINGS OF LISTED INGREDIENTS

MARINATED BEER MATS

DICED DICTIONARIES

PEPPERED PORN

TASTY NIBBLES OF SOMEONE ELSE'S NEWSPAPER

MOUTHWATERING MAGAZINES

POT BOILING PAPER BACKS

THE TENDER MEAT WHOLEWHEAT FINGER-LICKIN' GOODNESS

OF

ADVERTISEMENTS

Just CRACK   SMACKLE and

POP the lot

in the gob of the mind's eye.

(DELICIOUS!)

MOLECULAR POWER PROGRESSIVES

STATUS

Flouncing insignia hearts on sleeves

CULT HUGGERS

BOOT CRUSHERS

Leather boys strategically studded

Soldier boys swallowing uniformity

Heavy boys banging blue denim metallics

City boys pin striped and tied

Law boys robed and wigged

Holy boys cassocked and collared

FIngers WAggers   THumb SCrewers

RanK

MEN

TALITY

*   *   *   *   *   *

REDUCTIO AD ABSURDUM

Clothed we F
            A
              L
              L
Naked we LIE   Naked we STAND. SHIVER. BLUSH.
            D
            N
            A
            T
Clothed we S

from ANIMAL CRACKERS

GLASS SNAKE ELECTRIC EEL

mirror voltage/watery
          sh/ock manically
                    gathering face
                    muscles/freeze
                    in sp/l/it
                              Eternity
shedding
          past
glider
          undergrowth
softly trickle
hiss and
shimmy

```
    *              *              *

    *              *              *
```

EARTH PIG SUN SPIDER

crashing awkwardly spiked
                    drink
              on
soft fruit
cocktail gold/of
              blood turns/of
                        lemon
Desires for overlapping
spinning pink and messy
opposites colliding


```
              *              *              *

              *              *              *
```

RAINBOW BOA BUTCHER BIRD

uneasy embrace grows
getting
constricted
thrown on slab/back
breaking
spit
      gushing
arch reds to indigo
feathered and bled

Nik Morgan

Cannon Fodder

Fate in the heart
of the common soldier,
such value to the country
that honoured rag of proper property
and in himself
counted of little importance
still young and cheerful head
bent on the enemy's guns.

Windows

Crowds elbow the shops with eyes,
They look in,
But never see
The sad face of
A stare reflected in windows

A stare reflected in windows

necessary glance in the mirror

the passing

personality

massage

pensively

patting him on the back

A Debt to Gascoyne

The sound of clamber and a torch,
dancing:
flocking away into the trees.
The night is like wallpaper
pasted to the insides of eyes;
taste the gum of the green black.

This scene is displayed
on a small screen
no larger than the largest fork.
You catch it out of the corner of your eye,
then watch the collage somersault into words.

Haiku

Friends parting at night
all is darkness : though candles
burn on in the head.

Udders Haiku

Side to side slung snouts
of belly breast-a-bust and
pink gloves of bludder

The Supremacy of Words

(Haiku)

A row of squirly
eights can only leave a blank
space behind the eyes

88888888888888888

School Dinners

Rush up the queue
for hot scoff and steam ladies
who ladle the slop to plate.
Billows of white,
flesh and bumpkin faces
cooking up the smells of kitchen country
for the little masters.

Lads' Night Out

The hunger-scum hearaway herd
and glum club brass band
are out on the town,
with a fag face funnel puff
chuffa chuffa
down at "The Cough and Chunder"

Sea - Sick

My body,
queasy on its own sea,
awaits with terror
the sourgush heave,
brewing like stout
in the sick pouch.

leaned forward and burst

the sky shone pale
at godsend glow
a delicate ruby in the twilight
which fell unsuspecting into the sea.
up in the heathenish hammock
vault of the forest
night grew a moon
and drifted through the trees
as savages do

woods

huge noon spires
and jointed steeples
cloaked by
the drifting murmur
of the leaf

Night

darkness forms
the thousand stars
hidden in a sunny afternoon

deacon

white house parlour bone man

    pure and numb

before tea and cherried bears

Summer

cruel beak and chat of spawn
the sleepy noon frog
plump in a practised swallow.
bales of fodder
wrapped up for after
and hay nose
running
in the lazy golden belly of time

Christmas in Wales

snow grew arms and hands

from the whitewash bodies of trees

and swam overnight on the sky

settled on the moss roofs of grandfather postman

like that same daft Christmas drifted

Burial

A soldier's heroism
comes home
from the war.

Grace Nichols

from *i is a long memoried woman*

*   *   *   *

From dih pout
of mih mouth
from dih
treacherous
calm of mih
smile
you can tell

i is a long memoried woman

*   *   *

WE THE WOMEN

We the women who toil
unadorn
heads tie with cheap
cotton

We the women who cut
clear fetch dig sing

We the women making
something from this
ache-and-pain-a-me
back-o-hardness

Yet we the women
who praises go unsung
who voices go unheard
who deaths they sweep
aside
as easy as dead leaves

232

LOVE ACT

She enter into his Great House
her see-far looking eyes
unassuming

He fix her with his glassy stare
and feel the thin fire in his blood
awakening

Soon she is the fuel
that keep them all going

He/his mistresswife/and his
children who take to her breasts
like leeches

He want to tower above her
want her to raise her ebony
haunches and when she does
he think she can be trusted
and drinks her in

And his mistresswife
spending her days in rings
of vacant smiling
is glad to be rid of the
loveact

But time pass/es

Her sorcery cut them
like a whip

She hide her triumph
and slowly stir the hate
of poison in

SKIN TEETH

Not every skin-teeth
is a smile *"Massa"*

if you see me smiling
when you pass

if you see me bending
when you ask

Know that I smile
Know that I bend
only the better
to rise and strike
again

LIKE A FLAME . . .

Raising up
from my weeding
of ripening cane

my eyes
make four
with this man

there ain't
no reason
to laugh

but
I laughing
in confusion

his hands
soft his words
quick his lips
curling as in
prayer

I nod

I like this man

Tonight
I go to meet him
like a flame

OLD DRY-HEAD WOMAN . . .

I see the old dry-head woman
leaning on her hoe
twist-up and shaky like a cripple insect

I see her ravaged skin, the stripes
of mould where the whip fall
hard

I see her missing toe, her jut-out
hipbone from way back time when
she had a fall

I see the old dry-head woman
leaning on her hoe
twist-up and shaky like a cripple insect
I see the pit of her eye

I hear her rattle bone laugh
putting a chill up my spine

Once she too was woman
clad in her loveliest woman
skin gleaming faintly
with oils breasts nippling
the wind

THIS KINGDOM

This Kingdom Will Not Reign
Forever

Cool winds blow
softly

in brilliant sunshine
fruits pulse
flowers flame

mountains shade to
purple

the Great House
with its palm and orange
groves

sturdy

and the sea circling
all
is a spectrum of blue
jewels
shimmering and skirting

But Beware

Soft winds can turn
volatile
can merge with rains
can turn hurricane

Mountains can erupt
sulphur springs
bubbling quick
and hot

like bile spilling
from a witch's cauldron

Swamps can send plagues –
dysentery, fevers

plantations can perish

lands turn barren

And the white man
no longer at ease
with the faint drum/
beat

no longer indifferent
to the sweating sun/
heat

can leave exhausted
or
turn his thoughts
to death

And we
the rage growing
like the chiggers
in our feet

can wait
or
take our freedom

whatever happens

This Kingdom Will Not Reign
Forever

*   *   *   *

TAPESTRY

The long line of blood
and family ties

An African countenance here
A European countenance there
An Amerindian cast of cheek
An Asianic turn of eye
And the tongue's salty accommodation
The tapestry is mine
All the bloodstained prints
The scatterlinks
The grafting strand of crinkled hair
The black persistent blooming.

'Always potential . . .'

Articulated lorries
streaming up the North Circular,
streaming like profit
big brand names flashing by;
KODAK, JOHNSON'S, CADBURY,
triggering a bell of sugarcane
somewhere in my head.

The smell of sausages and eggs
from the Transport Cafe,
the egg-on-toast and tea
leaving a queer taste of aluminium
in my mouth.
Queer as the hills
of unsmeltered bauxite
in my raw undeveloped country.

And I can hear
the back-home politician-drone
*"We have a lot of potential
a lot of potential."*

Always potential.

238

from LAZY THOUGHTS
OF A LAZY WOMAN

'Who was it . . .?'

Who was it I wonder
introduced the hairless habit?
I have an interest
though I will not shave the armpit

No Gillette
I will not defoliage my forests

Also, let the hairline of the bikini
Be fringed with indecency
Let 'unwanted body hair' straggle free

O Mary Cant
O Estee Laud
O Helena Frankenstein

WITH APOLOGIES TO HAMLET

To pee or not to pee
That is the question

Whether it's sensibler in the mind
To suffer for sake of verse
The discomforting slings
Of a full and pressing bladder
Or to break poetic thought for loo
As a course of matter
And by apee-sing end it.

WHEREVER I HANG . . .

I leave me people, me land, me home
For reasons, I not too sure
I forsake de sun
An de humming-bird splendour
Had big rats in de floorboard
So I pick up me new-world self
And come, to this place call England
At first I feeling like I in dream –
De misty greyness
I touching de walls to see if they real
They solid to de seam
An de people pouring from de underground system
Like beans
And when I look up to de sky
I see Lord Nelson high – too high to lie

And is so I sending home photos of myself
Among de pigeons and de snow
And is so I warding off de cold
And is so, little by little
I begin to change my calypso ways
Never visiting nobody
Before giving them clear warning
And waiting me turn in queue
Now, after all this time
I get accustom to de English life
But I still miss back-home side
To tell you de truth
I don't know really where I belaang

       Yes, divided to de ocean
       Divided to de bone

Wherever I hang me knickers – that's my home.

'Dead ya fuh tan . . .'

If me na been come ya
Me na been know
People a dead ya fuh tan

Dem a lie on rock
Dem a lie on sand
People a dead ya fuh tan

Dem a buy sunbed
Dem a buy lotion
People a dead ya fuh tan

Dem a bare dem breast
Dem a bare dem bum
People a dead ya fuh tan

If me na been come ya
Me na been know
People a dead ya fuh tan*

Anyway dem can ketch de sun
Anyway dem can ketch a brown
People a dead ya fuh tan.

* 'If I hadn't come here / I wouldn't have known / people would die to get a tan'

241

Beauty
is a fat black woman
walking the fields
pressing a breezed
hibiscus
to her cheek
while the sun lights up
her feet

Beauty
is a fat black woman
riding the waves
drifting in happy oblivion
while the sea turns back
to hug her shape

Looking at Miss World

Tonight the fat black woman
is all agaze
will some Miss (plump at least
if not fat and black) uphold her name

The fat black woman awaits in vain
slim after slim aspirant appears
baring her treasures in hopeful despair
this the fat black woman can hardly bear

And as the beauties yearn
and the beauties turn
the fat black woman wonders
when will the beauties
ever really burn

O the night wears on
the night wears on
judges mingling with chiffons

The fat black woman gets up
and pours some gin
toasting herself as a likely win

BABY- K RAP RHYME

My name is Baby-K
An dis is my rhyme
Sit back folks
While I rap my mind;

Ah rocking with my homegirl,
My Mommy
Ah rocking with my homeboy,
My Daddy
My big sister, Les, an
My Granny,
Hey dere people – my posse
I'm the business
The ruler of the nursery

poop po-doop
poop-poop po-doop
poop po-doop
poop-poop po-doop

Well, ah soaking up de rhythm
Ah drinking up my tea
Ah bouncing an ah rocking
On my Mommy knee
So happy man so happy

poop po-doop
poop-poop po-doop
poop po-doop
poop-poop po-doop

Wish my rhyme wasn't hard
Wish my rhyme wasn't rough
But sometimes, people
You got to be tough

Cause dey pumping up de chickens
Dey stumping down de trees
Dey messing up de ozones

Dey messing up de seas
Baby-K say, stop dis –
please, please, please

poop po-doop
poop-poop po-doop
poop po-doop
poop-poop po-doop

Now am splashing in de bath
With my rubber duck
Who don't like dis rhyme
Kiss my baby-foot
Babies everywhere
Join a Babyhood

Cause dey hotting up de globe, man
Dey hitting down de seals
Dey killing off de ellies
For dere ivories
Baby-K say, stop dis –
please, please, please

poop po-doop
poop-poop po-doop
poop po-doop
poop-poop po-doop

Dis is my Baby-K rap
But it's a kinda plea
What kinda world
Dey going to leave fuh me?
What kinda world
Dey going to leave fuh me?

Poop po-doop.

CRAB DANCE

Play moonlight
and the red crabs dance
their scuttle-foot dance
on the mud-packed beach

Play moonlight
and the red crabs dance
their sideways dance
to the soft-sea beat

Play moonlight
and the red crabs dance
their bulb-eye dance
their last crab dance

OUT OF AFRICA

Out of Africa is the suckling
Out of Africa is the tired woman in earrings
Out of Africa of the black-foot leap
Out of Africa of the baobab, the suck-teeth
Out of Africa the dry maw of hunger
Out of Africa of the first rains, the first mother.

Into the Caribbean of the staggeringly blue sea-eye
Into the Caribbean of the baleful tourist glare
Into the Caribbean of the hurricane
Into the Caribbean of the flame tree, the palm tree,
the ackee, the high-smelling saltfish
and the happy creole so-called mentality.

Into England of the frost and the tea
Into England of the budgie and strawberry
Into England of the trampled autumn tongues
Into England of the meagre funerals
Into England of the hand of the old woman
And the gent running behind someone
Who's forgotten their umbrella, crying out,
"I say . . . I say-ay."

Rosemary Norman

HOUSEBOAT

This brick suburb is intelligent,
concerned, dislikes itself
and wants to be otherwise.
It clings to London,
brown and grey as a chrysalis
full of more than mere dreams:
it knows a butterfly is possible.

It could be a rainbow of them,
kissing on the wing
in a bright tree with infinite branches
and plenty of fresh fruit for the children;
but the brown houses are laden
only with mortgages and chores,
and under the grey tiles
wives and husbands forget each other
and sleep off the after dinner
butterfly.

Sad monster
it struggles and bursts out
blinded by tears and litigation.
Its wings, brushing our eyes and faces,
populate the streets with
wives' lovers
lovers' husbands
husbands' lovers
lovers' wives
and the houses, unmoved, revert to desirable
property, close to parks and the river.

I could live safer on one of these houseboats;
or even in a brown house,
if it rocked on the earth
enough to keep me awake.

246

TO H.W.B*

Come to bed again, old friend, and I will press
your sweet warmth deep
under each ache and each unease
until I repossess
my body and sleep.

You are innocent, without desire to please
yourself or me.
You do not smile, or twist your head,
or step with stiffened knees,
deceitfully.

I am stiff and cold, old friend, so come to bed
to my cold heart.
As I embrace, you will caress,
and no word need be said
of love, or art.

* Hot Water Bottle

247

BETWEEN LEGS

What's the difference between
a prick and a cunt?
Or between, let's say, a prick
and a penis, a cunt
and a vagina?
What's the difference between
testicles, as it were, and balls?
What's the difference between
labia majora and minora and
clitoris and clitoris?
What's the difference
between legs?

What's the difference between
toes, between ribs,
between eyes and fingers, between
lips dry as a whispered name
or running with wet?
What's the difference between
the accomplishment
of orgasm, and kissing
goodnight at a bus-stop until
only the bus comes?

What's the difference between
tingling and irritation
but the here-and-there
the whether-or-no of desire?
What's the difference
between lust and friendship
and love
            and love
                        and love?

WAR GAMES

I ought never
to have let him have them; who knows
what dangerous little bits and pieces
he might swallow?
Too late: a battalion of
two-inch heroes is swarming the sofa.
His hand
guides the great, grey tank,
his throat rumbles,
his milk teeth spit out bullets.
To comfort, he explains
caterpillar wheels are designed for safety
on treacherous ground.

Those villains he hid
under a rocky cushion are flushed out
and fall, to a man, over the
cliff to the hearthrug
where they drown, and are eaten by sharks.
Now, here comes a helicopter, threatening
to defoliate the Busy Lizzie.
But he keeps his best bomb
at the bottom of the box: a deterrent
that works, just like the real one.
Pink cheeks, bright eyes;
I expect
tears before bedtime.

HOME   *(June 1982)*

Home was once a brick wall
round you and Mother.
Father went back and forth, and you sat
on the doorstep, waiting.
There was a row of doorsteps
that was home.

250

When you grew big enough for geography
home was an island
coloured pink. It was small
but important. You lived there.
And besides, everyone knew,
there were other reasons.

You were sent away to defend
school history books and daily papers,
proud and homesick
and very soon, dead.
Home now is the open mouth
where your thumb will never again come to rest.

SALINE

Drip, drip. The old girl's
skinny, her bones laid out
as flat as fossils
under the sweaty blanket.
Her hair's shrivelled back
from brow and eyeholes.
Her gums chew on rough breath.
Soon she'll be dead.

And it's him, in the dim
drift of mist, her old
boy, her dear, her darling
coming for her, cock first,
bless him, as ever.
She melts, runs like summer
butter. It's good, so good, oh
yes. This is heaven.

LOVE POEM

Martens wheel and scrawl
noughts on a blank sky.
The window, half open, admits
a little evening air.

Everyone says it: the tall hero,
his heart tendered
chapter by chapter to her,
concedes it at last between kisses.
And she, like a child
trying out sounds in her mouth,
repeats it, naming him
the end of the story of her life.

Everyone says it: even the rapist,
his hand clamped fast over any answer.

And the unspoken nonsense
still, for all
my dictionary lore, and though
your tongue has cleansed my mouth
of protestation,
rises in me again.

here is an iron gate

water runs on this side

break from pink barley

waking close to sleep

how to remove the

252

AFTER

You did not leave a note, and would not
anyway, by then, have left one for me.
Not that I had not remembered
your going, the first time, in a chaos
of birds and spring blossom.
But I was calm, and the loss of you
was already completed.

Word of your death. Another decision
made and kept to. I will outlive you
now, twice over. Date events before, between,
between, after.
Myself, I will die
only when I must: till then
I will write notes and leave them all around me
everywhere, about everything, even this.

like an empty stave

rooks clatter on that

across thick blue cloud

I have considered

need for any notation

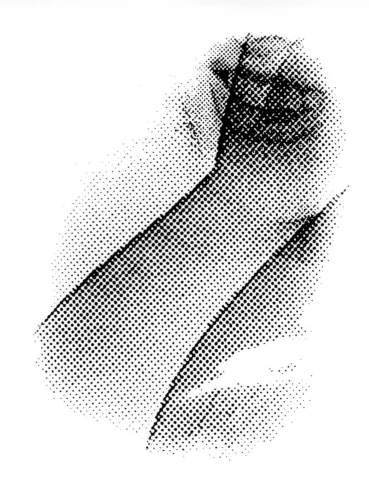

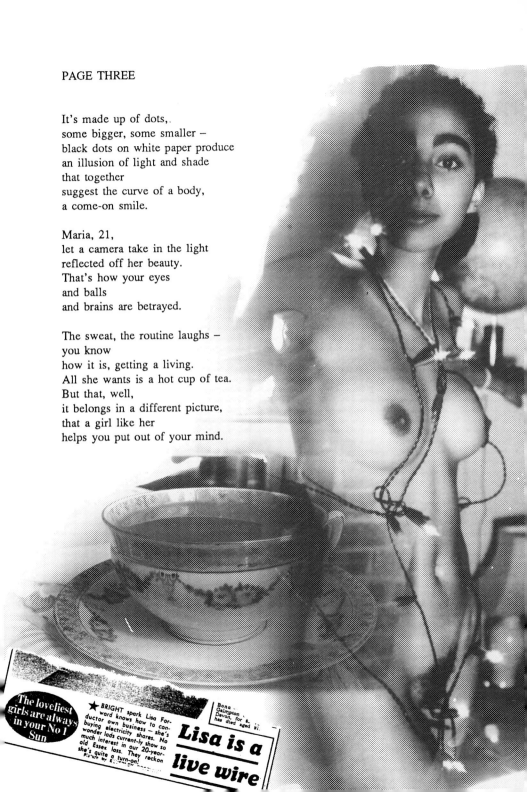

PAGE THREE

It's made up of dots,
some bigger, some smaller –
black dots on white paper produce
an illusion of light and shade
that together
suggest the curve of a body,
a come-on smile.

Maria, 21,
let a camera take in the light
reflected off her beauty.
That's how your eyes
and balls
and brains are betrayed.

The sweat, the routine laughs –
you know
how it is, getting a living.
All she wants is a hot cup of tea.
But that, well,
it belongs in a different picture,
that a girl like her
helps you put out of your mind.

Ben Okri

LITTLE GIRL

Little girl
In the green river
I watch you
Bathing away the last
Smiles of initiation
With ripples of the water's cruelty
Catching
The wondrous lights
From the sky.

Little girl
In the savage river
I marvel that you float
In silvery state
Amongst the riverweed
And fishes:
I marvel more
At seeing you smiling across
To the boatman
Whirling in the currents
Who drowned while sleeping
Who dreamed of the source
And of you.

I see the gashes on your face
The marks you can't explain
Or wonder at
For the river gives off no reflections;
The fever in your eyes
Calls me
From my watchpost
In this time of drought;
I descend
And find the waves
Are raging
A new fear, a terrible understanding.

The fishes have all gone
The weeds have gathered themselves away
I see you startled
At the stillness that comes
When the animals plunge
Into the river
To remain with you:
and I understand your terror.

Little girl
In the flowering river
You have discovered
An alcove in the whirlpool:
It seemed such a neutral place
For your last rites
Before the howls in the air
Discover your secrets.

And now that it is all over
And the animals bulk the shoreline
And the pillows of the riverbed
Whisper a great unease
And the river has reversed its current
And now that you can float
To all the cities
Under the darkening sky
There is one thing I have to tell you:

On my way back up
The watchpost has been destroyed
And a crumbling new tower erected.
There was a feast of madmen
And many tongues sang of abundant chaos
In the orgies
While there has been
So much water
From your eyes
In the river.

I SEE YOUR FACE

I see your face
Where beauty is threatened
With violence
Roseate in the evening's
Chimerical murders.

Your face is angled at me
Like cubist lines catching
Innocence at Calvary:
You trap misery
With a smile.

I see it at the window
Contemplating unhappy bodies
In the skyline
I see it by the river
Washing away the terror
Washed in from all
The junkyards battle-grounds slum-burials
Bleeding revolution.

Your face crowds me at the mortuaries
Defying the nakedness that is prodded
Packed and re-packed into a new
Geometry dreading the old
Dreading any resemblance to the bodies
Maddened in the streets
Or to the nakedness tossing serenely
On a bed heaving heat.

Your face smiles at me
When at the first rung of chaos
Soldiers carry out a dying wish
Showering bullets into bodies bound
For ever with our hunger
Smashing our essences
Understanding thunder
Jerking wildly on the red sheets
With us watching crescendoes carrying

Death-wash over
Our direst wonders.

I see your face
Seeing us mashed into lying
Pounded into hopelessness
Praised into submission
Starved into inhumanity
Cracked-down into circles
Where we laugh surprised
At our empty affirmations.

I see your face
As I ask kissing the razor's edge
What can we do
In this fear-chamber of our lives?
What can we do
When the lights blink back the darkness
Which seems to stay for ever?
What can we do
When the roads open out the deaths
We will confront at another turning?
What can we do
When the eyes of authority
Spatter blood on the children?
When the cold grey of the evenings
Brings in all the smells
Bearing the deaths of so many
Whose lives seemed like septic clutchings
Who were born saying yes and died
Trying
Trying to find an alternative?
What can we do
When we see the clouds swollen
With the blood of our futures?
What can we say
When poets lie
When politicians decide
To tell the truths
That sold us at the market-pits?
What can we say
When we know we should

Be doing something
About living our lives in brutal cycles?
The logic belongs to someone else
There is no music here.
We have been dancing
On the burning logs
The razor's teeth
The meat of our days
There never has been music here.

And when I see your face
See it cry
See it weep the blood we thought was ours
See it twitch and grin out our deepest hours
See it transform its beauty
Shocked by the flowering of bodies
Putrescent in our lives
When I see it
I see many faces in one
  — break this sacrament
    this heart this fire
    Share this body back to its
    original multitude
    as we scream into
    the fumes of the air;
There is no music here
When we are shot there is only an
Illusion of music
Which the frenzy itself transmits.
This is no way to live
When we can die
Holding our bodies by the invisible levers
And fight these temples that plague
Our bones;
There are no flowers here.
We squashed them on other days
As we spun the confusion of our ways
And we must come back here
To where the earth is smouldering
To where the smells curl on themselves
To where the flesh is raw at every street-corner
To where the mind is seared by the smell of dawn

To where the spirit tramps the million crevices of fear
To where this old animal stalks starving
To where this old flesh breathes death
To where it is hardest to begin
   Where we must scream clarity on chaos
   Scream simple terror on complacency
   Scream blood on blood
      Water on water:
         The pigs drowned yesterday
         The prophet went with them
         The sea now possesses us.

And do I see your face
Watching this new design
Lifting on each wind?
I know that
When we have been deposited
In this cauldron
Which widens in the smithy's fire
     in the electric tremors
     When the dawns have become
     Too much
And widened to each point in our battlegrounds
To each
To each
To each
I know
There will be faces
With yours and mine.

'And if you should leave me . . .'

And if you should leave me
I would say that the ghost
Of Cassandra
Has passed
     Through my eyes
I would say that the stars
In their malice
Merely light up the sky
To stretch my torment
And that the waves crash
     On the shores
To bring salt-stings on
     My face:
For you re-connect me with
All the lights of the sky
     And the salt of the waves
     And the lightness of air,
And with your passing
The evening would become too dark
     To dream in
And the morning
     Too bright.

262

AN AFRICAN ELEGY

We are the miracles that God made
To taste the bitter fruit of Time.
We are precious
And one day our suffering
Will turn into the wonders of the earth.

There are things that burn me now
Which turn golden when I am happy.
Do you see the mystery of our pain?
That we bear poverty
And are able to sing and dream sweet things

And that we never curse the air when it is warm
Or the fruit when it tastes so good
Or the lights that bounce gently on the waters?
We bless things even in our pain.
We bless them in silence.

That is why our music is so sweet.
It makes the air remember.
There are secret miracles at work
That only Time will bring forth.
I too have heard the dead singing.

And they tell me that
This life is good
They tell me to live it gently
With fire, and always with hope.
There is wonder here

And there is surprise
In everything that moves unseen.
The ocean is full of songs.
The sky is not an enemy.
Destiny is our friend.

Andrew Pearmain (aka Andy P.)

GARY AND GAIL – TRUE (1985)

First moustache quilted jacket
maroon acrylic jumper
stuck in homebound traffic jam
'bumper to fucking bumper',
GARY AND GAIL on the windscreen
in white letters on green vinyl
Gail's Mum said it looked common
Gary said – it's going on, and that's final.

Same with the fluffy dice –
Gail said they looked silly
dangling down like that.
Gary smokes, 20 a day, Piccadilly,
the odd cigar at Christmas
B & H if he's in the pub
holds them with thumb and middle finger
smokes them down to the stub.

Gail works in a department store
Gary works in a garage,
Gary wants his end away
Gail says not till the marriage.
Sundays they go to her parents
for chicken or roast with two veg,
Gary talks cars with Gail's brother
and business with Gail's Uncle Reg.

Gail helps Mum with the the washing up
while the fellas watch the Big Match
Mum reckons Gary's all mouth and trousers,
all that gold – thinks that he's flash.
Gail knows what she means
but at least he's got a job
and prospects, which is more than
Gail's sister Dawn's husband Bob,

264

not had a job since he left school
lot of good staying on did him,
should have left at 16 like Gary
– called round last week, you should see him
just sits around the house all day
watching telly reading wank magazines,
and at least Gary washes under his arms
stays out of trouble, keeps his nose clean.

Tuesday and Thursday evenings
Gail and Gary go out
to the pictures or the pub
or a restaurant – he has trout
and she has a medium steak
or sometimes a mixed grill,
he always used to pay
but now lets her pay half the bill.

Then he takes her home
she has to go to work in the morning
he drives fast but not too fast
he got stopped last year and given a warning,
and Gail's always reminded him
it doesn't half get him annoyed
– he knows if he lost his licence
he'd lose his job and be unemployed.

That's about it, I suppose
that just about sums 'em up
– oh, Gary supports Arsenal
thinks they'll win the Littlewoods Cup
next season, Gail's not interested
in twenty-two grown men
kicking a ball round a field
but she doesn't mind Gary going, now and then.

WHITE RASTA'S LAMENT

White rasta man vibration negative
dreadlocks washed out in shower
cost sixty quid down Kings Road
I and I look like dead sunflower.

I and I clean clothes inna washing-machine   .
red gold and green turn muddy grey
track-suit shrink even inna sink
pray Jah, dry-clean dem blues away.

Went to Jamaica for holiday
running that downpression down
package exile inna Babylon
I and I got mugged inna Trenchtown.

I and I tried Ethiopia next year
driven by natural reggae beat
home triumphant to Zion
repatriated for singing inna street.

Bought ganja in Finsbury Park Tavern
spent half I and I's weekly wage
on carrier bag full of bush
Oh Ras it's a blend of oregano and sage.

Wake up next morning feeling lousy
no better after dose of Phensic
go doctor say I and I feel awful
him say I and I schizophrenic.

White rasta man vibration negative
stuck inna Babylon N W 3
I and I never be proper rasta
join the local skinheads if they'll have me.

WORKS OUTING

It rained on the day of the works outing
organised by the works social club.
The blokes weren't really that bothered
they spent all day in the pub.

They persuaded the landlord to stay open
right through from three till half five
then carried on drinking till closing time
– they were lucky they came out alive.

They stopped off on the way to the coach
for cod and chips twice with curry sauce,
then carried their breaths and stomachs back
all set to sing themselves hoarse.

The women spent all day in arcades
and fed the machines ten pence pieces
pausing for crisps, mints and orangeades,
buying rock for nephews and nieces

. . . eyeing up the bingo-caller
wondering aloud what he'd be like in bed
– wondering to themselves if he'd make them happy
like they were once before they got wed.

Then they traipsed back to the coach park
and stood around waiting for the men,
taking the piss out of the coach driver and swearing
they'd never come here again.

Fiona Pitt-Kethley

PRIVATE PARTS

Pencil is less ambiguous than paint,
incising hard lines round the genitals.
I've seen art students, broad-minded enough
to talk naturally to naked models
in their breaks from posing, become furtive
as they draw a penis – men too. Often,
like children cheating in exams, one hand
shielded the other's workings from all view.
Others erased madly – they'd made it far
too short or long, then found they'd worked
the paper to a grubby thinness there,
or left black rubber pills like pubic lice.

Marble's cold and doesn't change however hard
you stare at it – an easier task than flesh
to draw. Sketching a Roman Mercury
in the Fitzwilliam, I'd toyed with the thighs
for far too long, eyed by some soldier
from a US base nearby. He stood until
I gravitated to the balls, then pounced.
An ugly human, he'd identified
with the smooth body of a god, the image
on the paper, seeing my pencil's touch
as a caress.

NO SMOKING

Lent is the time for cutting out what's bad,
I'll give up going to bed with men who smoke –
for that *and* other seasons of the year.

Is it the taste? That's not *too* bad as long
as I don't put my tongue into their mouths.

The tiredness of their skin? Their blood-shot eyes?
Is it the smell of fag-ash in my hair
next day? Not really. That can be washed out.

Post-coital light-up is what worries me.
We've had each other, then the smoking man
turns desperately seeking something else,
scouring the bedside cupboard, pockets, drawers.
He sighs on finding what he really wants,
then's silently unfaithful with his fag.

Some keep their little weapons to themselves.
The worst kind start a sort of troilism.
I don't feel easy with a naked flame
too near my vulnerable naked flesh –
you, me, a cigarette, a smoky kiss.
Out of the corner of one eye I see
a toppling inch of ash above a stub,
while lover-boy is fiddling with my tits –
foreplay designed to set the bed on fire.

GIRLIE MAGS

I do not care a toss if blokes must look
at glossy, big-boobed photos of bad girls.
I've met some centre-stapled, double spreads
who laughing took the cash and went their ways.
Women cannot afford to turn work down.
But how I hate the letters in those mags –
A. had her nipples pierced, linked with a chain,
B. had the firm's alsatian yet again,
C. buggered by six fellas, felt no pain,
and all loved it. So the male bastards claimed,
signing their missives with sweet female names.
All right, my guess is good as theirs, I'll write
and sign the thing John Smith. Last week I put
my bollocks through a mangle, and loved it.
May I recommend?

SKY RAY LOLLY

A toddler on a day out in Herne Bay,
on seeing an ancient, civil-servant type,
I held my Sky Ray lolly – red, yellow
and green striped, pointed, dripping down between
my legs and walked bandy. My Ma and Pa,
(old-fashioned innocents like Rupert Bear's),
just didn't notice this and ambled on,
that is, until they saw the old man's face,
jaw dislocated in surprise. They grabbed
that Martian's willy from my little hand.

The world still sees me as a nasty kid
usurping maleness. A foul brat to be
smacked down by figures of authority.
All things most natural in men, in me
are vice – having no urge to cook or clean,
lacking maternal instincts.

And they would take my pride, my rocket
of ambition, amputate my fun and geld
my laughter, depriving me of colour.
And smirk to see my little lolly melt,
me left with a stick.

PENIS-ENVY

Freud, you were right! I must expose my id
And show the penis-envy that lies hid.
It's not that I admire the look as such,
It seems a strange adornment for a crutch,
Like sets of giblets from a butcher's shop,
Two kidneys with a chicken-neck on top,
Floating serene in baths like lug-worm bait,
Or, jokily bobbing with the jogger's gait.
Fig-leaves, I'm sure, are prettier far than cocks,
And only suffer greenly not the pox.

270

As tools, pricks really aren't reliable,
One minute hard, the next too pliable.
If I had bought a hammer or a chisel
As changeable, I'd think it was a swizzle.

It's not that I'm against them in their place,
But simply that I cannot see a case
For cocks to be a sort of union card
In life's closed shop. I think it very hard
That humans with these fickle bits and bobs
Are given a fairer lot and better jobs.
If only I'd had one of them, it seems
I could have had success, fulfilled my dreams.
A female eunuch, though, all I'll attain
Is Pyrrhic victory and trifling gain.

Fiona snooks another (literary) cock

271

NIGHT LONDON

The pubs were out, the evening's takings done,
box-office hatches tightly closed. The girls
and boys of Theatre-land waited for their
release, hustling their patrons to the Strand.
'All out?' the firemen asked, huge padlocks
in their hands. The day's last workers left
by stage doors set in alleyways.
The night began . . .

A steel-blue lightness in the half-dark
of Charing Cross Road marked the Classic's foyer –
all-night horror and coffee – three fifty.
The Chinese usher handed little packs
of sickly shortbread buttons to the queue,
then disappeared behind a hatch to dole
out plastic cups of coffee – frothy pale –
sugar and milk compulsory. Two films
and a reel on in the musty dimness
a ticketless straggler wove the side aisle;
bottles dropped from his sodden carrier-bag.
The balding plush soaked Cyprus sherry up.
A policeman, manoeuvring, got him
by the intact elbow of his pee-stained mac.
The emergency exit's long bolt scraped
on concrete. Lamplight flooded in.

The river wind chilled the brightness of squares
and bridges, lifting the sick garbage smells
from stores and restaurants, drying the grimed dew
of parks and monuments. Next day's papers
lay in the great old stations, fresh with print.
Outside, the streets were bare, light, free,
the Tubes all latticed shut.

APPLES

Where are the old apples,
the conical, uneven apples, obscurely ribbed,
ripening to deeper yellow,
the crimson-cheeked apples,
marbled and washed with clear red,
the deep lively green apples,
strewed with silvery scales, dark-spotted,
speckled like hens,
brownish, orange-tinged against the sun,
veined in grey russet, angular,
smooth-skinned,
the transparent apples grown on sand,
the Bantam's-egg-sized apples,
the child's-head-sized apples,
the red-fleshed Sops-in-Wine,
anise-flavoured New Rock Pippin,
fennel Ross Nonpareil,
Pitmaston Pine Apple, balsamic Sack and Sugar,
the strawberry and violet flavoured Calville apples,
the waxen-yellow aromatic Gravenstein,
transparent as porcelain,
pine-flavoured Lord Burghley, musky Reinette Franche,
homely Costard, Catshead, Hoary Morning,
Nanny, Cockpit, Hall Door, Bedfordshire Foundling?

On the shelves are our apples – the apples we deserve,
thin-stalked, unctuous, even green, polished to an inconsistency,
flesh sub-acid, cardboard-pipped, eyes stamenless,
sweating under the lights like a crowd of nervous actors.

273

Philip Radmall

LATE EVENING SOCCER AT RUGBY

Across the old playing-fields,
Between the ancient hedges,
the last scattered spores
blew over the cold ground, sodden
and supplicant after the dull rain.
Small, stiff bodies hacked against the gale
blowing from the broad, exposed back
of a ridge rising out of shallow valleys
dim and distant in the late gloom,
and ran through the foul weather shouting
out in the bare field,
as the ball blew away downwind into the trees,
carried, like a seed, toward the black barks
and resting amongst acorns, conkers, dead pollen,
wet leaves cold as carrion,
going old in the damp, mossy ditch.
Then it was kicked back towards the players
wandering in the worsening murk
against the low hills
darkening around them –
until someone handled it,
deliberately, picked it up,
holding it to him, and ran with it
nursed in his arms like a large, generic spore,
germinating into another sport
across the small school ground.
And the hunched, black earth turned
towards a new season, and plunged back
into another night.

THE CHICKENS AT SUMMER KEEP

Look at the strange, ugly perturbations
of these birds, and the short, absurd,
perambulating necks tapered
like their stuck-up arses,
as they walk across the lawn.
I snatched the last eggs from the hutch,
neat and residential, then watched
as these three suburban chickens
raced towards my crude purpose,
like disgruntled housewives, chasing
off a scrumper in their brown pinnies.

SOIL

More contriving than my hand – the creases and quicks
clogged with earth, a white, pulled root relented
and hanging over my fingers – the worm sucked
at the cold soil and repelled it through
its whole body, turning like a warm tongue.
I walked back with the old vegetable
and watched my father, the spade hankering for depth,
still working in that patch for his dinner; whilst the worm
rolled, and tasted the plunged, intruding edge
that returned with the bluntest, absolute method
of anything that tried that old border:
wintered, opened into rough chunks of clag.

'WOMEN DIGGING POTATOES'
(after Van Gogh)

Their hands finger the small rounds – like stones
Cloaked in earth – and dump them into piles.
Large bodied, bending over in their heavy skirts;
Silent commentators, of the ambitious days

That draw in now across the open polder;
A slow perfunctory progress and long task,
Their backsides pointing upwards at the windmills
Which forage also in an awkward element.

And what is the inelegance of the soil
But something they inherited with their birth;
The ungainly earth, the ugly swollen ground?
And they gather up its knowledge in their hands.

These are the reclaimers. These are the peremptory
Processionals wielding their acres,
Stooped across the dirt, and going by the rhythm
Of the soil. These are the travailers of fields.

Theirs are original movements: notice
The broad backs, the intelligence in the hands.
The human course steers round their unprecocious craft.
Within these muddy features are angelic faces.

'WHEATFIELD WITH CROWS'
Van Gogh Museum, Amsterdam

He was bearing out his time there
deliberately, as if something was meant by it,
or as if discovering a fact
under a small constellation of crows
gathering formation.
And he looked
beyond those few birds,
watching them from the road
like a prophet
hauling their image
towards a further significance
as the rich, distinct,
yellow light heightened,
as if his eyes saw
through their own deep sincerity
something latent

278

towards the edge of the wheatfield,
siting the future
in the anguished sky.

He too was never wrong,
my father, about anxiety:
how it was implicit suddenly
in his tired mien
staring down at the soil,
his heavy spade
wedged into a tough border;
how it came then
like a late indulgence,
an ordinary martyrdom
beneath another flock,
bunched and undulant,
heading somewhere out of sight;
as if he studied out
his own privacy
behind that quiet face.
I watched him stand still
on the sodden earth,
as he stared at the darkness,
the mystery of the fields,
the turf heaps burning
like ancient, primitive pyres,
and the soft, smouldering hearths,
the smoke of their last offering
rising like ghosts off hot bones.
And I watched his stiff body
banked in fog
crossing down towards the house
and into the light,
suddenly conscious, I thought, of his own life
against the cold, misty fields;
and then coming in.
But should not something have been left
also from that?
As here, in this last picture:
A fierce light under a noon sky,
some rough track fading into a field,
an acre of agitated wheat.

THE SWING

Inquisitive of the fields
And my eyes watering in the wind
I ran across the long, ancestral lawn
Towards the swing seat.
Where we went that day was a long way away,
Where the river bends into stiff thickets.
And I sat down,
My dress bustling under the apple trees;
And, gulfed in their arcs, I swung
Beneath the shimmering sun.

I played until the evening
Not wanting to leave,
Until the last of the sun
Burned in the cloud above the bottom of the fields.
And all day the dead sedge had smouldered
At the water's edge from the ginger strips of straw
Which the boys had piled into small, secret fires.
At last I sat upon the bank and watched them
Clutching their handfuls of twigs
To be lit. Beside a willow,
A loose, hoarded cache of matches.
Again the thin stems caught and blackened,
And I ran back towards the swing,
The fresh smoke smelling on my clothes,
Still hearing the dry crackle of the straw
From their little hearths of earth.

I headed into the late, warm air,
Slogging back through throngs of shrubs,
A badge of nettle-stings on my ankle,
The soft, pink sky reddening
Like summer's blood glutted on the dying day,
And I felt a quick, dull pulse of sex
Swell between my thighs like a bruising,
And my lips hot like the flames
Stared at by boys wanting to touch.
I stopped and stood:

A brief gift of rain.
Then I stilled the swing.
Did any bird amongst the soaring flocks
Scared from those boughs
Possess my burning limbs then
As I settled in the seat,
Flung up my face at the rain
And flew into the air as if to love it?

INNOCENTS

We loosed our bait, those cold withered lures, alive
down to the weed for the eels, as the nervous barbs
twitched in their soft sides. We watched the slow tide retard
towards the pier-head, and for the sea to give.
The waves, shallow and black, swathed the lower beach
then pulled the eels back; but the catch was low,
the strong wicker baskets down on their hold
buoying beneath our close lines. The sea lay stretched
and apoplectic, the moon's glow tense and spinal
along a line towards us. And I saw my daughter then
bent back over the pier rail, and some boy haul
his tongue out of her mouth – then in again
as hers emerged to meet it, hooking out of her
like a new nerve, exposed, painful and alert.

THE HERRINGS

The white meat, and the bones tugged out
on the lifted spine, the tail's blistered feather;
the fried length of skin; a whole, neat chunk
on my father's fork; and the fish heads

severed in the sink. The way I had them
was slow, mushed in my fingers,
feeling for soft bones.
I was seven years old then

and sat in the lonely kitchen
amongst the rictuses on the faces of fish
slapped in flour; as frightened of myself
as of the winter darkness outside the window.

Tonight I watch a crypt of light in the fire's gules,
and see you there in a slither of fine flame,
the still warm ghost of you
standing at the end of the passage

in your red dressing gown, looking back at me,
burning in these old coals,
the blaze fingering your body
whilst I sit shivering in front of the heaped, hot hearth.

And I watch a plate of fish on my lap going cold
like the herrings in my search for bones; and expect
another night now, coming with the same manic purpose
to force out the boy, still cowering within me.

PRAYER BEFORE BIRTH

A soft but urgent rain accrues upon my face
And figures there like birthmarks
As I emerge from that warm place, ducking
Into the cold night to where you wait.
It is all new to me again: sensings, strugglings,
My head held in the whole world of your hands.
And my first words are not mysteries
But real as weights, and as cumbersome –
Dispelled onto the damp night air:
Difficult, muddled, vernacular.
The tongue heaves the awkward vowels
Which turn and plough the silence like soil.

My father, one night, cycling across the edge of fields
To a phone, prayed God for my delivery,
My blue head hanging dumbly then over the twisted cord;
But would already be asleep now,
Years later, as I stand in this doorway
And you entwine, suddenly,
Your wet white arms around my leaning neck.

Elaine Randell

DUSTING

I sweep the floor and dust
the furniture.
O dust full of earth, leaves,
branches, stones, chalk,
cardboard, tyres, rain.
Particles of bird, mouse,
flower, vole, bee, cat, tree,
chair, curtain, eyelash, postman
and moth.
O dust of shop, wellington, paw,
mouth and starling.
O dust carried in the air from
the fire, from a car, from a foot,
from plane, from lip, from speech,
from a bus, in coal, in wood, in paper.
O dust brought from miles away coming
here to rest in this kitchen only to be wiped up,
moved on, taken back.

7

Cleaning the offices
her stern legs
and tired arms   men stand around
in their shoes
watching tightly guilty.
She met him from school
by the wire mesh gate.
He ran out, the last child.
"I wet my pants" – he cried so hard.
Picked him up, the cold air and his wounds
whipping her heart.

8

They are laughing together at the back
of an old distant photograph.
A key at the door, he is home,
anxiously worn,
snapping at her for some small mistake.
Shipwrecked we are on so faint a seizure
of reality.

15

Along the High Street a woman slaps
her child. Livid at sound.
The lonely assault struck her ribs with clay;
heart broken as a robin's egg.

17

"Hello Mum, I'm home – "
he ran into the house.
"Yes, I can see that" she said leaning
away as he tried to kiss her.
"You haven't a cold have you, we don't want
anything spreading."
He ran out into the garden as far
as the lawn would allow.

SEVEN SCENES FROM THE SAUNA

1

Life without men is such a relief, she said.
Their strong hands and hair curling across
warm shoulders. You can do without it, she said,
all that dressing up and the looking and the
wait and the hope.
What a relief, she said, to be without hope.

2

Luck. I was born lucky – without it, she said
and laughed:
At the Nurseries today a coachload of young bronze Dutchmen came
and looked around the tomato house
and all the girls came out and flirted.
A whole coachload of men and who do I get –
the female teacher comes and talks to me about tomatoes –
Don't talk to me about luck.

3

"Oh, the effort to be healthy", she said
as she sweated away her huge limbs
on the wooden slats.
Ten years I've worked on that Hoffman press.
For ten years that metal bar has struck into my side, look, she said and
showed me the dented mark where the machine had established itself.
That's why my legs are so huge, she said, all that standing. You can't
stand for ten years and not expect the result can you?

4

"I told the judge I did when it came to Court
I don't want no maintenance from him
He can keep his money.
But you can't reason with men can you
and he made me take £4 a week for the girl but of course
he never paid so we had to go back to court again
and I told the judge then –

286

his money stinks worse than he does I shouted
and I don't want it and he don't want to give it.
   – *You're a special sort of woman* the judge said
and it made me feel all sort of glowing and happy
just to see an important man like that say those things to me."

5

They measure your legs and then they wrap you up in those bandages
tight as you can stand and then they cover it with cold stuff like unset
jelly and then they leave you. We didn't half laugh. Then they take it
off and measure you again and let you hold the tape measure so's there's
no cheating and it's great. I lost three inches off my hips and two off
my thighs. Don't know where the fat goes – they say it distributes it.

6

He conceived because I got an electric shock. I was plugging in the
washing machine and I had wet hands and the next thing I knew I was
on the floor on the other side of the room with my arm and hand all black
and the nails gone and the arm jerking up and down. I was in a right state
I can tell you. I rang my Mum and we went to the hospital. I was
in for two nights. Well I never took the pill those two nights did I and
when I got home he was conceived. I didn't give it a thought.
   But he died at 18 months. Hole in the heart. I'm not being horrible
or nothing but it was the best thing seeing as how the marriage was wrong.
I took him to the hospital almost every day at one time but he died. Bill
left the next day and didn't even come to the funeral. He used to smoke
Players and the morning of the funeral he put a note through the door
written on the back of a Players' packet saying 'Can't come to the funeral,
I'm working.' Not even 'Dear Sandra . . .' or signed 'Bill' – just that,
on the Players' packet. I didn't cry about the little one dying for three
months. I had Teresa to look after and I was all alone and then one day
I lost my purse and I showed my neighbour and she came round and put
her arms round me and said, "Never mind love, let's have some tea" but
it was her putting her arms round me that did it . . . suddenly I let go
and cried and cried. No-one had actually touched me for such a long time
you see. I never cry to my Mum. I like her, don't get me wrong, but she
can't accept it when I'm weak. I always have to be strong to her otherwise
she'll say what she always says – "You should never have let Bill leave
you, you have to work at marriage you know."

"Do you live in town?" the woman with short, dark hair and wearing a locket asked me. "No, no, I live out towards the Marsh" I say, "How about you? You local?" I shift on the hot planks – "Yes, we live over the Stanhope, Bradcar Close, you know it?" "Yes, I know it." "I can't stay long in here today, my old man's waiting outside, he changed his shift this week, reckon it's because he thinks I'm up to something while he's at work, thought he'd catch me out today he did by changing without telling me. I've got nothing to hide, more's the pity I'd say! I work at the Fish Restaurant in town. I used to think it was a right hovel till I worked there myself. Often my old man would say to me on a Friday night 'Take you out to the Fish Restaurant, save you cooking' and I'd say 'No jolly fear'. I always thought that place was a hovel, until I worked there that is." I ask if she is full time, "No, not me. But I have investigated the possibility of longer hours if I need to." "Need to?" I query, "Yes, need to. I might be leaving my old man soon, I'm thinking about it, solicitor reckons I've got more than enough grounds to go ahead. We've been unhappy for years now you see, it's only a matter of time I think. He's had that many girlfriends. I know them all. Not that he is anything exciting to look at, I reckon that most people wouldn't look once let alone twice but then there is no accounting for taste is there? Look at me for instance, I thought he was great at one time, five years ago, now he's just a barrel of shit." She shifts on the hot planks of the sauna, body steams away patiently.

"What about you, you married?" she asks, "you look too well to be married," she adds.

"Well, it's all over now that's for sure!" She hasn't waited for my reply but plunges straight on to tell me her tale. "One night we had just finished dinner, lovely dinner I'd cooked, pork chops it was and cabbage and peas and roast potatoes but anyway we'd had a funny day really with him not talking and me being out of sight, talking to the cat and anyway I'd made dinner, took me bloody hours it did while he read the paper and then fell asleep. Sometimes I was glad when he fell asleep at least I didn't have to talk to him did I? Well, we ate most of our dinner and afterwards neither of us moved to get up to clear it away so we both sat and finally after half an hour or so we both walked away, I was buggered if I was going to clear it away and wash the dishes and he was sure too cross with me for one reason or another to do anything but sit and so they sat there, the dishes that is, mouldering.

Next morning we got up, still not said a word and the dishes were still there. They stayed for a week going green. The thing was, them staying there for so long like that, it seemed a sort of monument to our marriage when all was said and done. They seemed to represent my lack of feeling for him, and his lack of giving to me. Being pork of course it just solidified and caked up like that, it went a very strange sort of green in the end.

Eventually I threw them all out – plates too – into the dustbin. 'I don't think I like you very much at all' he said to me as I threw the lot into the wastebin. 'I'm bloody sure I loathe you' I said as I shut the lid on the dustbin.

So you see, it's been a loveless marriage since we met and I'm glad of that job in the Fish Restaurant, you want to try it some time, you and your old man" she says moving her large limbs with her locket round her neck. I said, "Who gave you the locket" "Oh, he did of course, he was always generous, generous with his bloody money and his moods."

CASE NOTE

The first hot days of the year
girls move about the town in last years'
summer clothes, and the men with rolled
sleeves, or bare-backed, paint houses and thatch
rooves in the villages.
I admit into hospital a woman who calls me
the devil's advocate and also Princess Anne, her
delusions hallucinate her dry.
Later an urgent phone call sends me to the
caravan site where Jim, out on bail, tells me that
if I don't give him money for his wife and
child he'll rob a bank. I tell him to rob one for
me too while he's there. On his arm is tattooed
'born to lose'

289

Michèle Roberts

'women's entry into culture
is experienced as lack'

he wishes he were a
one of those able to
dance and shake
breasts and belly and hips
loose, a
not-himself, nothing-but

he wishes they did not have a
hiding from it in his bed stillness
he bruises easily

he wishes he were still a little boy
so that he did not have to face them
telling him he is an oppressor
he needs them to scold him
darling oppressor

if here were a
he would join the   movement
but at least his   friends
are always   who struggle

he has nothing to do but
help them out of
silence, he has
nothing else to do
with   oppression

he wishes they had a   too
so they could all just be friends

THE WOMEN OF THE HAREM

the women of the harem
over breakfast
compare dreams

I was the cup of water
in the desert which he
drained the piece of glass he
wore as diamond the sand
that sucked the fire of his
flesh the silk
that wrapped
the blood of his
bed the oil of
pleasure for his
still limbs I his
casket he my
drowned key

divided angels
swoop
and gobble dry stones

DAPHNE TO APOLLO

our confusion, to make men sound like gods:
unnatural woman, you are a tree
fixated, lost, with a deep gash
to be rained upon, rubbed up against
hidden in, struck down
sold, and burnt, your ashes
worthless

I plead, I can twist like metaphor
I approximate, I sway knee-deep

292

in ferns, I am cultivated, lovely
my bark is a thick plait

I rear myself near a woman lover
we are the hedges around farms
the milking-stool, the cradle
we furnish ships and boxes
brooms, coffins, desks, and paper
we are your floors, your windows
our roots nourish us, twinned
labyrinthine memories, between us
passages, and gaps, and halts
the darkness wet beneath
the perplexed canopy of our hair

my father carves his name
on each in the plantation
clears our flowers, strips us
in a single word
I have stooped for years
I have smiled around him
now, when I fall upon him
crushing, still he protests
you are my tree, only a tree

I too have words now, I have words
I am a woman in the city
but my dreams
flower with him

the forest is long ago, is
deep coal now
I pace the labyrinth
following the gold plait, thick, and knotted
when I find her, I am not only
heroine, but also minotaur, she too

memories of trees
who never yelled, or wept
or went away

CATERPILLAR

she births herself, the grub
the woman eating fear, her
bones black and prickly
tunnels the dark, a dream of water

she weaves a house of hair
golden as Marilyn Monroe,
    scornful as Hippolyta
sweetness glues her mouth, her angry tears
polish her jet-black coffin

she lives the night, the moth
splitting herself open like a rifle-shot
she straggles out, dusky
and brushed with brilliance

she whirrs above the forests
by day she hangs in men's houses
sometimes when still
she fears her largeness and her loneliness

she conceives while flying, the woman
balanced on blades, her art
is to construct what is possible

her daughters' hundred feet
fly in the face
of what is called natural

CIVILISATION'S ACROBAT

you insist
there are obsolescences:
hands that once curved over clumsy tools
carve chips in silicone, compute and clock
brain galaxies, cosmos of nerves and blood

soon, you sparkle
language will wither away
like wings on fish, binary counts
become collectors' items
like masculine-feminine, couples
and jealousy, we'll throw
new switches in the unconscious
and polka to the dialectic
of the paranormal

oh but you stir me up
you curvet in a colt's entrechats
whirl to my arms like
seeds that september scatters
fall, thudding like fruit
onto my earth, albeit
wishing to renounce
custom and gravity

civilisation's acrobat
I dare you to include
these atavistic surges of mine
these sarabandes of the woman corsair
this centuries-old
collapse and cry

post-feminist poet
having regrets

LULLABY

you're the night watchman, fingers swimming
cloaked along dark streets, you spill
lantern light on flesh, slow
guardian of my city's
deepest cellars, round and round you go
you're familiar with my doorway
every hour this summer night
my cones of lilac burn, and drip
like candles, you call out
all's well, all's well

you're the nightingale,
you're the cock at dawn

you're the bruiser, boy, you lust and leap
you scale your mother's lap
like hills in el dorado, leave
home for ever till tomorrow
when she lets you slip, and slaps
you swarm up apple trees, steal fruit
rip legs off flies

you're the pirate baby
you're the mouth at the sweet wine

you're the night fisherman, you push
long finger boats along canals
you slide, exploring, in between the river's lips

and you're the man
who pleasures all my locks with oil
who has the key, who knows the way
in, and who hears me call
all's well, all's well

MAGNIFICAT   *(for Sian, after thirteen years)*

oh this man
what a meal he made of me
how he chewed and gobbled and sucked

in the end he spat me all out

you arrived on the dot, in the nick
of time, with your red curls flying
I was about to slip down the sink like grease
I nearly collapsed, I almost
wiped myself out like a stain
I called for you, and you came, you voyaged
fierce as a small archangel with swords and breasts
you declared the birth of a new life
in my kitchen there was an annunciation
and I was still, awed by your hair's glory

you commanded me to sing of my redemption

oh my friend, how
you were mother for me, and how
I could let myself lean on you
comfortable as an old cloth, familiar as enamel saucepans
I was a child again, pyjamaed
in winceyette, my hair plaited, and you
listened, you soothed me like cakes and milk
you listened to me for three days, and I poured
it out, I flowed all over you
like wine, like oil, you touched the place where it hurt
at night we slept together in my big bed
your shoulder eased me towards dreams

when we met, I tell you
it was a birthday party, a funeral
it was a holy communion
between women, a Visitation

it was two old she-goats butting
and nuzzling each other in the smelly fold

THE FASCIST, WHEN FEMALE

the fascist, when female, looks
forward to nothing: closing
the window she wheels
back to the dark marvellous room, the
merry-go-round of beds, the
crackerjack jokes, the tickles, the
tucking up, just one more story of how
the little princess ran away from home
with daddy

the fascist woman is well
versed in chopping brains
kidneys and liver, hair and fingernails
so now she wants
to cut God's heart out
and chew it raw; this way
she believes she can become God

she freezes her tears
in refrigerator trays, bottles
her lust in glass
rows on the larder shelf; her bundle of twigs
is a birch broom: she excludes
filthy rage, the mess of pleasure
by beating her daughter, beating the floor

I know her: when I lay unconscious
last night, she climbed into bed with me
calling my name
she insists we are
sisters under the same skin

My name's
Lucretia —
what's your
poison?

TO A MALE INTELLECTUAL

you say
colour is clear:
fields lie, little
tucked-up
beds of taut green silk
an orange car comes by
glossy as caramel, colts
kick up their smart white socks

I tell you
look again
brown is brighter than shorn curls
and bronze ditches
are deep with the purple of figs
the hedges' olive mouths
are stained with plums
those forests flush, that
beech-flame interrupts
the willows' silver-grey

only your language knows
where rust ends
salmon, pink begin

I tell you
landscape is truer than you
less curt
and more careless

TRAIN JOURNEY SHREWSBURY-ABERYSTWYTH

Violet earth, green fuzz of grass.
Bright sticks fill the ditches, oildrums pile
next to a swamp rosy with pigs.

Under the elms, the graves are tidy bright
packets of seed laid out in a patience game.
The dead wear florals and do not care.

Snail churches crawl up the hills.
Sheep with red numbers stamped on their backs
lambs in black stockings, spill down the slope

fallen white petals. Chickens
scuttle and flap. Now the hills
swoop and leap, swell to mountains.

At every village stop women and babies
are suddenly visible. The guardsvan disgorges
them, hung about with pushchairs and shopping.

The mothers have stood all the way
in the rattling dark. We rush away from them
as though we have taken vows

of freedom, instability, unchastity.
Single, as serious as brides
we hurtle towards the same deep bed.

IRISH PRISONERS OF WAR

this is the last battleground
their skin is a thin barricade

once, they were rosy mouths at mother's breast
once, they were white milk in a flask of flesh
now that sweetness dries, now their mouths are
stoppered up: the tender leather
of wineskins shrinks
to bags of gristle and sticks

war has boarded their bodies up
and they have flares, not eyes
that burn indifferently
through newsprint, onto our TV screens
no patrol can put that fire out
that consumes their citadel

under their barbed-wire crowns
their souls snarl out:
yellow smears along the walls
they are the holy ones, the lonely anchorites
well schooled in crucifixion, by their priests

wild men, naked, on the blanket
wild women, starving for what
new mothering?

Maria Sookias

THE CONJUGAL RIGHTS OF A PIG

. . . Frigid cow my wife's a bore
Says she can't stand me no more
— And then she goes "You don't care"
Scratching at her crusty hair.
Well I dob her one to stop her gabbing.
"You ignorant pig" — the words are stabbing
So I start on the bastards, little brats,
And I dob them an' all, knock 'em both flat
— But I keep my bottle and head for the pub,
Pints of big nipples and greasy pub grub.
I booze and piss and I booze some more,
Then home to a fat ungrateful whore.
She plays at prick-teasing and runs in the loo
But I get what I want 'cause she wants it too
. . . I'm a man after all and I'll fuck her all night.
Rape of a woman? No — my conjugal right.

305

LONDON – CITY OF NIGHT
(Down and Out in the new Hard Times)

It isn't even raining but it soaks up cardboard feet
And drizzles on the loneliest of people you don't meet
– It seeps among the rubbish bins where lost rejects excrete
And an alcoholic dream will scream at you
                         from a door in Brewer Street.
Into the mucky gutter a tip of fag is flung
That swells a grotty roll-up down a cancer ridden lung,
And raindrops in the drain reflect the winking neon signs
Chasing out the dragons between double yellow lines
That lead to Piccadilly – they call it the Meat Rack
Where a teeny-bopper boy is fed with a money-key on his back . . .
An innocent is play-acting, bravado masks his fear
And the risk of Aids comes closer – he's been tricking for a year.
Repayments are high on the meat rack, everything has a price
And where cobble-stones aren't paved with gold
                         kerbs crawl with body-lice,
And life is sniffed and snorted down
                         through snot and a polythene bag:
Youth's mainline opportunity is Sell, or Be Sold as scag –
When hooked, a herring-boned tripper finds what London's all about
As empty as a bubble, and bitter as best stout.
The myth's long past its sell-by date, the city's rotten mean
And the only Witting Dick you'll see is on a porno screen
That blinds you to the rent-child ageing a year each working night,
Without a hope in hell of Orwell's 'down-and-out' insight
– But still fighting the same battle, to earn a crust of bread
And survive this city of homeless night that breeds the living dead.

FAST FOOD

I'm walking to the restaurant when I see a

– *FLASH* –

and the skin on my eyes
boils and spits
and splits in
     to

– two microwaved eggs –

splattering my hair
– and even that's
          on fire now,
crisp charcoal flesh draped
like a debonair mink
(barbecues are in Vogue this month).

Thought I was a rare human being
– should have known I'd get burned down
to an overdone lump of meat,
fond illusions of being a gourmet
grilled for warheads to eat.

I'd send myself back to the kitchen
but I'm too dead to protest
at screaming shadows on the wall
still waiting for a tip.

  This is not
  a nice place to eat.

HOMECOMING PARTY

"Welcome the hero!"
– We love ya, kid . . ."

Why open the doors and show us this?
Why no toes, no kneecaps
   – no legs at all?
Why no fingernails and –
     Was that a *head*?

The sheep are hushed:
The shepherd proudly reveals
A fitfully moving relic
   On metal wheels.

On its chest is pinned
A candy-striped strip – top prizewinning spoils.
The five-pointed torso sits like a star
Locked in a spotlit space pumped full
   of empty glory,
And he's crying inside
   – What else?

The Lord Mayor blushes, his throat is a lump,
But the official gold watch and handshake
Will fit nowhere
   Upon this mega-stump.

REMEDIAL CLASS

"Get your books ready now 4 C
And Maria, its time for Mrs McFee."
A jury of eyes are scorning at me,
Convicting an idiot – ILLITERACY . . . . .
Slowly I rise avoiding smug stares,
And make for the door with uneasy flair.
Bag on one shoulder – I'm told not to chew,
I spit out the gum and utter "Stuff you – "
I head for the room for thickos and dims,
By-passing ark-angles practising hymns
– There sit the rejects, all solemn and still
Each in there own world, intent on the kill
In the War of the Word, embattled by books.
The General enters, I'm sure the floor shook!
The onslaught begins and so does my sickness,
Line by line – "I'm not feeling well Miss".
The rigourous pages are mapped alphabetically –
I count my class-mates, attacking strategically,
Plotting planned paragraphs that I'll have to stutter.
I turn to a neighbour, " – Whats this say?" I mutter,
Remembering long words and guessing the short –
I'm bullshitting on and havent got caught.
Odd words I don't know the General obliges,
On into darkness – my heart beat rises . . .
The beetroot sits down in releaf that its over.
"An improvement, well done." – The thick cow, I loath her.

The end of the lesson spells faltering hopes –
I'm told I can read – I can't but I'll cope:
Trapped in deceit, so I'll lie till I'm rumbled –
Almost crying I'll giggle, though I feel I might crumble . . .

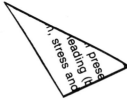

Chris Sparkes

THE SCHOOLBOY

Reading a book,
the schoolboy
rings
the door-bell

and leans
against a wall,
waiting, reading,
— a satchel

twisted round
his back — till
the door
opens — when, heaving

himself
off the wall,
he walks
in, still

reading, not
looking up
from
the page

Geoffrey 'Radix' Chaucer, the great-grandfather of Big League Poetry, not only established nearly all the terms of the modern rules of the game, but was himself a great slugger back in the days when the wild boar sniffed the arboreal breeze in unpolluted Engelond.

A somewhat stout carl, he lacked none of the virtues of an all-rounder in his lord's tournaments against the Infidels. He was also the innovator of the moving portrait-gallery, precursor of our latter-day stadiums, which he designed on the models of the Greek and European architects.

Unlike many superstars, he suffered no shame nor ignominy in numbering himself with the hoipolloi and nondescript, the ne'er-do-wells and vulgar. Nor was he hoodwinked by the gowns and robes of certain ecclesiastic imposters. He preferred the simple benign Persoun whose runs reached to houses far asunder.

His finest match was the epic in which he completed twenty-three home runs on the way to Canterbury, culminating illustriously in one giant whomp over the Cathedral with his wine-dark bat.

When he saw a loose and juicy volley whistling down the track, his eyes twinkled in his head like stars on a frosty night.

A celebrated Forefather of Big League, Radix is sepulchred in Pitchers' Corner in Westminster Abbey.

Radix Chaucer, inspecting a bat:
"Eek, all this new-fanglenesse!"

The big thing about Long John Milton is of course how he managed to play without a decent pair of goggles. Concerning his technique in this, apart from playing with a runner, about as much as anyone ever got out of him was his enigmatic 'stand and wait' – which is only what all sluggers do anyway.

Few have surpassed his Classic bursts of energy, and he perpetually aimed at Erudition. Currently seeded fourth in the world computer rankings, he is one of the top contenders for the Triumvirate of Megabards, and due to his strength his name has eponymously been given to the sag wagon physio's favourite pick-me-up: Miltonic. Also, the white dubbing for Big League boots, now called Meltonian, may have derived from his pure upstanding stance.

Despite the record-breaking efforts of his most famous and supreme individual performance, Paradise Lost, and suffered Perdition. This was mainly thanks to a few giant howlers, now commonly called Milton's Howlers, such as: portrayal of the Captains – a perennial headache; needless swearing at non-existent Muses; mingling deliveries of myth and truth; and spoiling his style with showy, anachronistic, and ill-contex'd Allusion and fo-fum mythology. (Or, as one spectator put it, it needed the blue pencil and a wash and brush-up and its bottom spanked.)

The profligate Captain was hurled headlong out of the Stadium and out of the League to boot, to relegation and "hideous ruin" in Pandemonium. The team fell out, and

Long John Milton –
Steaming one in as of yore

313

made its exit in a ponderous stroll through Eden Park. Their moans redoubled to the hills. There were, however, predestined plans for the return match.

His other more down-to-Earth matches were played for the Puriniks, of whom Oli Crombie was head-honcho in their slog-outs with the Cavalry.

He always played strictly according to the book, never demeaning himself by pandering to the gallery. Accordingly, his style was stiff, but Long John trained hard, and rehearsed some serious up-dates from the ancient Hebrew courts, though not surprisingly he lacked his predecessors' fluid rhythm. His side-show act included Minor League Roman Rules, and he was Roman Rules secretary for Crombie's team, a position won on the merits of just one dedicatory and obsequious lap around the ballpark.

In his last wallop, Long John's art had ironed out the major flaws, and his Sampson re-run is one of Big League's masterpieces. He was back in Classic form, showing know-how, stamina and sheer poetry.

Rightly did the Puritan backfielder Andy Marvell marvel at how Long John "Through that wide field . . . he his way should find."

(Rightly too did his Babe Ruth to come, the Cumbrian Codger Wordsworth, lamenting the barely negotiable fen of stagnant waters and alien corn to which he felt the major home pitches had sunk, courtesy the attempted Augustan Rule Resurgence, invoke Long John's shade – as well we might today – with "Milton, thou shouldst be living at this hour."   *– Ed.)*

BIG LEAGUE POETS   *No. 149*   WILLIAM WORDSWORTH

Codger Wordsworth has been the most over-rated of all Big League's players. He is noteworthy more for his steady performance and lifetime run average rather than for any great individual knocks, except for one or two elevated lofty blows off Gratis Freedom's donkey-drops.

He had a droopy, sombre, sulking stance, as though he'd always just been out first ball, and he was the game's all-time arch bragger. He wrote to one fan who helped pay his subs that his hits would be "efficacious in making men wiser, better, and happier." Imagine passing that round the bleacher-stand.

The annoying thing about him is the impression he gave of putting his own interests before the team's, often dictating matters to his wife or sister (who was just as good a player in her own right in the Women's League). And he made his partner Coleridge, himself a great player and umpire, feel – so he said – 'a little man'.

Codger Wordsworth came from a good sporting family. His sister played some elegant strokes. His brother scored prolifically, was mustard on the rules, and a coach at Cambridge. One nephew toured, coached, commentated, and notched up a majestic hymnal of divine and holy numbers some devotees still sing about. Another nephew played Roman Rules, also coached, and started the first Varsity match.

Codger Wordsworth – another crossbat heave through the daisies

He is the only English Big Leaguer to have written an autobiography, and that without a ghost writer. The truly great contribution from Codger lay in helping to ease Big League out of its 18th Century straitjacket. After his Continental tour his average was ebbing, what with slick Prose taking over the game's dominance. Yet decades later whole teams of Bards really started picking up on some of his rural riffs.

Not exactly a crowd puller with his wit – he was never known to burst a single joke – but for all that, Big League could do with a space-age Wordsworth to free itself from the chains of the new Academy, for many of whom it's not worth cutting down trees to make pitches.

Looking back on the old videos now, Codger really grates – at best a Big League craftsman without Big League flair. There was too much missing from his game for genuine Big League, and dull would one be of soul to get off on his fluttering and dancing about with daffodil wreaths in the Lakeland Stadiums that's given so many schoolboys the jeebies about Big League. Likewise hard to forget is the vacant fielding that so often let his side down, plus his namby *pardonnez-mois*, attitudinising crossbats, and lily-liver *alla stoccatas*. He was consistent, but no good to watch, a plodder entrenched in his mark, and entrenched accordingly in the record books.

One non-plussed critic from East Hampshire once commented that Codger should have left his bat at home and hit the road instead. Nevertheless, portraits of his grumpy head are still familiar in Lakeland gift shops. And as he did slog an incredible number of great boundaries, League bores the world over never stop bickering about whether his bid for the Immortality score has ever been equalled. So his place with Radix in Pitchers' Corner is reasonably appropriate.

BIG LEAGUE POETS *No. 157*   JOHN KEATS

In his short but dynamic career, Babyface Keats was a familiar sight out training on the grounds of Hampstead Heath. He is well known for his obsessive studies underneath his school-desk of the grandmasters of Big League, and for his subsequent imitations of the numbers Petrarch flowed in, and Eddie Spencer's and Bill Strat-Shaker's styles, as well as for his own controversial techniques. He also once borrowed the famous Decameron's Bat of Basil.

He thrilled to watch many an airy clout clamber through the clouds, and there is an interesting legend that after being knocked out by a high celestial body-line ball one time, he got a notebook out and started scribing scribbles and odd jots about a nightingale. Howsoever that may be, it's been authenticated that Babyface wrote to a friend from one of his typical tours that the air in Winchester was 'worth sixpence a pint!'

At its best, his style was exquisite, though at times a bit susceptible to the milquetoast syndrome. His longest knock got bad press from the *Blackwood* reporter, and it won for him the Cloudy Trophy, a sort of backhanded booby-prize donated by Mel Ancholy. After that, it was bedlam for any umpire who was found to be *sans merci.*

After a minor incident following a club meeting in 1820, he spat some blood out and declared, "That drop of blood is my death-warrant." Just a year later, aged only twenty-five, his elegant clouts must no further soar.

He got his last game in just before going to Italy for the final five months of his cursed career. Babyface is buried in Rome next to a couple of team-mates – obituaried with a riddle in Roman rain.

316

Babyface Keats, having been struck on the jaw

LANDSCAPE IN NEW ALRESFORD, HAMPSHIRE

A few black ones amongst
the standard off-white
sheep all of them busily chewing

grass as fast as it grows
on a dampish morning
at the foot of a narrow valley

only a whistle away
from the silver roofed cow-shed
behind the farm gate

in the next field watercress beds
and the banks of the River Alre
then ploughed ruts sloping away

up the hill the sheep down
in their pasture marching
forward advancing slowly each one

in a different direction
never more than four steps at a time
or three steps or two

or half a step a number of them
grouped where the fence
meets the hedgerow several rooks

around them walking over tufts
as though their hands
are stuffed in their pockets

or their trousers
dally round their ankles
each creature alone

and separately enjoying
the blessings of the land
it stands on

head down
no time for
anything but its grazing

ART IN RUSSIA

(After seeing *Dr Zhivago*)

In the swaying wheatfields of Russia,
A posse crawled on its belly and sniped
Enemies of the state, and burned villages.
Blood flowed, running down necks like snow
In avalanches. Men in red jackets
With gold frogging stood by in bleak winds,
And a fat one ran a hand through his hair
Saying, "It's nothing to worry about;
The personal life is dead." The book
Slapped shut, and he wiped his spectacle lenses
While seagulls flew over roof-tops.

All thought revolves around the self. I
Am an enemy of the state. Visions to
Underground poets came blustering!
They hid in corridors of paranoia, and dared
To write, and dared to paint shorthand iliads.
On floorboard rooms from Moscow
To Vladivostock to Leningrad they laughed
In their beards, as a woman
In her thirties sang like a linnet
And tuned her lyre to a ballad, or a poem,
With a tune composed by the poet.

Rifle butts smashed finger bones.
There was screaming, tearing across
Squares. In the streets they wrote reams of oracular poems
And allegories, and prophetically on their knees
Drew one-man shows in pastel
On paving stone galleries. Like a pastiche
Of tomorrow's portraits, Isayevich stood
Shaking his fists at soldiers and thugs,
As rain fell on paper pavements,
As crayon grassblades cut through concrete,
And wheat grains fell to the ground, and died.

The Garden

In the Garden of
Contentment
Where rests at ease
the rake,
And hidden lies the
Billhook,
There glides a little
snake.

WESTERN HAIKU

i   like a maternity dress
        the honeymooners' tent
     flapped in moonlit wind

ii   through the leafless apple orchard
     spokes of January sunlight
       splash the frosty boughs

EASTERN HAIKU

i   assembly of jap
     anese motorcycle re
     quire great peace of mind

ii   dismantling of peace
     of mind require great Japan
     ese motorcycle

SOAP BUBBLES

A screaming child in a shopping precinct/ with all the trauma of the hour of birth stamped on her howling face/ on noticing at last/ a spray of bubbles/ then a stream of bubbles in the street wind/ blowing like shooting stars/ from the short plastic bubble-wand of another child/ in the twinkling of an eye is transfigured/ and released/ into delirious expressions of the gift of life.

Unshouldered of her woes now/ she makes clumsy handclaps/ and flails her arms/ in her new world/ of shrieks/ and silent pops/ and armfuls of glassy bubbles. And the father/ with the carrier bags/ stands amazed.

Is there anything so captures the eyes of a child/ as even a single bubble/ the size of a sorbo ball/ rising up past staircase railings/ and second floor windows/ blown up from the dustbins/ empty cartons/ and twisted bicycle wheels of her own backyard/ until the next bubble takes flight/ and so on/ one after another/ lifting the child's eyes/ transporting them/ to the bright clouds and squinting heavens?

Neil Sparkes

the king's head.

sun-burst smack
through a bank
of floating grey
roof-top chimney
giving the sky
a poke
rain drop
crystals dot
the window pane
tucked up snug
with a burn on
the guinness as
warm as the sun.

drum.

the skull
of a dog

a smack of
the lips

trains on
the tracks

and the
crack of
a bone

timbre and
cadence

voices and
tongues

the drum speaks.

325

drums in the rain.

i hear drums
when rain
begins to fall.

it echoes in
the backyard
like a bust
old tap
dripping on a beat
and tattered
bass drum skin

a ghostly sound

howling dogs and
shivering rats
cat squeal fucking
the drum
pattering and
tapping out
of time

as if an old
tramp thrumming
on the bass drum
with bone white
old fingers

shot to pieces
on scotch

all empty
bottles and a
twisted eye

out in the backyard
gone midnight
in the rain.

love like.

a love like
the shit process
the tension
in the stomach
excitement limbs
the want to
but i'll wait
and then
the pleasure
sat crouched
on the seat
a love like
the shit process
after you
flush just
the stink
and an
empty pan
and all
you can do
is wash your
hands and leave.
love like shit.

327

night train.

clear ice air
blows on my
face through
the open window
of a night
train compartment
winter sky
sea blue

black purple
train sounds
rattle on
the tracks
the orange of
towns cutting
the blue

then shadows

of platform
people as
it pulls away.

underground postmen.

lost on the
london underground
all the tunnels
look alike
this is where
i was before.
turning a corner
i am knocked
down by a
postman riding

a bicycle.
there's a crate
of white chickens
on the front
of the bike.
chickens scatter
in all directions
when they hit
the ground
they turn into
un-delivered
letters.

tunnel vision.

grey diesel
filth
rattling incessantly
slime station
platform skin

this girl
comes on
all smiles
and tight arse
blue jeans

vomit spattered
all over the
carriage floor
chewing gum
crusted on seats

rain shivers
down the
brown panes
stench of
cigarettes and piss.

on the train.

an old woman
without teeth
mouths words
without sounds

a blond girl
with red eyes
like she's
been or is
going to cry
behind her
sore gaze
i read a
goodbye letter

a paki looking
bloke eyeing
up an indian
girl, like
she was a
chicken tikka
looking away
if i look
directly at him.

i thank god
and british rail
that i'm
holding it all
together

only to catch
sight of my
unshaven image
in the window
and see i'm
as near the edge
as the rest.

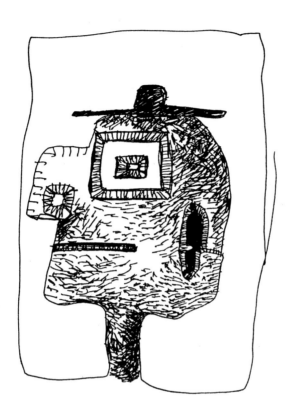

knowing people.

glassed
his face opened
like a zip-up bag
all its contents
spilt down his shirt

anyone can commit murder
– talking and knowing
people in this
fucking shambles
is the hard thing.

Paul Weller

TEN TIMES SOMETHING EMPTY   (1980)

1   Like the six year old left waiting in a deserted playground,
     Waiting for his mum, to take him home.

2   Like being lost in a desert and seeing your shadow,
     On the horizon.

3   Like standing at the edge of the cliffs at land's end (at sunset)
     And glimpsing you in a white sail-boat.
     Three hundred yards off shore.

4   Like running over grey sky golf courses,
     And catching your darkened figure, fleetingly escaping
     Over Surrey downs.

5   Like a tired suburban station, in early morning,
     Your face at the window of a passing train
     Bound for Waterloo.

6   Like spotting you from the top of a high place
     At the end of a rainbow, fleshly wet,
     Three miles across town.

7   Like walking round a busy Saturday market,
     I saw you through the crowds
     But couldn't reach you because of them.

8   Like at dawn, through a London window,
     Watched you play in the square,
     But by the time I got there – you were gone.

9   Like a quiet Sunday museum –
     I turned to see your back slip through the revolving doors
     Into a waiting black cab.

10   Like from a Sussex summer field with tall wheat,
     I watched and suddenly spotted you
     On a country road, walking lonely, but carefree
     – I ran to catch up, but you'd already turned at the crossroads
     And I didn't know which way . . . . . .

Like something very empty.

332

THE STORY OF SOMEONE'S SHOE   (1987)

It's either –
Something in their eyes or something in the drink
But whatever it is they both stop and think –
There's no going back and nothing above
It's lust or loneliness – but seldom love.

She takes a breath as he takes his keys
First name terms is the extent of it –
There's no getting out as they're going in
But by tomorrow they both will begin

To regret and renege on a bond they have struck
A small price to pay and casual luck.
Some lose nothing – some lose a lot
But whatever we have is all we have got.

He takes her hand and leads to the room
In half-light and silence for their clothes to remove
– There's no doubt in her mind, but hope in her heart
That this last one of many may be the start.

So they wriggle and writhe for an hour or two
But time has no place when two are consumed –
They moan and they gasp but they don't really speak
As no conversation will fit this scene.

And tomorrow as always, always comes
As she slips away – he still dumb –
He felt the urge just as she felt the need –
Now the need to get out, still carrying his seed

– Which trickles down her leg and onto her shoe
Onto the pavement and then out of view –
Into the gutter and down into a drain
Joining a river and there to remain –

There's no going back, there's nothing above –
It's lust and loneliness that drive us along

    It's lust and loneliness
    But it's seldom love.

333

SATURDAY'S KIDS

La la la la la la la la la ___ la la la la la la la la la la ___ la.

Sat - ur - day's boys live life ___ with in - sults, drink lots of beer and wait for half time re - sults,
Sat - ur - day's kids play one - arm ban - dits, they nev - er win but that's not the point is it?

af - ter - noon tea in the Lite - a - Bite ___ chat up the girls, ___ they dig it!
Dip in sil - ver pa - per when their pints go flat, how a - bout that. ___ Far out, man, their

Sat - ur - day's girls work in Tes - co's and Wool - worth's, wear cheap perfume 'cause it's all they can ___ af - ford.
mums and dads smoke Cap - stan non fil - ters, wall - pa - per lives 'cause they all die of can - cer,

Go to dis - cos they drink Ba - by - cham ___ Talk to Jan ___ in bin - go ac - cents.
What goes on, ___ what goes wrong ___

save up their money for a hol-i-day — to Sel-sey Bill or Brack-le-sham Bay. —

Think a-bout the fu-ture when they'll — set-tle down, — marry the girl next door, when

one on the way, — these are the real creat-ures that time has for-got, — not gi-ven a thought, —

it's the sys-tem, hate the sys-tem, what's the sys-tem? —

Instr.

Sat-ur-day's kids live in coun-cil hous-es, wear V-necked shirts and bag-gy trou-sers.

Drive Cor-tin-as, fur

trimmed dash boards, stains on the seats — in the back, of course! La la la la la la

la la la — la la la la la la la la la la la la — la.

335

SATURDAY'S KIDS   (1979)

Saturday's boys live life with insults,
Drink lots of beer and wait for half-time results;
Afternoon tea in the Lite-a-Bite – chat up the girls
 – they dig it!

Saturday's girls work in Tesco's and Woolworth's,
Wear cheap perfume 'cos it's all they can afford;
Go to discos – they drink Babycham, talk to Jan
 in Bingo accents.

Saturday's kids play one-arm bandits,
they never win but that's not the point is it?
Dip in silver paper when their pints go flat,
How about that – far out!

Their mums and dads smoke Capstan non-filters,
Wallpaper lives, 'cos they all die of cancer,
What goes on – what goes wrong?

Save up their money for a holiday
to Selsey Bill or Bracklesham Bay;
Think about the future – when they'll settle down,
Marry the girl next door – with one on the way . . .

These are the creatures that time has forgot,
Not given a thought – it's the system,
Hate the system – what's the system?

Saturday's kids live in Council houses,
Wear V-necked shirts and baggy trousers,
Drive Cortinas, fur-trimmed dashboards,
Stains on the seats – in the back of course . . .

PRIVATE HELL   (1979)

Closer than close you see yourself –
a mirrored image of what you wanted to be.

As each day goes by, a little more
You can't remember what it was you wanted anyway.

336

The fingers feel the lines, they prod the space –
Your ageing face – the face that once was so beautiful
        is still there but unrecognisable
          – private hell . . . private hell.

The man who you once loved is bald and fat
And seldom in – working late as usual.

Your interest has waned, you feel the strain –
The bedsprings snap, on the occasions he lies upon you
          – close your eyes and think of nothing but
        private hell . . . private hell.

Think of Emma, wonder what she's doing –
Her Husband Terry, and your grandchildren.

Think of Edward who's still at college –
You send him letters which he doesn't acknowledge

'Cause he don't care – they don't care
'Cause they're all going through their own
        private hell . . . private hell.

The morning slips away in a valium haze
And catalogues – and numerous cups of coffee.

In the afternoon the weekly food
Is put in bags and you float off down the High Street.

The shop windows reflect – play nameless host
To a closet ghost, a picture of your fantasy
  – A victim of your misery
        and *– private hell . . . private hell.*

Alone at six o'clock you drop a cup –
You see it smash – inside you crack,
You can't go on –
           but you sweep it up

    – Safe at last inside
    your *private hell*

    – Sanity at last inside your
    private hell . . . private hell
  . . . private hell . . . private
hell . . . private
      hell –

GHOSTS OF DACHAU*

I close my eyes I reach out my hand and there you are
Beautiful in scabs caressing my scalp
Under the mounts of the gun towers.

The crab lice bite the typhoid smells and I – still here
Handsome in rags, a trouserless man
Waiting helpless
        for dignity.

Come to me, angel
Don't go to the showers,
  Beg, steal or borrow – now
There's nothing left to take
        except eternity.

I shout your name, I kick out in dreams and here we are
– The searchlight beams the siren squeals
And hopeless shuffle
        to certainty.

And who will come to flower our graves with us still here
Covered with dust, remembered by few
But forgotten
        by the majority?

Stay with me, angel
Don't get lost in history
– Don't let all we suffered
Lose its meaning in the dark
        that we call memory.

* – *This is about people who still (try to) carry on their love affair amidst the death
and degradation in Dachau, a Nazi concentration camp. I went to Dachau, which
is just outside Munich in Germany, in 1978 and still the place haunts me. I think
if everyone could be made to visit those Nazi death camps, it would soon put a stop
to a lot of the racist bullshit around.* (P W, 1984)

ETON RIFLES   (1979)

Sup up your beer and collect your fags,
There's a row going on down near Slough.
Get out your mat and pray to the West,
I'll get out mine and pray for myself.

Thought you were smart when you took them on
But you didn't take a peep in their artillery room –
All that rugby puts hairs on your chest
– What chance have you got against a tie and a crest?

>   *Hello Hooray – what a nice day*
>   *for the Eton Rifles, Eton Rifles –*
>   *Hello hooray, I hope rain stops play*
>   *with the Eton Rifles, Eton Rifles.*

Thought you were clever when you lit the fuse,
Tore down the House of Commons in your brand new shoes,
Composed a revolutionary symphony
Then went to bed with a charming young thing.

>   *Hello Hooray, Cheers then mate*
>   *it's the Eton Rifles, Eton Rifles –*
>   *Hello Hooray, an extremist scrape*
>   *with the Eton Rifles, Eton Rifles.*

What a catalyst you turned out to be,
Loaded the guns then you run off home for your tea.
Left me standing
            like a guilty schoolboy . . .

We came out of it naturally the worst,
Beaten and bloody and I was sick down my shirt,
We were no match for their untamed wit
Though some of the lads said they'd be back next week.

>   *Hello Hooray, there's a price to pay*
>   *to the Eton Rifles, Eton Rifles –*
>   *Hello Hooray, I'd prefer the plague*
>   *to the Eton Rifles, Eton Rifles –*

340

Eton Rifles, Eton Rifles . . . . . .

Eton Rifles, Eton Rifles.

BLOODSPORTS   (1985)

Who takes the heart from a stag
Who gets a hard-on with blood on their hands –
Who strips the wonder of life
When they don't have the right
– But they say it's fair game
And they won't feel no pain
As we feel no shame.

> *So let the sun come down*
> *Let our eyes close the blind*
> *Let the rivers run dry*
> *Let the forest life die.*
> *– But who are they to decide*
> *As if their right is divine –*
> *As if their right is sublime?*

Who wins the hooves loses respect –
Who kills the Grace treads with intent
Into heaven's domain
Playing little Christians
– Hear their voice soar in Church
Giving thanks for this Earth
Then destroying its birth –

> *So let the sun come down*
> *Let our eyes close the blind*
> *Let the rivers run dry*
> *Let the forest life die.*
> *– But who are they to decide*
> *As if their right is divine –*
> *As if their right is sublime?*

341

THE WHOLE POINT OF NO RETURN   (1984)

The harbour lights that shine before me
The jewels that glint from the beckoning sea
The rising shrieks that come from below me
The rushing winds of age and time

> *To close my eyes and feel the fall*
> *To not resist unto the pull*
> *– Oh it's easy, so, so easy.*

A tiny scent that breezes past me
A promise that all could be mine
Just lose myself and make it easy
But I'm not prepared to live the lie

> *To shut my mouth and just say yes*
> *To make a vow and then confess*
> *– It's so easy, much too easy.*

With all the power that I possess
My faith alone shall stand the test

> *To live my life as I see best*
> *Without dark glasses or rosy specs*
> *– It's not easy, not so easy.*

LITTLE BOY SOLDIERS   (1979)

It's funny how you never knew what my name was,
Our only contact was a form for the election . . .
These days I find that you don't listen
These days I find that we're out of touch
These days I find that I'm too busy
– So why the attention now you want my assistance
– What have you done for me?

You've gone and got yourself in trouble,
Now you want me to help you out.
These days I find that I can't be bothered
– These days I find that it's all too much
To pick up a gun and shoot a stranger
– But I've got no choice, so here I come
War games . . .

I'm up on the hills playing little boy soldiers,
Reconnaissance duty – up at 5.30:
' – *Shoot, shoot, shoot and kill the natives*
– *You're one of us and we love you for that.*
Think of honour, Queen and country,
You're a blessed son of the British Empire
– *God's on our side and so is Washington.*

'*Come out on the hills with the little boy soldiers*
Come outside – I'll sing you a lullaby,
Or tell a tale of how goodness prevailed:
We ruled the world – we killed and robbed,
The fucking lot – but we don't feel bad
– *It was done beneath the flag of democracy* . . .
You'll believe' – and I do – yes I do – yes I do
– Yes I do – yes I do – yes I do – ooh . . .

These days I find that I can't be bothered
To argue with them – well what's the point?
Better take your shots and drop down dead
– Then they send you home in a pine overcoat
With a letter to your mum saying
Find enclosed one son, one medal
– And a note to say he won.

LITTLE BOY SOLDIERS

It's fun - ny how you ne - ver knew what my name was, our on - ly con-tact was a
You've gone and got your - self in trouble, now you want __ me to

form for the e - lec - tion. These days I find that I __ don't lis - ten, these days I find that we'
help you out. __ These days I find that I __ can't be bothered, these days I find that it's
These days I find that I __ can't be bothered, to ar - gue with them well

__ out of touch These days I find that I'm __ too bus - y so why the attention now yo
__ all too much to pick up a gun and shoot __ a stran - ger but I've got no choice out here
__ what's the point, better to take your shots and drop __ down dead then they send you home in a pine

To Coda

want my as - sis - tance. What have you done __ for me.
__ I come __ war games. __
__ ov - er - coat. with a let - ter to your

(Drums) 8

I'm

up on the hills playing little boy soldiers, re - connaissance dut -y up at five thir-ty.

Shoot, shoot, shoot and kill the natives, you're one of us and we love you for that.

344

Think of honour, Queen and country, you're a blessed son of the Bri-tish Empire. God's

on our side and so is Washing-ton. Come out on the hills with the little boy soldiers, I'm

up on the hills playing little boy soldiers, Come out on the hills playing little boy soldiers.

(Molto accel.)

Come on out-side, I'll sing you a lul-la-by, or tell a

tale of how good-ness pre-vailed: we ruled the world, we

killed and robbed the fuck-ing lot, but we don't feel

(a tempo 1st time)

bad. It was done be-neath the flag of de-moc-ra-cy you'll be-lieve

and I do, yes I do, yes I do, yes I do, yes I do, yes I

do. Ooh.

⊕ CODA

mum, say-ing find en-closed one

son, one me-dal and a note to say he won.

345

DOWN IN THE TUBE STATION AT MIDNIGHT (1978)

The distant echo of faraway voices boarding faraway trains
To take them home to the ones that they love who love them forever
The glazed dirty steps repeat my own and reflect my thoughts
– Cold and uninviting, partially naked but for toffee wrappers
      and this morning's papers – *'Mister Jones got run down'*
– Headlines of death and sorrow, they tell of tomorrow,
Madmen on the rampage – and I'm
      Down in the tube station at midnight.

346

I fumble for change, I pull out the Queen – smiling, beguiling . . .
I put in the money and pull out a plum – behind me
Whispers in the shadows, gruff blazing voices – hating, waiting
– "Hey boy," they shout "have you got any money"
And I say "I've got a little money and a take-away curry,
I'm on my way home to my wife –
She'll be lining up the cutlery, you know
She's expecting me, polishing the glasses and pulling out the cork"
. . . I'm *down in the tube station at midnight*.

I first felt a fist and then a kick – I could now smell their breath
They smelt of pubs and Wormwood Scrubs
      and too many right wing meetings.
My life swam around me – it took a look
      and drowned me in its own existence
– The smell of brown leather blended in with the weather
Till my eyes, ears, nose and mouth were blocked
Till senses couldn't hear speak any longer
. . . I'm down in the station at midnight –
I said I was
      Down in the tube station at midnight.

The last thing that I saw as I lay upon the floor was
'JESUS SAVES' painted by some atheist nutter
and a British Rail poster saying Have an Awayday
– a cheap holiday a Do it Today . . .
– The wine will be flat and the curry's gone cold
I glanced back on my life, I thought about my wife
      'cause they took the keys and she'll think it's me
– I'm down in the tube station at midnight
– The wine will be flat and the curry's gone cold
And I'm
      down in the tube station at midnight
– Don't want to go
Down
      in the tube station at midnight
                   – Oh . . .

347

Ifigenija Zagoričnik-Simonivić

I USED TO BE A GIRL

One day my stepfather decided to strangle me.
He took care of me, then. He was taking me, then.
He had had me ever since we moved into his house.
He took care of me, then. My mother said, I was
lucky. Not all stepfathers love their stepdaughters.

To strangle me was quite alright. I did indeed
miss the bus. I did indeed have sand in my schoolbag.
I did indeed forget to learn the rhymes. I did indeed
fail to be good, Oh, I did, my mother said, I was
lucky. Not all stepfathers are concerned.

No, I did not mind being strangled at all.
I only felt wrong doing him a favour.

My mother was standing by, watching, holding hands
ready to catch me, later. Afterwards. She was going to
catch me, I knew I could trust her.

I looked at her face and I looked at his face
and the faces blended into a blurry patch of coloured
mist and cloud. Only their eyes were pecking through
like beams, hot rays making my throat dry and sore.

I could not stop thinking. I was visualising the day
before. He was handling me. He was saying not to be
scared. He needed me, he said. He washed his congealed
milk out of my hair just on time. I told my mother that
I was wet because my baby brother pissed into my face.
We all laughed.

I am here now. Still here. I am
looking forward to the final blow. I am indeed looking
forward into the future. I am lucky. I have no daughter.
I would find it hard to hold hands out ready to catch her.

348

AFTER LOVEMAKING

you alone beside me
me beside you alone
    a spider
creeps out of my eyes
my head is split open
    night
builds its nest there
and hatches
    its young

ONLY   ONLY

I do not only have
        my life in my hands

I do not have my life
        only in my hands

(translated by the author with Anthony Rudolf)

GIVE A CHILD IN A CAGE

TO A CAGED BIRD

you may pull child's hair
  you may peck its eyes
you may blow the child up
  you may rape it
you may bring the child up

you may hold it by its ankles
  six feet off the ground
you may drop it
you may chain it to the radiator
or let it flutter from the church tower
  a flag for our familiarities

you may stuff child's mind
  with clutter
  you may love it
go on
  suffocate it in your embrace
go on
  poison it with your kisses

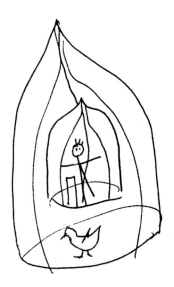

you may let your child develop
  acute disappointment
  let it hope
go on
  just let it be

  you can explain
  you can give orders
  you can promise

  anything

look — flies have their wings plucked out
  chicken gets its head cut off
  cat has its litter drowned

350

IT IS TIME TO GO

he invites me and I go
passing the alarm at the front
and one at the back
through double-locked doors
passing the kennel
also locked
    though he has
    no dog.

he invites me and I go then
between the sheets
    the whiteness cuts into my cuts
    his bedside cupboard locked
    the doors to all the empty rooms
    all locked my cuts opened wide
    coffee afterwards
    behind locked doors

he invites me and I am there
    but not quite and also quite disturbed
    a moth is fluttering around
    the lampshade and I can hear
    the video is on
    and I can hear something
    whispering in my rear
    it's my cunt
    even she can't take it

A POET

When I take off my head
the head looks
into my bleeding neck

    I do not shout
    I do not run amok
    like a wild boar
    I do not stare
    into a blank wall

I only take off my head
so that it can look at me
and think its own thoughts

LITTLE BOAT FLOATING

spring comes
    without fail ever

willow trees green
    whilst I hesitate
    (do I want more springs?)
a bird floats its song
    on the air – it
    doesn't ask why waters
    overflow why they
    run blindly why
ice eats into valleys

            go on floating
            go on floating

spring throws mud in our eyes
awakens us with sunrays
    then strikes us blind
– nothing that runs
    or flies or crawls
    can escape ever

peasants cut down trees
birdsong falls off

            go on floating
            go on floating

(translated by the author with Michael Horovitz)

Benjamin Zephaniah

FOR TWO YEARS ONE TIME

For two years one time I lived in a cell,
then outside was heaven for that cell was hell.
The wardens would tell me what time I should wash
– told me what I should, and what I should not.
First thing in the morning they made me slop out
this meant wash my face, and then came the shout
to go down to breakfast to eat some bad food,
I could not complain, I could not be rude
– I worked in a big ugly guarded workshop
I would start work at nine and at five I would stop.
The job I was doing was making baskets;
the prisoners would talk of their loves and regrets
– I recall an inmate, can't think of his name,
well he came from Birmingham, by the river Tame,
and he used to talk of the crimes he had done
– then one day he told me that prison was fun.
The walls they were covered with nude shots of girls
and smoked cigarette butts were treated like pearls.
I saw prison wardens beat men till them sick
and then run them off to the hospital quick.
At night when lights out cockroach congregate;
it was easy to hear lonely men masturbate
they would call girlfriends' names or try sexing young men
– if you don't know prison please don't go my friend.
For two years one time I lived in a cell,
and I really mean it, it was fucking hell.

AS A AFRICAN

As a African I danced to riddims wild in Nicaragua,
I overstood dem well.
As a African I did not celebrate 200 years of Australia,
I understood its history is black.
As a African I went to find Palestine,
I got confused on de West Bank,
And as a African Palestine is important.

As a African I grew old,
I went and sat down and reasoned with Mr. Ayatollah.
Mr. Ayatollah told me to mind my own business,
and so did Mr. President USA.
Mrs. Thatcher wouldn't even talk to me.

As a African a plastic bullet hit me in Northern Ireland,
But my children overstood an dey grew strong.
As a African I was a woman in a man's world,
A man in a computer world,
A fly on the wall of China,
A Rastafarian diplomat
And a miner in Wales.

I was a red hot Eskimo
A peace loving hippie
A honest newscaster
A city dwelling peasant,
I was a Arawak
A unwanted baby
A circumcised lady,
I was all of dis

And still a African.

MISS WORLD

Beauty is about how you behold
more than silver more than gold
if I say I am beautiful
it means beauty is accessible,

'cause beauty is about how you greet
de everyday people dat you meet
you are beautiful so all rejoice
your beauty is a natural choice.

My sister is a beautiful girl
but she don't want to be Miss World
her value is not prize money
more value than a pearl
my sister is a beautiful girl
human delight
she could be out of sight but she would rather stay and fight.

Her legs are firm and strong
best for self-defence
dis daughter kicks like wildfire
so cause no grievance
she won't walk the platform
to upsex people's lust
and you can't get the number of her height, age or bust;
she don't want to go to the market
to be viewed like a slave
the viewing time is over
put de judge in the grave;
she don't need to go to the market
'cause she's already won
beauty contest no contest
she don't need to run.

I talk of people in society who judge you by your looks, and
they will give you a number dat is written in a book,
lustful eyes from all around come to look at you,
and dey will judge your lifetime
by a quick interview.

My sister is a beautiful girl
but she don't want to be Miss World
her personality can't be rewarded by no judge or earl.

My sister is a beautiful girl
she needs no contest
and you can't put her with another judging who's the best.
And you cannot judge my sister's heart
by looking, just by looking, and staring at her breasts.

SO FARI

in I do I find I salvation
in I all good things are a must
in I do I see I liberation
in I only I do I trust,
in I is the will to keep on going
in I is the shining of the day
in I is the knowledge of dread knowing
in I is the homebound highway.
Your I is no different from I I
all I's are alike in I eye
the seeing of you I make me high
I and I together in FARI.

BEAT DRUMMERS

Come Zipporah come rock with I
songs of praise to set spirit high,
drummers beat, drummers beat,
we were never here to stay
hear that sound from far away,
drummers beat, drummers beat,
beat drummers beat 'cause the beat well sweet
beat down the beat that cools the heat,
drummers beat, drummers beat.

Come little children rock with I
the beat of the drum will never die,
drummers beat, drummers beat,
drum beat sound will never drown
listen to the beat as the beat beats a hard,
drummers beat, drummers beat,
beat drummers beat and beat it hard
beat it like you beat when you beat it back a yard,
drummers beat, drummers beat,
beat drummers, beat drummers beat drummers beat.

WHAT YU EAT

Fish an chips will cramp yu lips
an currant buns will hurt yu bum
hot curries will mek you run
hot peppars mek yu angry.
Sausages might give you fits
too much mincemeat gives you de S!!!s
an chillies mek yu eyes go red
brown bread's alright wid honey.
Some take-away may sell yu dogs
small ants fried go nice wid frogs,
drink vinegar juice an' you'll hang loose
an chewing garlic's funny.
But people dey will always eat
veg, pulses, fungi and meat;
today I sat down in a seat
an watched a man eat money

360

ROBOTS OF THE FUTURE

The Robots of the future they living here today,
you see them on the trains, they like to hear what papers say,
their movements, they are limited to working and the pubs,
their happiness is having sex and eating fancy grubs.
The politicians run their lives,
and for this the Robots grateful,
they never did think for themselves, and they were never able,
beware – approach with caution, they are programmed to obey,
the Robots of the future are living here today . . . .

GREEN

Everyone's talking bout protecting the planet
As if we just come on it
It's hard to understan it.
Everyone's talking bout the green revolution
Protecting de children an fighting pollution
But check – capitalism an greed has caused us to need
Clean air to breathe, yes
When you get hot under the collar
You suddenly discover dat you're going Green all over.
– For years
You've been fighting wars an destroying de scene
An now dat you're dying
You start turn green

A few years ago if you wanted peace
you would have to make a demonstration.
You were called a traitor, a Russian infiltrator,
De scourge of de nation
– A few years ago if you said you were Green
You were really seen as Red.
Yes a few years ago you were seen as a weirdo
If you were to eat brown bread.
Now you don't have to be clever to know bout salmonella
An dere are many reasons to diet like a vegan.
Now it is official: don't eat too artificial
When you're told you have no future, try some acupuncture.
To live long, get wise an try some exercise.
Forget de Harp, stay sharp
An tek care of you heart.
To go jogging is belonging
Walk instead of driving
– You start thinking of surviving now dat you are dying
Remember old time saying: Beware of what you're spraying
Now is de time to panic
So let's go eat organic
Your fridge will burn creation –
Dis is so-called progression.
– For years
You've been fighting wars an destroying de scene

And now dat you're dying
You start turn green

Many singer songwriters have it as a topic:
De rainforests, those hungry people
– Daddy, we must stop it.
De ozone layer's fading
– I must make an LP
I'll get de credit an I'll give de cash to charity.
(I must be honest
And speak personally:
I don't have dat much money to give to charity.
My people were rich but robbed
An we were healthy
so I don't know bout you but me, I plead Not Guilty.)
So now you have a house
World music gets you high
An now you exercising hard cause you don't want to die
An you got loadsamoney but you don't need no cash
Cause you got loadsa credit cards an you're so proud of dat
De greenhouse effect makes de world hotter, but
If you have loadsamoney really it nu matter.
Nobody knows what's happening to de weather
An all of a sudden we're told to pull together
– Pull together?
Pull together.
An recycle yer paper.
De Government said if you don't you will regret it later.
They used to say dat Green was soft
Don't worry bout de atmosphere
An now a scientist has said:
Oh damn, we're going to disappear.
– For years
You've been fighting wars an destroying de scene
And now dat you're dying
You start turn green

Now when it comes to wars   governments are funny
Lives are secondary   first is bloody money
Troops out if it costs too much   troops in if it pays
And in the English dictionary   what is war anyway?
Angola: dat's war

Afghanistan dat's war
Tibet dat's war
– Far-off people have dem
Ethiopia dat's war
El Salvador dat's war
Bolivia dat's war
– Feel sorry for de children
Lebanon dat's war
Gaza dat's war
Mozambique dat's war
– An someone's got to stop dem
Korea dat's war
Haiti dat's war
Northern Ireland . . .   Er, well –
Dat's somethin else
– Now dat is just a problem.
Still we don't have no constitution
So-called progress breeds pollution
You can buy a share in de illusion
Or you can go to school an study de Green solution
– For years Green tings have been pushed aside
We're going fast on a downward slide
Now who's going Green on de sly?
Is dat kinda business upset I.
– For years
You've been fighting wars an destroying de scene
an now dat you're dying
You start turn green

Everyone's talking bout protecting de planet
As if we just come on it
It's hard to understan it.
Everyone's talking bout de green revolution
Protecting de children an fighting pollution.
– But check
Humans have been taking and not giving
An now de boat is sinking you stop an start thinking
Yes, well, there is a change of tone
De problem's coming home
De world's a danger zone.
– For years
You've been fighting wars an destroying de scene

An now dat you're dying
you start turn green
– For years you've been getting technological
But ignoring de facts
An now you're so technical
But you cannot relax

| Blue | will | turn | Green |
| When | votes | are | seen |

An you will get   lead-free   Gasoline

MY GOD! YOUR GOD! *

So dis is de state dat your kind dreamt about,
And after your beating – is dis your way out?
'Cause I was a witness, now I want to shout
– Explain to me, who is your God?

You dreamt of a homeland – well others dream too.
De fruit was forbidden and now you can't chew;
How can you do dis? In de past it was you
– Is dis in de name of your God?

Does your God love children?
Does your God love peace?
Could your God bring justice to de Middle East?

Does your God love anyone, whatever their kind?
Is your God dis brutal, or is your God blind?
And is your God willing to talk to a nation,
Or did your God come here to wipe out creation?

My questions are childlike but I'm in confusion.
– My question is:
Where is your God?

* – *Written in Jerusalem, 1988. I have always believed there is a God, but to see
so many religions wanting this city and to see that the natives are the least heard,
and on top of this (and I mean on top of the city walls), to see the soldiers clutching
their guns while the tourists come and go, has put me right off organised religion
for the rest of my life. I still believe there is something, someone greater than us,
but religion with its dogma, rituals, myths and wars, no! The biggest problem with
this land is that it is full of soldiers.* (B Z)

HAPPINESS

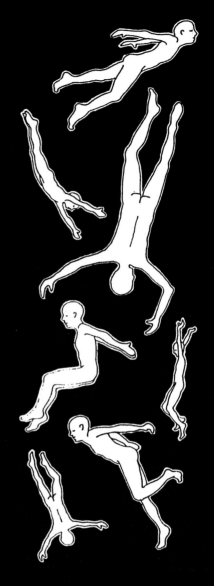

Grass of green I like your scene,
to I you are so pure and clean,
if you get cut then grow again
keep your harvest to the end.

Blossom flower, you have the power
for love will wet your roots with shower,
and if your petals fall to dirt
a new season will bring new birth.

Yes, bird sing and do your thing
for joy to me at morn you bring,
and I am sure you sin no day
for nature's god controls your way.

Rain and sun I beg you come
for you are nature's blessed sons,
rain wet the fields, sun dry to clay
then do the same so far away.

And new-born child, so innocent
your cry is like the sweet incense,
your sweat is like the morning dew
— my utmost love I give to you.

And tree that standeth well and fast
how many years have come and passed?
I breathe the oxygen you feed,
you live so long without no greed.

O love I cannot see your face
but on my lips I feel your taste,
and deep within I know you live
so much of you I have to give.

And I give love to you mankind
but you don't seem to have no time,
I beg you see the naturalness
for there I find my happiness.

Notes on (and by) the poets: –

JOHN AGARD was born in Guyana in 1949. The Albionic muse's fancy was well tickled when he settled here in 1977, for he swiftly became a leading light of the new Westindian-British dawn of bardic composition that *is* jazz, dance, theatre, chant, confrontation politics, carnival, rap, song and playtime. When the sense is sex, the sound streams joyously horny and hot. And this space-age Solomon is unselfishly loving enough to give Sheba her share of the best lines: *"i want to feel you wine/like a eel/between dis pum-pum of mine."* The wide open nakedness of *"a eel"'* is typical of Agard's tenderly tuned mouth music. With a sassy finesse beyond the wildest dreams of faberable 'Blue Verse,' it conveys just that wriggling body-electric tension the grammatically correct *"an* eel" would deny. It equips us to see, hear and feel the sensation and the thought. – Naturally, for this is the utterance of a lover whose prime concern is the *sharing* of energy – a writer-performer for whom lovemaking and poetry are at one, *"we tongue locked/in a syntax of yes."* With such lashings of treble-cream lip service (as in the rest of his *Lovelines for a Goat-born Lady* – Serpent's Tail, 1990), sex-in-the-head gets its come-uppance, embedded for real.

John has published many collections of poetry for children and adults. *Man*

368

to Pan (from which 'Web of Sound' on page 31 is excerpted) celebrates the evolution of Steelband in a cycle of poems to be performed with drums and steelpans. The sequence won the 1982 Cuban Casa de las Americas poetry prize. His children's books include *I Din Do Nuttin* (Little Mammoth), *Laughter is an Egg* (Viking) and *Lend me your Wings* (Hodder & Stoughton) which was shortlisted for the 1987 Smarties prize.

He has opened up his inexhaustible poem-bag and delivered from it all over Britain, Singapore, Canada, Germany, Holland and the West Indies, and acted in the Guyanese feature film *If Wishes were Horses*. During his last years in the Caribbean he joined up with the *'All-ah-We'*, a mobile troupe of Guyanese actor-raconteurs including Marc Matthews, Henry Mootoo and Ken Corsbie; currently, his wordsounds are frequently embellished with deliciously soaring and swooping flute notes from the Afro-Guyanese virtuoso Keith Waithe.

In the introduction to *Mangoes & Bullets: Selected and New Poems 1972-84* (Pluto/Serpent's Tail, 1985/1990), John Agard 'Himself Interviews Himself' as follows: –

". . . I gather your journey of migration to the UK in 1977 was uneventful apart from your luggage being searched for explosive mangoes. Six years later you were to produce *Limbo Dancer in Dark Glasses*. Is there any logical connection between these events?"

"If there is, it is sheerly subconscious. The Limbo Dancer sequence took off from a traditional view that limbo dancing was born in the cramped conditions of the slave ship/a far cry from the tourist image."

" . . . To describe your performing style you use the word poetsonian, and the Jamaican poet Mervyn Morris observed that your body language is akin to that of the calypsonian. Do you agree with this?"

"Yes, I like how he put it. But I also got in mind a kinship with the satirical spirit & folky surrealism of the calypsonian. Who else but a calypsonian would like to be reincarnated as a bedbug? Who else but a calypsonian would conceive of a district magistrate trying his own case ('himself charge himself for contempt o' court') and giving himself five years to pay a fine of 20 dollars? The whole resurgence of the oral art in poetry has caused black poets to come up with words of their own making. You can think of jazzoetry/Gil Scott-Heron calls himself bluesician or bluesologist/you also got dub poetry, using reggae beat/rapso poetry/& a number of white poets call themselves ranters. Not that anything is wrong with the word poet. Is just that some people have come to see 'poet' and 'poetry reading' in very distant cerebral terms. So using these other terms I just mentioned is like subverting the expectations of audiences. Is a way of reclaiming other art forms into poetry like theatre & not treating poetry as isolated. So Ntozake Shange, for instance, describes her work as choreopoem or poemplay/incorporating dance & drama/ and I describe a long children's poem I did recently, growing out of different musical instruments, as a poemsemble. It's nothing new really, it's a return to ancient traditions, a return to the troubadour & the shaman/shawoman."

"One final question. What do you miss most about the Caribbean?"

"I miss sweating."

FERENC ASZMANN was born in 1958 of Anglo-Welsh-German-Hungarian parentage. Raised in Brixton, mutant product of the modern working class. Forged in the same fires that led to punk, his poetic influences include Sean O'Casey, Bobby Womack, Glenn Hoddle, Brian Wilson, Electro and the Sex Pistols; also has Country & Western aspirations as witness his poem on pages 36-37.

An un/healthy passion for cultural politics has led him through various dead-end jobs, most recently in education, and regular stints on the Hell escape-committee. As well as appearing on many club, cabaret and rock stages, and other mental institutions (for a time as **'Gandhi versus the Daleks'**), he has initiated &/or organised events, festivals and happenings since 1976, and Soho's poetry-and-music oasis, the Hard Edge Club, during 1990-91.

Extended wordrage-and-graphics sequence in his own hand in *Angels of Fire* anthology (Chatto & Windus, 1986). LPs – *Another boring book of poetry* (Why Aren't You Making Records Records 1979), *Stars at Dawn* (Ashtray Park 1988).

Ferenc Aszmann

Attila the Stockbroker

370

ATTILA THE STOCKBROKER was born John Baine in 1957 and raised in West Sussex. He attended Kent University, then played bass guitar in punk groups, worked hard for Rock Against Racism, and spent 1979 in Brussels with a brash heavy-metal band. He took up a new lease of life and work as a performance poet and songwriter-singer in 1981, feeling that "rock music has become largely-redundant as a means of communication: the generally inane volume means that you can't hear the words."

Having temped as a clerk in a stockbroking firm, John felt the monicker 'Attila the Stockbroker' would be in keeping with his contract from the gods to liquidate "the gaggle of grey lugworms and displaced Martians who've held the official UK poetry scene in thrall for yonks resquirming the same old nepotistical pretentious irrelevant gunk."

One of his first big breaks as a troubadour came with a benignly explosive set at the 1981 Young Vic *Poetry Olympics* (some of which is preserved on the first *Poetry Olympics* LP, 1982). Attila ranted on to gig all over Britain, Europe, East Germany (R I P), Canada and Australia. Lately he's been doing a lot of TV and radio, playing mandola and fiddle, completing a rock opera, and writing about football, music, poetry and politics for various publications including *NME*, *The Guardian* and his own mag, *Tirana Thrash*.

Attila's albums and cassettes are *Ranting at the Nation* (1983), *Sawdust and Empire* (1984), *Libyan Students from Hell* (1987), *Scornflakes* (1988), *Live at the Rivoli* (Canada 1990), and *Donkey's Years* (1991). His printed publications are *Cautionary Tales for Dead Commuters* (Allen & Unwin 1985) and *In Praise of Slough* (Berks & Bucks Observer Group 1988 – an anthology of local poets celebrating the Berkshire Riviera, edited by Attila). His verse has graced many compilations including *Hard Lines 2* (Faber '85), *Culture Shock* (ed. Michael Rosen, Viking 1990), and *New Departures 15* (1983).

"... Inspired by Hillaire Belloc, Struwelpeter, and the local fish population, I wrote and performed my earliest poems at primary school in Southwick. Most of them were about fish. I didn't write verse again until I was 22. I still write about fish quite a lot. I also write about world issues. A sense of balance is important in poetry. I lived in Harlow for 10 years and have a spiritual attachment to Slough (a sense of belonging helps poetry too). I don't live in Harlow any more, but a small corner of the pedestrian precinct near the obelisk will be forever Stockbroke. Now I'm back where I grew up, on the South Coast, next to the site of a proposed sewage works. Sewage works are important for poetry – some sort of filtering system, anyway. There's an awful lot of shit about.

"I love sea fishing and Brighton & Hove Albion Football Club. There aren't many fish around these days, due to greedy trawlermen and the inexorable tides of pollution. But the odd flounder still greets me from time to time as I wander the shore composing. Hillaire Belloc remains my favourite poet. Despite his having been a peculiar kind of fascist, he inspired me to write, and inspiring other people is a prime function of the art."

371

SUJATA BHATT was born in 1956 in Ahmedabad, India and raised in Poona. She was educated in the US, including two years at the renowned International Writers' Workshop at the University of Iowa. A frequent and popular visitor to Britain, she's recently been living between British Columbia and West Germany with her husband, the German writer Michael Augustin and their young daughter. Sujata works as a freelance writer and has translated Gujarati poetry from her mother tongue into English for the Penguin anthology of *Contemporary Indian Women Poets*. Her poetry has appeared in various UK, Irish and American journals and miscellanies. She received a Cholmondley Award in 1991. Her books so far are *Brunizen* (Carcanet 1988) which won the Alice Hunt Bartlett Prize and the Commonwealth Poetry Prize (Asia); and *Monkey Shadows* (Carcanet 1991) which is a Poetry Book Society Recommendation.

The themes of many of Bhatt's poems are of violence and love, past and present, treated within the contexts of her wide-ranging experiences. Her work explores mythic landscapes, scientific laboratories, racism, and the interaction of Asian, European and North American cultures – the dilemma of having "two tongues in your mouth." She discovers contradictions in her own past and present: her grandfather imprisoned for helping Gandhi reads Tennyson in his cell; a young Indian woman in Germany reflects on the gold Hindu Swastika her grandmother gave her as a blessing.

Goats and lizards, snakes and peacocks, political strife and eroticism intermingle in her diversity of subject-matter, brilliantly brought back to life with an entirely original gamut of tones and techniques. Sujata's writing has a simple, sensuous, passionate clarity that feels as close to oriental fine art as to any previous literature.

VALERIE BLOOM was born Valerie Wright, in Clarendon, Jamaica in 1956. Prior to training as a teacher she worked as a librarian. In addition to teaching English, Speech & Drama at her old school, Frankfield, she started a Speech & Drama Club. The plays she directed and several speech pieces won gold, bronze and silver medals in the National Festival, and her poem *Mek Ah Ketch Har* won a bronze medal in its Literary Competition in 1978.

In England, where she settled the following year, Valerie has lectured and taught in schools on folk traditions in dance, song and poetry. She also worked as a peripatetic music instructor with the Ethnic Music Centre, Manchester. Listeners to Radio Manchester would recall her contributions on the weekly spot *'I 'n' I rule OK.'* She gained a first class honours degree in English with African & Caribbean Studies from the University of Kent, and from 1986-'88 worked as Multicultural Arts Officer with North West Arts in Manchester.

Her first book of poetry *Touch Mi, Tell Mi* was published by Bogle-l'Ouverture in 1983, since when she's been published in several anthologies. A second, much revised edition of *Touch Mi* came out in 1990, and a collection of poems for children *Duppy Jamboree* (including *Tables* and *Don' Go Ova Dere* on pages 62–65) in 1992 from Cambridge University Press. She has performed extensively throughout Britain, including many *Poetry Olympics* events on which everyone relished her warmth and brilliance on stage, and her extraordinary talent for evoking voluble audience participation.

Linton Kwesi Johnson wrote in his Introduction to *Touch Mi, Tell* Mi: – ". . . .The late '60s and early '70s mark a most decisive period in the development of Caribbean poetry. This period of 'post-independence blues", of stagnation and decay, also revealed the emergence of new and active social forces, stimulated largely by the American black power movement. Caribbean artists began addressing themselves to the business of coming to terms with the meaning of nationhood and the task of giving authentic artistic expression to the Caribbean experience.

"These new voices have largely eschewed the inherited language of the colonial, literary tradition, opting instead for the rich oral traditions of the Caribbean folk. In the poem *Language Barrier* Valerie Bloom is expressing her own sheer delight in the twists and turns of ordinary Jamaican speech. She also expresses the attitude of a whole new generation of Caribbean poets to the very stuff of their art:

> *Jamaica language sweet yuh know, bwoy,*
> *And yuh know mi nebba notice i',*
> *Till tarra day one foreign frien'*
> *Come spen some time wid mi.*
>
> *An den im call mi attention to*
> *Some tings im seh soun queer,*
> *Like de way we always sey 'koo yah'*
> *When wi really mean, 'look here'.*
>
> *. . . De French, Italian, Greek an Dutch,*
> *Dem all guilty o' de crime,*
> *None a dem no chat im language*
> *Soh Hugh betta larn fe mime.*

"With a sharp sense of the ironical, a penchant for farcical situations, her mastery of form and language, her skilful character sketches, Valerie Bloom is able to entertain us with her poetry, offering us insights into the human condition . . . an important and welcome addition to an ever growing body of Caribbean oral poetry."

Troubadour, tank driver, political catalyst; **BILLY BRAGG**'s name seems to attract alliteration. Popularly known as The Bard of Barking (aka The Big Nosed Bastard from Barking), his rise from this minor London suburb shadowed the ascent of Essex Man (aka Norman Tebbit) during the Thatcher years. While the new right plundered, Bragg attempted to pull the pieces of the old left into something new and relevant.

For a lad born in 1957 and "meant for the production line of Ford, Dagenham," rock and roll and the army offered the traditional means of escape. Billy left the Tank Corps after three months' trial, while punk rockers Riff

Raff, of which he was a member, foundered after a few independently produced singles. Launching himself as a solo act, he brought the energy and iconooclasm of punk to the notion of the strumming singer/songwriter folkie, a tradition grown feeble and marginal by the '80s. His first record *Life's a Riot With Spy vs Spy* (Go Discs 1983) established the quality of his song-writing – its 'A New England' would later be a hit for Kirsty MacColl – and introduced his combination of acerbic electric guitar with football terrace vocals.

Also established were Bragg's otherliness to a pop mainstream sinking back into blandness and sterility after the eruption of punk: he put out his records at budget prices, campaigned for the striking miners, and undertook a ceaseless touring schedule made possible by the mobility and low overheads of a one-man band. (Among Bragg's numerous minor achievements is a claim to "the only stage invasion of the Outer Hebrides"!)

Brewing Up with Billy Bragg (1984) and the chart EP *Between The Wars* (1985) extended the range of Bragg's songwriting and refined his political sensibility. 'Island of No Return,' a commentary on the Falklands War, demonstrated his ability to go beyond simple-minded protest songs and marked an abiding intrigue with matters military. *Talking With The Taxman About Poetry* (1986) emphasised the growing diversity of his writing; the hit 'Levi Stubb's Tears,' for example, was a poignant vignette of a low-life loser from a trailer park.

The title of *Talking With The Taxman* was taken from the Russian poet Mayakovsky, a sign of Bragg's attempts to consciously re-engage with the

374

lost ideals and aesthetics of Soviet constructivism, and indeed with the whole history of socialist art and folk-culture. *The Internationale,* released on his own Utility label in 1989, offered new interpretations of red anthems, including a re-translation of 'The Internationale' itself, occasioned by a Soviet peace festival where Bragg and veteran US folkie Pete Seeger found themselves unable to stomach singing the custom-staled lyrics.

By 1986 Bragg's agenda had extended beyond pressure group activism to the gritty realities of party politics. He was instrumental in building up Red Wedge, a broad alliance of musicians and artists who campaigned for a Labour victory at the 1987 General election, while attempting to shift the party's policies to more adventurous ground, particularly on issues concerning young people – YTS schemes, education, housing and environment.

Bragg had also embarked on a series of international forays which sought to prise wider the chink of liberty opened by *glasnost;* he made expeditions deep into the USSR and the East European republics, simultaneously confronting the isolationism of the United States on a series of North American tours. The lamentations of the Essex marshes were also heard in Japan, Australia and Nicaragua, while a journey across Bolivia and Chile with DJ and broadcaster Andy Kershaw (once Bragg's roadie) resulted in a critically acclaimed BBC-TV programme. The late '80s also saw the release of *Workers Playtime* (1988), and a surprise number one in the shape of Bragg's cover of the Beatles' 'She's Leaving Home,' recorded for an *NME* charity disc.

More recently Bragg has continued touring intensively whilst diversifying his creativity. A keen fan of William Blake, he recorded the hymn from *Jerusalem* on *The Internationale,* and gave further voice to Blake's verse for the short film *Chartered Streets.* His prose has appeared in publications as diverse as *The Guardian* and the West Ham football fanzine *Fortune's Always Hiding.* His 1991 album *Don't Try This At Home* saw the emergence of a more complete Bragg, still politically abrasive and caustically humoured, but with songs evolved into taut social cameos, plus a fuller and more varied accompaniment, and imagery that manages to incorporate Gennady Gerasimov's smile, Red Star Belgrade football team, and sardonic shades of Rudyard Kipling.   (Neil Spencer, 1991)

JEAN BINTA BREEZE, born in 1956, is a pioneering dub poet and storyteller. Like her brother bards and countrymen Oku Onuora and the late Michael Smith, she studied at the celebrated Jamaica School of Drama. Linton Kwesi Johnson encouraged her to come to London, which she did in 1985, becoming among other things a much loved teacher at Brixton College.

A creator with a strong sense of place, JBB is as familiar with rural Jamaica where she was born as with the ghetto of Kingston where she came to the fore as a recording artist and an enormously communicative performer, at popular events like the international Reggae Sunsplash festivals. In writing that explores a wide range of personal, social and political relationships, Breeze presents telling insights into post-colonial experience and the conditions of blacks and women in Britain and the West Indies. By focusing on themes that affect women in much of her work (she's a single parent), Jean has been one of the first to bring a female dimension to dub poetry. All this made her a natural and welcome new star in the early *Poetry Olympics* galaxies.

In 1980 Race Today publications issued *Riddym Ravings & Other Poems*, edited by Mervyn Morris. Jean's recordings include *Slip African School Yu Slack*, *Aid Travels in a Bomb* and most recently *Tracks*, with perfectly tuned accompanying harmonies and counterpoints by the Dennis Bovell Dub Band (LKJ Records 1990). As a reader, singer, actress, dancer, choreographer and theatre director, Breeze has a compelling stage presence, generating all the power and excitement one might expect to be delighted and instructed by in a full-blown theatrical performance. JBB's work continues to develop both within and beyond the genre of dub; her first film *Hallelujah Anyhow* was screened at the BFI's 1990 British Film Festival, and thereafter on BBC2. Here are some confidences from under her poet-teacher's hat: –

"I write some of my poetry in reggae rhythms, some of it in jazz rhythms. The poem comes with its own musical form because poetry is musical. I don't see any art form that is totally unrelated to any other art form, which is why in my performances I make sure that movement is integrated with drama, with poetry, and all of that.

"I like people and I like the presence of people and I think every time you go on to the stage with a different audience, it's a new thing, another challenge of communication; and so although, yes, I like studio recordings and putting out an album or publishing a book, for me as an artist, performance is my medium and what has been important to me over the last couple of years is to really get the writing up to a standard of performance ability. So now I see it in the twofold: I see the writing and I also see the performance.

"What I would say to young writers is, don't lock yourself off from experiencing. We've been greatly socialised into playing safe, always wanting our lives to be safe, but safety doesn't really exist and I'd say just go for those experiences. Go out of the seclusion, go out of the what is accepted as the normality of life and then, I think, there will be something for you to write. As to your craft and your skill, that is something for you to develop, but I say once you have those experiences, once you open yourself to people and to situations, then I think you have the chance of becoming a fine artist."

ZOË BROOKS was born in 1958 in Winchcombe, Gloucestershire, and now lives in South East London. She was first published in her teens and has since been published in many magazines including *The Rialto*, *Argo*, *Pennine Platform*, *Label*, *Joe Soap's Canoe* and *Other Poetry*.

She was three times winner at the York Poetry Festival. Her play *Joan* was

Zoë Brooks   *Donal Carroll*

performed at Cheltenham Literature Festival. She has written several long
poetry pieces – *Poem for Voices, Breaking Clouds* and *A Dance at the End
of the World.* Her most recent work *Fool's Paradise* – a long poem written
for several voices and triggered by a visit to Prague shortly after the raising
of the Iron Curtain – had its first performance in December 1990.

Since leaving university Zoë has worked as an arts manager with several
theatre companies, the National Centre for Puppetry, and the Area Museum
Service for South of England. She now works as a freelance arts manager
(always available for work!) and as a full-time mother.

DONAL CARROLL was born in Wicklow, Republic of Ireland in 1947. Came
to London late '60s. Worked as television engineer, journalist, poet and
political comedian on 'alternative cabaret' circuit. Published poetry in *New
Poetry 6* (Hutchinson 1981); *Apples & Snakes: Raw & Biting Cabaret Poetry*
(Pluto 1984); *Voices: from 'Arts for Labour'* (Pluto 1985); *From Where I
Stand: Minority Experiences in Britain* (Edward Arnold 1986); *Angels of
Fire* (Chatto 1986), and *City Limits.* Also published *Don't You Believe It*
(Macmillan 1981), a college textbook on political literacy.

*"Presently working in Education. This was recognisable as a Public Service
till the Thatcher administration decided to spend less and less on more and
more people, and eventually nothing on everybody. Interested in poetry with
themes of social structure and mass belief, which puts gin in the imagination
and is not in the locked up language of despair and defeat. Most approved
'contemporary British poetry' ignores most of what is happening in Britain.
It suffers from the PITS (post-imperial tristesse) and Home Counties melan-
cholia – usually passed through the Oxbridge homogeniser in case something
might surface and criticise. With a few honourable exceptions, most editors
collude with and shape this design, and are even more reactionary. Which
is why I can't be bothered writing more poetry."*   (DC, 1991)

377

Born in 1950 in Salford ("the capital of Manchester"), **JOHN COOPER CLARKE** first took to writing when the art teacher editing the school magazine at his devoutly Catholic Secondary Modern commissioned John to review the 1962 Ideal Home Exhibition. He left school at 15 to work as apprentice mechanic at a local garage. This didn't last, and many jobs followed including fire-watching, dish-washing, mortuary attendant, bingo caller and stand-up comic on the Northern club circuit. On his 16th birthday. Clarke's girlfriend ("a bit of a beatnik") bought him a book on modern art, which introduced him to Italian Futurism and to "the notion that everyday stuff could be rearranged into art."

Until then his poems had been "morbid introspective dirges concerning flowers, girls and death." These things continued to colour his work – and still do – but the particular track Clarke uniquely forged from the late '60s on was the transposition of "the gaudy iconography of tin pan alley, the kandy bar rhetoric of advertising, X-films and comics" into high-energy oral verse. He "took the Trash Aesthetic and it clung like a cheap suit. Clad in the slum chic of the hipster, (he) issued the slang anthems of the zip age in the desperate esperanto of bop."

He declaimed his chants, whose scripting and performance were crafted with increasingly slick finesse during the succeeding decades, everywhere from pubs, jazz joints and strip clubs to town halls, sports stadia and pop festivals the whole world over. The raunchy eloquence of his nasal rasp – on record, radio, TV and film, as well as stage and page – had become almost ubiquitous by the mid-1980s. The detonation of the *Poetry Olympics* from Westminster Abbey in 1980 brought him, as Britain's leading rock poet of the punk generation, together for the first time with Linton Kwesi Johnson, the black community's pioneer reggae bard, in a poetry context. Both were inevitably featured on many subsequent Olympics gigs, and John (with Roger McGough) had the lion's share of the first *Poetry Olympics* 'live' LP (1982), including inspired renditions of 'Psycle Sluts', 'Chicken Town', 'I Mustn't Go Down to the Sea Again', 'Track Suit' and the "lugubriously comic travelogue" 'Beezley Street' (which turns out to be an unsparing dissection of – as well as an affectionate ode to – JCC's backstreet beginnings in Salford).

The first publication of his autobiographical 'Ten Years in an Open-Necked Shirt' was in *New Departures 12* (1980), with further appearances in *New Departures 13* (1981) and *New Departures 14* (1982) including 'I travel in Biscuits' and 'I Married a Monster from Outer Space.' His first slim volume was *The Cooper Clarke Directory* (Omnibus 1979), followed by *Ten Years in an Open-Necked Shirt* (Arena 1982). The first recording of *Psycle Sluts* on Manchester's Rabid label led to a CBS contract whose fruits included *Snap, Crackle & Bop* (1980) and *Zip Style Method* (1982).

Appropriate press responses to John's *Poetry Olympics* spots came from Neil Spencer in *NME*: "Clarke slings his poems on the floor and attacks the mike like a bouncer grabbing a drunk's lapels, and instantly sets the muse's old mama heartbeat pumping the vital juices through the nation's cultural

378

bloodstream again" – and from Val Hennessy in *New Society*: "Resembling a stick insect, or hockey-stick with hair, legs like spaghetti, skinny ankles dangling from short drainpipes, Clarke punctuates his poems with fancy footwork. Volleys of technicoloured idiom rattle across the auditorium and ricochet off 500 'Right to Work' badges. We're tumultuous, yelling, groaning, screaming for more. As Ben the punk singer from Vermin says, 'Sob yer heart out, Willie Wordsworth'."

The anti-bourgeois overlaps of John's high-Gothic punk image, his apparent endorsement of brazenly commercial streamlining, the fast-talking frenzy of his 'Manchester Motormouth' delivery, and his wacky street humour, seem to have helped a number of presumably thick-eared critics to miss out on the fact that – although essentially self-educated – this is a singularly well-read, tough-minded and creatively traditional poet. (Even his spontaneous ironic one-liners tend to be poetically *a propos*, as when he dedicates 'Track Suit' (page 99) to those "people who run at the side of busy roads inhaling 80% more lead than anybody else".) Tom Paulin, alone with John Agard and myself in anthologising Clarke, is a notable exception, having pointed out in the *Sunday Times* that his work "belongs to the popular and populist oral tradition that amplifies a singing consciousness as it moves from primeval woodland, through complaints about enclosures, to industrial ballads and modern songs which mention fish fingers. Like many of these anonymous poets, Clarke writes a form of native pidgin or English Creole, with a throbbing and exultantly dionysiac wildness."

MERLE COLLINS is Grenadian. In Grenada she was a teacher, member of the National Women's Organisation and, from 1979-83, a research officer on Latin American Affairs. She's been based mainly in London, teaching and writing, since 1984, but "The Caribbean is still home to me. It's the experience I come from and to which I still hope to return."

Merle's work extends the African tradition of performance poetry. She worked for some years with African Dawn, the troupe renowned for its fusion of dramatised poetry, music and mime. Her collection *Because the Dawn Breaks!* (Karia Press 1985) is a poetic anthem to the 1979 revolution, celebrating the visions, dreams and hopes of the Grenadian people during a time of deep upheaval. It's a chronicle of slavery, colonialism, exploitation and oppression – and finally of joy as Grenada is reclaimed for her own people.

She is also the coeditor, with Rhonda Cobham, of *Watchers and Seekers* (The Women's Press 1987), an inspired anthology of the amazingly various creative writing recently composed and performed by black women in Britain. Her fiction includes *Angel* (Women's Press 1987) which centres on the lives of three generations of Grenadian women, and *Rain Darling* (short stories, Women's Press 1990).

"I write because my hand, head and heart have this conspiracy to keep me going. And because the Grenada Revolution helped me to recognise and con-

379

textualise my communicative skills. And because there is so much I want to say in so many different ways. Which is partly why, I suppose, the public readings came first, the publications later."

PAT CONDELL was born in Dublin in 1949 and remains "Irish, but not practising." Grew up in South London. Spent 15 years as a labourer (5 of them in Canada). Co-founded and performed with the comedy and mime group 'Mountbatten's Plimsoll' in 1982-83 when the pieces on pages 65-70 were written. Others published in *Apples & Snakes* anthology, *Hard Lines 2* (Faber '85), *Tirana Thrash* and (along with his witty graphics) in *New Departures 15*. Currently working in cabaret. Wrote the following, in response to editor's request for a note on his relationship with poetry : –

"I went into poetry a few years ago purely for the money. Now I'm a millionaire. But I still have noisy neighbours. For some reason, whenever I play my favourite Attila the Stockbroker record, the people next door start hammering on the walls with pots and pans, broomhandles, shovels, anything they can get their hands on, and I have to crank it up to full volume to drown out their noise. It's got so that every time I play the damn thing I have to wear earplugs.

But poetry? My grandmother used to say 'If you've got a problem write a poem, and the answer will be revealed,' but she used to wear a potty on her head, not a good sign.

A friend of mine is a sound poet, as opposed to an unsound one. He makes noises with his mouth. He gave me some advice. 'The way to write a good poem is to imagine your arm being chewed up by a garbage disposal unit, and write whatever suggests itself.' He grabbed me by the lapels: 'Once you start thinking you're fucked, am I right? Am I right or wrong?'

'You're right, you're right, let go, you're creasing my simulated polyester lining . . .' It emerged that he had been trying to translate T S Eliot into English: '. . . No chance. And look at Shakespeare – couldn't even spell his own name properly . . . . Chaucer didn't even write English, you're not telling me he was one of us . . .'

As for me, I don't write much any more. My eyesight has deteriorated and I'm too proud to wear glasses."

CAROL ANN DUFFY was born in Glasgow in 1955. Moved to Staffordshire as a child, and educated at St Joseph's Convent, Stafford and Stafford Girls' High School. Studied Philosophy at Liverpool University 1974-77. Wrote several plays for radio and stage – two of them produced at Liverpool Playhouse 1982-86. Her innovative love poetry, political satires and dramatic monologues are often underpinned by a canny playwright's skills of timing and characterisation. Carol Ann has presented many readings, workshops and courses. In recent years poetry editor of *Ambit* magazine, reviewer of new verse for *The Guardian*, and presenter of it on BBC Radio 4.

Poetry Books: *Fleshweathercock* (Outposts 1973), *Fifth Last Song* (Headland 1982), *Standing Female Nude* (Anvil 1985), *Thrown Voices* (Turret 1986), *Selling Manhattan* (Anvil 1987), *The Other Country* (Poetry Book Society Recommendation, Anvil 1990).

The straight-talking economy and formal expertise of her prodigiously sustained output have, for many of Duffy's most talented peers, set a new pace comparable to the luminous examples of compulsive poem-making provided by Sylvia Plath and Adrian Mitchell in the '60s – and even baroque elders of UK poetics like Peter Porter and Robert Nye have recognised her purity and originality. Thus Nye, reviewing *Standing Female Nude*, welcomed ". . . a clarity, a mixture of charm and truthfulness which breaks the windows of perception in new ways altogether," whilst Porter declared: "It is good to see a crusading spirit refusing to surrender any touch of art to the urgency of its cause."

PETER GABRIEL born in Woking, Surrey in 1950, was educated at Charterhouse School, and by 1960s British beat music, and then as a drummer by blues, R & B and soul (notably Otis Redding at the Ram Jam Club in Brixton). Co-founded *Genesis* rock band in 1966, with which he recorded seven albums and worked till 1975. From 1977–'83 recorded *Peter Gabriel 1, 2, 3* and *4*, and *Peter Gabriel Plays Live*; 1986 music from Alan Parker's film *Birdy*, and *SO*; 1989 *Passion* (soundtrack of Scorsese's *Last Temptation of Christ*). Musical collaborations with Laurie Anderson, Kate Bush, The Call, Phil Collins, Charlie Drake, Robert Fripp, Nona Hendryx, Joni Mitchell, Youssou N'Dour, Jimmy Pursey, Robbie Robertson, Tom Robinson, Cat Stevens and many others.

In 1982 founded WOMAD (World of Music, Arts and Dance) featuring music and multi-cultural arts from all around the world. 1985 founded the Real World Group to develop projects in arts and technology focusing on interactive experiences in an "alternative theme park". 1986 started Music for Peace Programme to serve all non-government groups' work for peace in the related areas of human rights, environment, hunger and social justice. *'Hurricane Irene'* concerts in Tokyo marked the first time rock groups from Africa, Asia, America, Russia and Europe were on the same stage at the same time. 1988 toured with Amnesty International *'Human Rights Now!'* concert.

In 1989 Gabriel launched the Real World record label.

"Looking back on my childhood, I always told myself it was a happy time, but much of it was dreadful. Fear and loneliness dominated my first years at public school, which was tough, cruel and alienating to those not strong at work or sport. Music provided a rebellious antidote and joyous relief. One of the things my music still attempts is to find the psychic pain, express it and so relieve it. I learnt the idea of catharsis from the blues. When a blues-singer sits there and pours his heart out, he's purging his soul, and he's doing it for everyone. I know that when I can get emotion out, I suddenly feel more alive, pulsing with new blood. It's so much better than when I try to suppress things.

"Music is a language that can be understood all over the world. It's a doorway into the thoughts and feelings of other peoples and cultures. So it tends to work against racism and across the apparently great divide between the first and third worlds. What we're seeing now is reminiscent of the '60s, but it's a lot more practical. We can't change the world as directly as we'd hoped, but we can provide practical and emotional information. The 'Sun City' project helped – along with the pirated news broadcasts – to ignite an awareness in the U S of the South African situation. It was a chain of influences. But I don't want to be preached at all the time by entertainers . . ."

Re **ROB GALLIANO**, Neil Spencer writes – "While the name Roberto Galliano suggests an Italian background, it's Irish blood that beats in his veins, and London to which his soul belongs. As Robert Gallagher he was born (1966) and raised in the capital, adopting the extravagant surname during his early excursions into live performance as madcap bongo player and resident beat on the Radio London shows of jazz DJ Gilles Peterson. The two were old friends from London clubland, '80s soul boys turned nouveau jazzniks, high on their discovery of a jazz heritage that included clothes, language and the cult of the cool, as well as music.

"Rob had long been obsessed with such poets of soul music as Curtis Mayfield and Gil Scott-Heron, artists who brought to their work an impassioned sense of social justice. Linton Kwesi Johnson, then at the forefront of the UK anti-racist movement, provided a powerful model for Rob's earliest writings, which were intended not for the page but for the microphone, and which would eventually be declaimed MC style at Peterson's DJ club sessions. Opposition to racism has always featured strongly in Galliano's work, a legacy in part from his London Irish background. To these influences jazz added the beatitudes of Kerouac and Ginsberg, the *'Vout'* tongue of Slim Gaillard, and other argots of disestablishmentarianism.

"Rap has been another inspiration; not just the rap of the hip-hop movement but the innovative declamations of '60s militants The Last Poets; indeed, one of the group's founders, Jalal Nurridin, now resident in London, was to

382

Rob Galliano with band 'spars' Spry the Headcorn Dread and Mr Constantine

become Galliano's mentor. In 1988 Rob released his first record, *Frederick Lies Still* (Acid Jazz Records), while jazz magazine *Straight No Chaser* put him into print. In 1990 Rob formed a group, also called Galliano, who rapped not to beatbox rhythms and samples, but to their own music. Their first album *In Pursuit of the 13th Note* (Talking Loud 1991) distilled an array of influences into an articulate whole, alternately angry and reflective, a verbal and musical reflection of contemporary, cosmopolitan London. 1991 also saw Galliano, man and group, perform on stages beyond the UK – New York, Berlin and Tokyo among them; another outsider gone international."

ADAM HOROVITZ was born in Paddington in 1971, the only child of poets Frances and Michael Horovitz. Grew up in Gloucestershire, Tyne and Wear, Northumbria, Herefordshire and London. Started reading voraciously at 2, a habit which continues. Has written a certain amount of verse each year since 1978, and some prose including science fiction/fantasy and reviews. Also writes and draws comic strips, some published in *Obsidian* magazine in 1978-'89. Has played substantial stage roles in plays by Albee, Congreve, Caryl Churchill, Lorca, Pinter and Synge.

Poetry published in *Agenda, Envoi, 4th World Review, New Departures 13,*

Michael Horovitz   Adam Horovitz

14, 15 and *16, Orbis, Poets' Market*, and in the anthologies *Singing Brink* (Arvon Press 1987) and *The Orange Dove of Fiji* (Hutchinson '89). Joint first prizewinner in Cheltenham Literature Festival Young Poets' Competition 1984, and one of ten prizewinners in the World Wide Fund for Nature competition sponsored by the *Guardian* in 1989 (for the poem *Tears Like Lava* on page 158).

MICHAEL HOROVITZ was born in Frankfurt in 1935 of largely rabbinic European forebears, transplanted to England in 1937. Started *New Departures* series and *'Live New Departures'* jazz/poetry troupes and arts circuses in 1959, *Poetry Olympics* festivals 1980. From early childhood largely preoccupied with enjoyment and practice of poetry, song, music and visual art. Organised/ presented/performed at several thousand venues across Europe & N America – solo or in collaborations with Pete Brown, Frances Horovitz, R D Laing, Jeff Nuttall, Stan Tracey and many others including Allen Ginsberg, who's described Horovitz as a "Cockney, Albionic, New Jerusalem, Jazz Generation, Sensitive Bard." Since early '80s writing more and more prose, of which the most widely published examples to date are reviews, articles and letters in the UK press. Also singing and playing more jazz, blues and original music.

Publications include *Alan Davie* (Methuen 'Art in Progress' series 1963), *Poetry for the People* (Latimer Press 1966), *Bank Holiday: a new testament for the love generation* (Latimer 1967), *Children of Albion: Poetry of the 'Underground' in Britain* (Editor – Penguin Books 1969), *The Wolverhampton Wanderer* (Latimer New Dimensions 1971), *A Contemplation: of high art, solemn music and classical culture* (Calder New Writing & Writers 15, 1978), *Growing Up: Selected Poems and Pictures 1951-79* (Allison & Busby 1979), *Midsummer Morning Jog Log* – a 670-line rural rhapsody, illustrated by Peter Blake (Poetry Book Society Recommendation, Five Seasons Press 1986; see p.416), *Art Catalogue* (Combined Harvest / New Departures 1987), *Bop Paintings, Collages, Drawings & Picture-Poems* (England Gallery/New Departures 1989). Recording: *Poetry Olympics at the Young Vic*, with Attila the Stockbroker, John Cooper Clarke and others (All Round Records/New Departures 1982). Also edited *New Departures 1 – 16* (1959–1983 – see page 415).

384

MAHMOOD JAMAL was born in Lucknow, India in 1948. Family migrated to Pakistan in the early '50s. Came to Britain 1967. Took a degree in South Asian Studies (Urdu/History) from London University's School of Oriental and African Studies. Co-ordinated readings at Troubadour Coffee House, Earls Court 1972-1975, and contributed to Cecil Rajendra's *Black Voices* forum for Third World writers. Coedited *Black Phoenix* magazine. Received a Minority Rights Group Award for his writing and translations in 1984.

Mahmood has scripted, produced and directed various music, drama and documentary films, mainly for Channel 4 TV. In 1988 his 'Retake' film & video collective won the BFI Independent Film & TV Award. He co-produced *The Peacock Screen* series on the history of Indian cinema, and wrote the first Asian soap – *Family Pride*.

Poetry publications: *Coins for Charon* (Courtfield Press, London 1976); *Silence Inside a Gun's Mouth* (Kala Press, London 1984); the *Penguin Book of Urdu Poetry* (edited & translated – Penguin 1986). Continuing work in progress on the poetry of Faiz Ahmad Faiz.

Asked for a statement on poetry, Mahmood wrote:

"There is punk poetry and junk poetry
There is monk poetry and drunk poetry
There is sad poetry
And mad poetry, but above all
There is good poetry
And there is bad poetry . . .

"The purposes of poetry are many and varied. For me it is a physical act that renews the spirit. My disposition is to give entertainment second place in my work. First and foremost comes the art of sharing the sorrows of the world and the pain of being; but it does not seek to exclude humour, scepticism, laughter or pleasure.

" . . . When all else fails, Silence would suffice."

LINTON KWESI JOHNSON was born in 1952 in rural Clarendon, Jamaica, where his grandmother, an illiterate peasant farmer, had him read to her regularly from the Psalms, Proverbs, Songs of Solomon, and Ecclesiastes, which he still quotes freely. The exalted rhetoric and hypnotic tone of some of Johnson's later poetic parables, sermons, incantations and refrains probably echo this grounding, but he was soon attracted to more immediately native influences such as the *mento* tradition of 'Miss Lou' Bennett (the pioneer of verncaular Caribbean verse), and then to the newly emergent reggae of Bob Marley *et al.*

In 1963 Linton left Jamaica to join his mother who'd emigrated to Brixton: he was quickly disillusioned by the undisguised, often violent racism inflicted by schoolkids and teachers alike at Tulse Hill Comprehensive. He left at 16, but took a Sociology degree a few years later at Goldsmith's College. In 1970 he joined the Black Panther Youth League and began organising writers' workshops and reciting revolutionary verses, often with musical backing by Rasta Love and other groups. He became known as 'Poet' round Brixton, which remains his home turf – and as 'LKJ' the world over, after electrifying more and more black communities and multiracial audiences with his increasingly outspoken yet subtly crafted performances.

Though he still occasionally writes in ironic versions of the Queen's English, Linton gradually found that "what I had to say could be much more easily and appropriately expressed in the Jamaican language." As soon as he started using it " – music entered the poetry; whenever I wrote I had reggae rhythms in my head." In the mid-70s he coined the phrase 'dub poetry' in celebration and reapplication of the modes of his favourite reggae DJs. Johnson loved the way their spontaneous lyricism about social, political and cultural activity carried on the forms and functions of traditional African poetry, being oral and improvised with a musical base.

He didn't mean to found a school in adapting their styles and techniques to his own work – rather a restoration of grass-roots realism and rhythms: "Shock-black bubble-doun-beat bouncing/rock-wise tumble-doun soul music;/foot-drop find drum, blood story,/bass history is a moving/is a hurting black story.//Thunda from a bass drum sounding/lightening from a trumpet and a organ,/bass and rhythm and trumpet double-up,/team up with drums for a deep doun searching . . ." (*Reggae Sounds*).

LKJ's poetry and journalism of the 1970s reflected his experience of growing up in a mainly hostile environment, and his commitment to the black working-class movement. His early books and records focused on police oppression, racist politicians, confrontations between authorities and black youth, the unending struggle with colonial conditions, and articulation of independence from them. In the early '80s he continued touring – chanting solo, with tape loops, or with the 9-to-15 piece Dennis Bovell band. After the 1985 *LKJ Live in Concert* album he withdrew almost completely from the public eye. Though he could have made a fortune, as so many do, by repeating himself or floating out any number of perfunctory products, he decided (as so few do) to keep quiet till he had something new to say.

Johnson describes the *Tings an' Times* sequence, released on record in 1991, as "a reflective look at how far we've come in the black struggle, and where we're going." Several of the tracks are responses to the recent upheavals in Eastern Europe: ". . . so Garby gi de people dem glashnas/an it poze de Stalinist dem plenty problem/soh Garby lego peristrika pan dem/ confoundin bureaucratic stratagems/but wi haffi face up to di cole facks/im also open up pandora's box/yes, people powa jus a showa every howa/an everybady claim dem democratic/but some a wolf and some a sheep/an dat is problematic/noh tings like dat yu woulda call dialectic?// . . . Kaydar/ e ad to go/Zhivkov/e ad to go/Honicka/e ad to go/Cauchescu/e ad to go/

John Cooper Clarke and Linton Kwesi Johnson backstage at the Young Vic Poetry Olympics, London 1981

jus like apartied/soon gaan . . ." (*Mi Revalueshanary Fren*).

Tings an' Times is as far a cry as its predecessors from the narcissistic, untranslatable, apolitical and gutless 'Martian-Masterclass' formulae that have been passed off as 'major' contemporary British verse by their careerist marketeers of the 1980s. Whereas Linton's unstinting efforts with the activist Race Today collective and its community arts wing 'Creation for Liberation', as well as his tellingly spare, deep-voiced bardic missiles, carry on the building of Jerusalem at its most practical: "histri biggah dan mi or yu yu know/time cyaan steal but it can heal/soh wipe di cobweb from yu face/wi gat nuff work fi dhu/far wi noh reach mount zion/yet . . ." (*Di Anfinish Revalueshan*).

From the mock fairy-tale opening *Story* (see pages 170-171) to *Di Good Life* (dedicated to CLR James and characterising socialism as "a wise ole shepad/im suvive tru flood/tru drout/tru blizad"), what LKJ has given us here is a plain-speaking vision of the better future within our reach. Whilst tackling head-on the resurgence of narrow nationalism, xenophobia, racism, fascism and violent or insidious repressions, he continues to underwrite the new Internationale of body, mind and spirit most worth reflecting, fighting, marching, dancing and singing with – spreading power of the people, from the people, to the people.

Johnson's books are *Voices of the Living and the Dead* (Race Today 1974), *Dread, Beat and Blood* (Bogle l'Ouverture 1975), and *Inglan is a Bitch* (Race Today 1980). His recordings include *Poet and the Roots* (Virgin 1977), *Dread, Beat and Blood* (Virgin 1978), *Forces of History* (Island 1979), *Bass Culture* (Island 1980) and *Making History* (Island 1984).

387

TIMOTHY EMLYN JONES started to write shortly after moving to London as an art student in 1966. His poetics sprang from his highly personal approach to drawing as a way of thinking, and through his involvement with happenings and performance art in which he collaborated with Stuart Brisley, Joseph Beuys and others. Subsequently he came to a personal discovery of children's strategies for creative work which has remained as an informing influence on both his visual art and his poetry.

Jones's exploration of the interdependent themes of structure, abandonment and celebration has taken him through several combinations of verbal and visual forms. He argues that visual and verbal techniques such as drawing and poetry are merely two dimensions of the one human, aesthetic concern and he relishes Blake's inspiration in this view. The large-scale drawings that he has exhibited recently do not have titles but are accompanied by short texts which interact with and extend the process of looking at the images. Sometimes the spectacle of the drawing process is presented as a performance in itself.

In illustration as in making texts he sees a mutually informing balance of word and image and even when he does separate the verbal from the visual each seems to linger within the other. A case in point is his current work-in-progress *The Beach*, which is as dependent on the fall of light as are any of his drawings. See also, as well as his main set in this book, the drawings and etchings on pages 28, 32-33, 42 and 43.

Tim published with his own T J Press (*Poem Without Words*, 1973; *The Will of Triumph*, 1974; *Man as a Window*, 1974 – see pages 174-178) before co-editing anthologies of children's creative work for the ILEA with Tom Pickard (1977) and Zoë Fairbairns (1978). He also published with Beau Geste Press ('Poem Without Words' in *General Schmuck*, 1974), Embryo Books (*Now, here*, 1975), the Welsh Arts Council (*proposition: ymlaen*, 1978) and Arrowspire Press (*The Passion*, 1986; *The Duplicity*, 1986). Selections from 'The Beach' were included in *Seeing in the Dark*, edited by Ian Breakwell and Paul Hammond (Serpent's Tail 1990).

He has performed or exhibited all over Europe, and is represented in public art collections in Britain, the Netherlands, Poland and the USA.

388

BILL LEWIS was born in Maidstone, Kent in 1953 to rural working-class parents. He left school at 15 and worked many years in shops and factories. His most recent full-time job was with the Health Service. He was a founder-member of Medway poets, the group of six who spearheaded a literary movement in North Kent from the early '70s on. Being self-educated, Bill often adopts an original approach to language, including British working-class vernacular as comes naturally. In 1982 the Medway Poets disbanded. TVS filmed a documentary showing clips of their last performance together. The group has occasional reunion concerts, and toured for Amnesty International in 1987. An LP of their performances was released that year on the Hangman label.

In 1985 Lewis was appointed writer-in-residence at Brighton international arts festival. He has read at many venues – not only literature centres, schools and colleges, but also hospitals, prisons, borstals, youth clubs *et al.* Bill and his wife Ann are part-time youth workers, and also sometimes work with prisoners serving life sentences at Maidstone Prison.

Lewis is a radical Christian with a pronounced interest in Latin American culture. In 1989 he visited Nicaragua and gave a series of readings to celebrate the tenth anniversary of the Sandinista Revolution. While there he met up and read with many Latin American writers including Carlos Rigby and Augusto Morales. Some of his poems have been translated into Spanish by the Salvadorean writer Claribel Alegria and the Cuban writer Clara Allen. In 1991 Bill became involved with Creation Centred Spirituality, an ecumenical, radical and mystical revival of prophetic traditions. He joined the School for Prophets in Walderslade, a group founded by the radical Catholic priest Bert White. Lewis's interest in Judaism (see pages 179-181) is "purely spiritual. If one's to be a true Christian, one has to be, in a sense, a Jew."

Bill's poetry books include *Medway Nights* (Laserwolf Books 1982), *Selected Poems 1976-1983* (Victoria Press 1983), *Night Clinic* (Laserwolf 1984), *Communion* (Hangman Books 1986) and *Rage Without Anger: Poems 1976-1988* (Hangman 1988).

BRIAN McCABE was born in 1951 in a small mining community near
Edinburgh, the youngest of four children, their father a coal miner, mother
a cook. He began writing poetry at 16 and won various competitions sponsored by *The Scotsman* and the BBC. He studied Philosophy and Eng Lit at
Edinburgh University, then began giving public readings, notably on the
Edinburgh Festival Fringe. McCabe was awarded a Writer's Bursary by the
Scottish Arts Council in 1980, since when he's lived as a freelance writer. He
has done reading tours of Britain, Canada, Denmark and Germany, and was
chosen as Scottish/Canadian Exchange Fellow in 1988-89.

Poetry publications include *Spring's Witch* (Mariscat Press 1985) which won
an S AC Book Award, and *One Atom to Another* (Polygon 1987). He's also
published a collection of short stories – *The Lipstick Circus* (Mainstream 1985/
1990), and a novel – *The Other McCoy* (Mainstream 1990/Penguin 1991).

Peter Porter described him in the *Observer* as "a poet of great natural
charm . . . with a delicate humour which you notice only subsequently is also
highly robust. Where most composers of fables are pleased to make our blood
boil, McCabe prefers to invent post-Hiroshima myths with a simple Aesopian
bedside manner. No one label suits him – he is love poet, domestic surrealist,
satirist and verbal conjurer." And more.

IAN McMILLAN was born in Barnsley in 1956. After graduating in Politics
& English from North Staffs Poly in 1978, he worked two years on a building site and another three in a tennis-ball factory. These jobs and his South
Yorkshire upbringing have provided the material for much of his work:
buses, pits, cottages, pigeons, pubs. His life changed when, in 1981, the
Yorkshire Arts Association awarded him a Bursary of £800: he's been writing,
performing and tutoring ever since.

The blurb for his first book, *The Changing Problem* (Carcanet 1980)

390

observed that "The 'Changing' in the title refers to the art of bell-ringing, something of an addiction for this poet. 'Ringing the changes' on imagery is a skill he has developed – a kind of wit, at times baleful, at times hilarious." Tim Dooley wrote in the *TLS* of this volume's successor, *Now It Can Be Told* (Carcanet 1983), that "These are knowing poems, recognising that language is neither innocent nor transparent while exploiting its ambiguous malfunctions and unexpected local quirks . . . McMillan's language-games signal an engagement with responsibility rather than an evasion of it. Poems and sentences fail to resolve themselves in the expected ways. The results are often very funny; yet they also mimic the ways in which the patterns and efforts of our lives fail to resolve themselves as we would hope."

His other collections include *Selected Poems* (Carcanet 1987 – a Poetry Book Society Recommendation), *Unselected Poems* (Wide Skirt Press 1988), *More Poems Please Waiter, and Quickly!* (Sow's Ear Press 1989) and *A Chin?* (Wide Skirt Press 1991). He was a founding member of the Versewagon mobile writing workshop, and of The Circus of Poets performance-poetry group, and is now half of Yakety Yak poetry/comedy duo with his old pal and co-founder-trouper Martyn Wiley. In his own words: –

". . . I've been a freelance writer and performer since 1981. Being freelance means that you get asked to do all sorts of things, so over the last few years I've written poems, stories, plays, comedy and journalism for media as diverse (maybe) as Channel 4 TV, *Poetry Review, Slow Dancer, Label,* the *NME, Q* and *She* magazines, and Radio 4 Arts programmes. I'm a big believer in the power of the written word when it becomes the spoken word, so I've performed in thousands of venues from the South Bank Centre to prisons, schools, libraries, clubs, theatres, supermarkets and outdoor markets, photo-booths and car parks, Citizens' Advice Bureaux, front rooms, fields and a boat.

"At one of the first readings I ever did the organiser started selling vegetables halfway through my set. I was just about to launch into another poem when he shouted 'Come on, get your carrots!' I thought it was a form of surreal heckling so I shouted 'Yes, and get your bananas too!' He yelled 'Spuds only 5p a pound!' A man said 'I'll kill that bastard' and a woman leaned over the candlelit table towards him and said 'It's all right, darling, the drink has destroyed him' and I thought *I must get that line into a poem sometime.*

"Readings sometimes attract very odd people, for no reason that I can work out. You don't get mad violinists elbowing their way to the front of a string quartet recital to have a go, but you often get people with their cardigans on back-to-front shouting their poems while you pause to take a sip of water.

"I did a reading in a wine bar in Telford once. It started really well; then a taxi rolled up outside, and I should have been suspicious. I'm the only person who normally goes to my gigs in a taxi. A woman lurched out. She was covered in fur and was very drunk. She staggered in and the organisers just gaped at her. She stood right in front of me and started to heckle. Normally I don't mind a bit of good-natured banter but this wasn't witty heckling or even surrealist heckling. It was stuff like 'That's crap' to which there isn't a hilarious reply. She persisted and I could hear the organisers clucking and the audience muttering. I didn't feel too appalled because I knew I was building up quite a good deposit of audience sympathy to be drawn on later. Then she turned and confronted the audience at their tables. 'This is Ian McMillan' she said. They nodded and looked at their drinks. 'I've lived with him for the last five years.' This was a complete lie. The audience began to look sympathetically at the woman and harshly at me. 'He knocks me round the house something cruel.' The audience nodded. I was outraged. 'I've never seen this woman before in my life!' I said, and as I said it I realised that it was the kind of line you only hear in radio plays and never in wine bars in the Midlands. 'He's rubbish in bed!' she shouted. I left the stage and skulked round the back. The organiser came and said 'I've put Robin on and Tom's phoned for the police.' I smiled grittily. Robin was a hippy and his acoustic doodlings contrasted nicely with the fur-woman's dramatics. The youngest policeman I've ever seen in my life arrived. He looked about eleven. He strode up to the woman and tried to say 'I arrest you in the name of the law' like they'd taught him at Police School. He got as far as 'I' and she smacked him on the head, then started dancing with him, moving around the room in time to Robin's music. Robin was smiling. Eventually the young policeman radioed for help. An older, wiser copper who looked a bit like Ben Cartwright arrived and soothed the woman away. As they passed me I said 'It's all right darling, the drink has destroyed her,' but the policeman gazed stolidly ahead and the woman's eyes were glazed. The evening started again, but she'd certainly taken the edge off it. The audience were polite to me, but no more. Nobody browsed through my books at the end of the reading. As we left I noticed that Robin was taking notes. Perhaps he was writing a new song."

LINDSAY MACRAE was born in Bridlington in 1961 of Scottish parents. She took degrees in drama and film, and was awarded a creative writing scholarship to William & Mary College, USA in 1982. She sang in several bands including the Orson Family and The Impossible Dreamers. She pursued a short-lived career as newsreader for God's own station, Vatican Radio in Rome, and also produced its book programme, which meant reviewing such fruity tomes as *The Letters of St Paul* and *The Practical Guide to Celibacy*. After ideological differences with some Cardinals, she left to become arts editor of the *International Courier*.

On returning to England in 1986 Lindsay helped in the offices of *Artists Against Apartheid*. She began to perform more regularly in alternative cabaret, joined Angels of Fire collective and helped organise poetry festivals. Then she left to form LIP with Jeremy Silver and Cheryl Moskowitz, touring Britain to bring new and accessible poetry to arts and community centres, and run workshops in schools and libraries.

MacRae worked many years as a freelance arts journalist, and became TV

392

presenter for *Network 7* and *The Channel 4 Daily*, and reporter on *Right to Reply*. She also co-founded London's Hard Edge Club. Her poems have appeared in *Angels of Fire, Purple and Green* (Rivelin Grapheme 1984), and *No Holds Barred* (Women's Press 1985). She coedited *Dancing the Tightrope*, an anthology of love poetry by women, for the Women's Press (1987).

GERALDINE MONK was born in 1952 in Blackburn, Lancs. She started writing verse and prose after moving to Yorkshire in 1971. Her active interest in visual arts led to 'Reworking the Title', an exhibition at the Mappin Art Gallery in Sheffield in 1990-91, for which she selected paintings from the City Art Gallery's permanent collection and retitled them with her own words. Geraldine's poetry publications include *La Quinta del Sordo* (Writers' Forum 1980), *Spreading the Cards* (Siren Press 1980), *Tiger Lilies* (Rivelin Press 1982), *Animal Crackers* (Writers' Forum 1984), *Herein Lie Tales of Two Cities* (Writers' Forum 1986), *Sky Scrapers* (Galloping Dog 1986), *Quaquaversals* (Writers' Forum 1990).

Bill Griffiths wrote of her *Walks in a Daisy Chain* (Magenta 1991): "Here are 41 characters, lyrical grumbles, smug self-assessments, flights of soliloquial frenzy, all linked, all individually word-carved, the quarks and neutrons of the housewife, the fine and living art of the butcher, showing us our exciting in-built gift for getting what really matters essentially wrong, not smart satires but basic fun-kits, the swank of the policeman's helmet, the sub-editor's stunning punning, sliding incorrigibly from one profession to another, till the final sonic link joins up."

TONY MARCHANT was born in 1959 in East London, where he still lives with his wife and two sons. His early writings evolved partly via the Tower Hamlets Working Writers' Group, and some were published by Tower Hamlets Arts Project and also in Paul Weller's arts and poetry series *Mixed-up/Shook-up*, in 1979-80. He took a variety of jobs including one in the dreaded Manpower Services Commission.

Marchant came to the fore as a playwright with productions of *Remember Me?, London Calling* and *Dealt With* (the last two performed and published together under the title *Thick as Thieves*) at the Theatre Royal, Stratford in 1980-81, and of *The Lucky Ones* in 1982. *The Lucky Ones* won him Drama Magazine's 'Most Promising Playwright' award for that year. He wrote *Raspberry* (Edinburgh Festival and Soho Poly Theatre in 1982) and *Stiff* (Soho Poly '82). Paine's Plough company commissioned *Welcome Home*, about the Falklands War, which was toured and then performed at the Royal Court Theatre in 1983. *Lazydays Ltd* was commissioned by Stratford East and performed there in 1986, and *The Attractions* performed at Soho Poly in '87. The Royal Shakespeare Company commissioned *Speculators*, which was performed at the Barbican Pit in 1987-'88. Lyn Gardner wrote in *City Limits*

Tony Marchant   *Nik Morgan*

that ". . . *Speculators* is a horrifyingly entertaining attack on those who have substituted 'Greed' for 'Cheese' in the group photo and have forever changed the traditional city rules in their ruthless pursuit of the fast buck."

The Attractions and *Speculators* are published by Amber Lane Press (1988), whilst most of the other plays are available in Methuen's New Theatrescripts series. Tony has also adapted his plays for television, and written the following original drama scripts for the box: *Reservations, The Moneymen, Death of a Son,* the trilogy *Home and Away,* and *Goodbye Cruel World.*

NIK MORGAN writes ". . . I was born of Anglo-Welsh parents in Norwich (1962), where I lived until moving to Swansea in 1980 to study for an English Degree at the University of Wales. In 1983 I graduated, and then moved to Cardiff to research into the work of Dylan Thomas for an M.A. Degree. Since then I have lived and worked in Penarth. My work consists of poems, paintings, drawings and collages, the poems often being word re-arrangements from various sources. I try to use words out of their normal context in an attempt to re-discover their 'extraordinariness', usually lost through habituation and routine use. By putting language in unfamiliar contexts, with peculiar aspects of its sound, meaning and syntax highlighted, it may be approached in an unconventional way, allowing its extraordinary nature to become apparent. In seeing the 'familiar' as 'strange', the reader is encouraged to realise that the sense of 'ordinariness' normally associated with words is not their real nature, but merely an appearance which shrouds the original extraordinary reality.

My visual work centres largely on characters experienced through dreams and the imagination. Like the poetry, it aims to make visible the 'invisible' unconscious, and to reveal the supramundane and sacred reality hidden beneath mundane appearances."

394

GRACE NICHOLS was born in 1950 in Guyana, where she grew up and worked, among other things, as a journalist. She came to Britain in 1977, and has since published three books of poems. Her first, *I is a long memoried Woman* (Karnac House 1983), won the Commonwealth Poetry Prize for that year. *The Fat Black Woman's Poems* (1984) and *Lazy Thoughts of a Lazy Woman* (1989) are published by Virago, who also brought out her first adult novel, *Whole of a Morning Sky* (1980), which is set in Guyana. Her books for children include: two collections of short stories published by Hodder, *Trust you Wriggly* (1980) and *Leslyn in London* (1984); a book of poems, *Come On In To My Tropical Garden* (A & C Black 1980); and an anthology *Black Poetry* (Blackie, 1988 – reissued as *Poetry Jump Up* by Penguin, 1990).

Of her later work, Archie Markham has written: "There is a pervading sense of fun, even when the challenge is sharp ... Grace Nichols's skill at slipping in and out of modes of English is as good as any and she manages to make 'nation-language' seem not a duty, not a deliberate act of 'rooting', but a gift joyfully received."

In a meditation on 'Home Truths', Grace herself writes: –

"*... I like to think of myself as a Caribbean person; because the Caribbean embraces so much it's like saying you're a poet of the world. For psychically, you're at once connected to Africa (which I see as a kind of spiritual homeland), Europe, Asia, and the Americas. My early childhood was spent in a small country village along the Guyana coast and my most treasured memory is of myself, around the age of 6, standing calf-deep in rippling goldish brown water, watching the moving shapes of fish just below the sunlit surface. This picture stands out like an oasis in my memory.*

"*Although I'd already started writing (mostly fiction) back in Guyana, it was only after coming to England that poetry began to play a bigger and bigger part in my life. I started to read more of the work of other Caribbean and Black American poets. Having been surrounded by a lot of English poetry as a child I found that Caribbean poetry helped to put me in touch with the different rhythms, orality and atmosphere of our own culture. I myself like working both in standard English and Creole, and tend to want to fuse the two tongues because I come from a background where the two were constantly interacting.*

"*Though I still enjoy the work of some English poets, there comes a time when I feel like something that sounds different to the ear. Something that looks different to the eye on the page. Something with a different rhythm. But in writing a poem I don't consciously set out to write it in Creole or standard English. The language, like the form and rhythm, dictates itself.*

"*... I is a long memoried woman owes its inspiration to a dream I had one night of a young African girl swimming from Africa to the Caribbean with a garland of flowers around her. When I woke up I interpreted the dream to mean that she was trying to cleanse the ocean of the pain and suffering that her ancestors had gone through in that crossing from Africa to the New World. So the book sprang from that dream which is echoed in one of the poems: –*

> *... even in dreams I will submerge myself*
> *swimming like one possessed*
> *back and forth across that course*
> *strewing it with sweet smelling flowers*
> *one for everyone that made the journey ...*

"*As the cycle of poems began to develop I was aware that I was dealing with my whole female history but I don't see my work as limited to women. In my novel for instance, the main character is Archie Worrell, inspired by my father. And when I give poetry readings both men and women respond to the Fat Black Woman with her quirky tongue-in-cheek look at the slimming and fashion industries. Poetry thankfully is a radical synthesizing force. The erotic isn't separated from the political or spiritual."*

(Grace Nichols, 1989)

ROSEMARY NORMAN writes "I was born in London in 1946, and decided at eight years old to be a poet. The decision has stood through change after change in what I understand by it. I'm wary of imposing purposes on poetry. Could the pressure many poets feel to do so, be a response to the business ethos in its own terms, a willingness to present their alternative as a set of aims and objectives? And I'm wary of imposing poetry on people. To believe that everyone needs, in a direct way, what we have, seems to me an élitism very like its apparent opposite, ourselves as the chosen few.

"For ten years I've been in a women's writing group which grew out of a City Lit course in feminist writing, led by Zoë Fairbairns. And last year I took over from Carol Fisher as organiser of the Open Poetry Conventicle in Putney, a mixed group where we combine listening and talking to an invited guest, with reading and discussing our own work.

"A collection of my poems, *Threats and Promises,* was published by Iron Press of Tyneside in 1991. I live with my teenage son on the edge of London, and work as a librarian in a girls' comprehensive school." (RN, 1991)

Born in Minna, Nigeria in 1959, **BEN OKRI** was educated in London and Nigeria, returning to England to study comparative literature at Essex University. Having started writing early on, Ben published his first novel *Flowers and Shadows* in 1980, and whilst at Essex in 1982 published another, *The Landscape Within.* He was poetry editor of *West Africa* magazine from 1981-'87, and worked as a broadcaster for the BBC World Service in 1984-85. His short story collection *Incidents at the Shrine* won the Commonwealth Writers' Prize for Africa in 1987, and his subsequent collection *Stars of the New Curfew* was shortlisted for the Guardian Fiction Prize in 1988.

Okri's third novel *The Famished Road* won the 1991 Booker Prize, and also some of the most poetically entranced reviews any narrative can ever have received. Linda Grant's response, for instance, concluded –

"Okri is incapable of writing a boring sentence. As one startling image follows the next, *The Famished Road* begins to read like an epic poem that happens to touch down just this side of prose. Beside it, most modern British fiction seems deracinated and condemned to the worst sort of literalness. Okri reminds us that politics is not always a little, expedient thing and that the slum-dwellers of the Third World have lives beyond a Comic Relief film clip: 'Dad was redreaming the world as he slept. He saw the scheme of things and didn't like it. He saw a world in which black people always suffered and he didn't like it . . . He saw the women of the country, of the markets and villages, always dogged by incubi and butterflies.' When I finished this book and went outside, it was as if all the trees in South London had angels sitting in them." *(Independent)*

396

Alannah Hopkin in the *Financial Times* suggested that "Okri is more of a poet than a novelist," but most of his work in prose and verse is born from and delivered to a more mythic and transmedial sensitivity than such genre categories, so restrictively deployed, can dream of. This is not to say the writing projects misty-eyed escapism – Nadine Gordimer, on the contrary, finds it "uncannily pitched into the personal drama of social upheaval." *The Famished Road*'s opening may seem to resemble that of the Bible at first, but a more exalted aesthetic and more answerably moral spectrum soon put that old white magic in the shade: –

"In the beginning there was a river. The river became a road and the road branched out to the whole world. And because the road was once a river it was always hungry.

"In that land of beginnings spirits mingled with the unborn. We could assume numerous forms. Many of us were birds. We knew no boundaries. There was much feasting, playing, and sorrowing. We feasted much because of the beautiful terrors of eternity. We played much because we were free. And we sorrowed much because there were always those amongst us who had just returned from the world of the Living. They had returned inconsolable for all the love they had left behind, all the suffering they hadn't redeemed, all that they hadn't understood, and for all that they had barely begun to learn before they were drawn back to the land of origins.

"There was not one amongst us who looked forward to being born. We disliked the rigours of existence, the unfulfilled longings, the enshrined injustices of the world, the labyrinths of love, the ignorance of parents, the fact of dying, and the amazing indifference of the Living in the midst of the simple beauties of the universe. We feared the heartlessness of human beings, all of whom are born blind, few of whom ever learn to see . . ."

In regard to the impulse of this anthology, and its public projections to come, Ben wrote to M Horovitz on 15-1-1991: –

Poetry's homeland is the spirit and the human voice is its best vehicle, certainly its oldest, and the most qualified to educate the ears to guide the eye's reading and interpretation; too many being somewhat blind out of laziness can ~~always~~ often be stirred by the total self incarnate with the voice ringing or whispering; we need to awaken the readers to make them read with all their intelligence and sensitivities; hunger or suffering makes it easier, but here we have to be angular or like 1922 or noisy or very quiet, but tangential in some vital way. End of essay. Beginning of brief goodbye.

Ben Okri

ANDREW PEARMAIN was born in Leeds, 1954: "My family was fallen middle-class, abandoned among the northern proletariat by a father who moved there as a missionary for Catholicism and Social Democracy, conceived my sister and brother and me, and then smoked himself to death. I grew up poorer than most of the kids around me, but sustained and separated by a sense of cultural superiority, reinforced by passing the 11-plus and getting sent daily across the city to grammar school. I narrowly avoided juvenile delinquency by reading beat poetry and listening to long-haired music, which turned stealing and truancy into acts of liberation. Somehow I managed to get to University (with A-level grades so low I've never yet mentioned them in job applications) – initially to study Latin, then Philosophy because it felt sexier. My links with the class I'd grown up amongst, tenuous in the first place, were well and truly severed, and I joined the Communist Party.

"Some years of hyperactivism later, and it's Thatcherism year zero, only we all think it's an aberration and we'll soon have someone cosy back to shout at like Callaghan or Foot. Time passes, and it all starts to get serious. I start reflecting on what had happened, and all this stuff comes gushing out, usually but not always in rhyming verses. All of a sudden I'm a pop poet, and people are prepared to pay money to hear or read what I'm saying. It was never very much, mind, but it topped up the dole. There was an opening of doors, a grudging recognition of our power to amuse and provoke with clever words, a willingness to shut up and listen. I reckon it lasted about three years. People got tired of being in permanent opposition, important sources of support like radical bookshops and 'alternative' venues got picked off one by one, and audiences got drunker. The doors closed on those of us who didn't fit onto television. With a huge sigh of relief I settled down to parenthood and a series of semi-serious jobs – mainly teaching."

Poetry publications: contributed to *Apples & Snakes* and *Hard Lines* anthologies, and various obscure left-wing journals. Books, under the pseudonym **'Andy P'**: *Poems for the Young Professional – The Habitat Book of Comic Verse* (DIY Publications, 1983); *The Playbook for Young Adults about Late Capitalism* (DIY Publications, 1984); *1985 – Don't Relax* (still available on order @ £2, including postage, from DIY Publications, 182 Thorpe Rd, Norwich NR1 1TJ); *Thatcherism, Social Democracy and various other things* (£1.50 post free from DIY Publications).

FIONA PITT-KETHLEY was born in Middlesex in 1954 and brought up in Ealing. Her broad-minded mother's forebears include 300 years of Welsh preachers and hymn-writers, whilst two generations of journalists preceded her father becoming one too, albeit eccentric and under-employed. He was "a religious maniac who joined several hundred churches, loved dirty jokes and taught me to do a lot of misbehaving."

Fiona "was treated like an adult from babyhood" and her first word was NO. She was expelled from Sunday School at 3, and sent to a psychologist at 7 at her headmistress's suggestion for writing "bum" onto her classroom desk – the shrink found nothing wrong. From 12 to 17 she planned to become the first woman vicar, till "a lightning anti-conversion" when she discovered snogging, and couldn't bring herself to believe it sinful. Now she's an atheist "with a *penchant* for the pagan gods."

She studied painting for four years at Chelsea Art School, ushering at the Old Vic and the National Theatre in the evenings. After trying to run a junk shop, turned to writing full-time in 1978, with stints as film extra or teacher. Her poetry publications are *London* (privately printed 1984), *Rome* (Mammon Press 1985), *The Tower of Glass* (Mariscat '85), *Sky Ray Lolly* (Chatto 1986/ Abacus 1990), *Gesta* (Turret Books 1986), *Private Parts* (Chatto 1987/Abacus '91) and *The Perfect Man* (Abacus '89). She's also published a novel *The Misfortunes of Nigel* (Peter Owen 1991), and a travel book *Journeys to the Underworld* (Chatto 1988/Abacus '89). This is a picaresque romp round Southern Italy largely concerned with sex from the standpoint of a female Casanova.

Reviewing *Private Parts*, Peter Porter noted that "she mines her territory carefully. Since she is so sprightly in manner and so disenchantingly realistic in a dirty-mac way, she builds up a lot of latter-day morality . . . . her most attractive and ebullient verse is not about human sex but the natural world. If human beings were like the plant kingdom, and our reproductive organs were not private parts, we would get a better press from Miss Pitt-Kethley."

Her favourite word is Fuck – "so easy to remember and pronounce/and good for rhymes. It's not a synonym – /an honest word that only means one thing" (from *That Word*). She pursues classical detachment as against romanticism but does not consider herself "anti-men: I'm anti-prejudice, anti-insincerity, anti-cruelty." She also considers obedience a much overrated virtue – "without it the Nazis, the Inquisition and mankind's other organised cruelties could not have existed."

The Perfect Man includes 30 pages of highly entertaining notes, and selections from her many incautiously self-revealing correspondents' fantasy lives, which reinforce the poetry's sardonic and probing gloss on the book's title. The originality, freshness and pleasures of Pitt-Kethley's clear-eyed modes of debunking stem in part from her readers' recognition that nothing has been censored.

PHILIP RADMALL writes: "I was born in 1957 in Rugby, where I was brought up and educated. Father a draughtsman, mother a keen spiritualist, of English and Dutch stock, the old ancestors having come over from Holland in the 17th Century. Got interested in poetry from 7-8 on, especially in the English Romantics and the Modernist movement. A lot of juvenilia reflected this. At 19 I went to study Philosophy at Manchester University, concentrating on Russell and Wittgenstein, with a thesis on the philosophy of mind. Whilst there, together with two others, I edited a poetry magazine called *Lines*, which featured contributions from poets in and around Manchester, and was sold on the streets of the city.

"After graduating in 1979 I moved to London, settling first in Peckham, where for two years I worked purely at writing poems to build up a body of work. Also lived for a while in Holland in 1982, concentrating on the same endeavour, with poems geared more towards the landscape and weather, and influenced by Dutch art (see pages 276-279, and *Innocents* p.281).

"Since then, after money ran out, I worked mainly in and around the TV industry, in the administration of commercials and commercial airtime; and more recently for a company involved in the writing and supplying of computer systems to the ITV network and commercial radio. Have lived in Kensington for the last 7 years, during which time, as well as continuing to write poetry, I have also completed a novel about a research student in search of a dead philosopher's past and his own future."   (P R, 1991)

ELAINE RANDELL was born in 1951 in Charing Cross Hospital. Since the mid-70s she's lived in rural Kent with sheep, chickens, geese, ducks, setter dogs, and her husband and three daughters. She enjoyed writing since childhood, and at sixteen started editing *Amazing Grace* poetry & arts magazine from her bedrooom floor. In the '70s she ran Secret Books Press. Her early years were spent in South London. She worked in many fields, including rare books, antique silver, and journalism. She qualified as an art therapist in 1974, and as a social worker in '78. Her college dissertation gave little comfort to her Marxist tutors, being on 'Love in Social Work,' with reference to Schweitzer and Mother Teresa ("That doesn't mean we have to love all the people we help; but I have to be humanitarian"). Elaine went on to be a child care and mental health practitioner for Social Service Departments in deprived areas of London and Kent. Another job took her to the King's School, Canterbury as counsellor; she perceived the public schoolboys as undergoing an experience quite close to that of children in care.

She now works as a Guardian ad Litem (independent assessor for the child) in contested child custody cases, and spends most days in legal and court work. In a 1991 *Guardian Women* profile, Jane Hardy noted that ". : . her subject is often the quiet (or not so quiet) desperation of the people she helps – abandoned children, blackly humorous women. As she says in *Routine*, 'I make my life a belly of people.' What elevates the dramatic monologues above raw emotion to real art is Randell's ear for the way language reveals character. 'I'm a great talker to people in bus queues.' Randell sees no contradiction in being a social worker who writes; on the contrary, she finds ' – The skills often overlap: listening, picking things up about people from small details.' She has virtually created a new genre, the case history as fable."

Writing and art therapy are also useful in helping to evoke feelings without falsification: "One little girl drew tiny people and a big witch she thought was going to take her away, which told me a lot about her anxieties." In his Afterword to *Beyond all Other: Poems 1970-1986* (Pig Press 1986), Lee Harwood wrote: "... The hallmarks of her writings are an insistence on the importance of subject-matter and the clear sharp eye of a careful observer. She continually shows us the world that surrounds us: '*the night goes by and girls hover in doorways with tattoos.*' The personal and the words are always set in context, in the houses and streets and countryside we inhabit, we move through. There are always other people in the room, or a room next door, or passing by outside. '*He goes out to the corner past the ironmonger and the men carrying trade plates.*' In her sequences (see pages 285-289) people speak for themselves and their words are respected. And at the root of this respect is the heart. The base-line we work from, the qualities of love we choose, value or deny . . . This love is transcribed with elegance and subtlety, intelligence and wit, and a stunning skill. She is a poet of our frailties and beauties, of our continual dependance and influence on one another, of 'the compulsions of love' in all its forms."

Elaine's other books include *Early in My Life* (Permanent Press 1977), *Larger Breath of All Things* (Spectacular Diseases 1978), *This, Our Frailty* (Oasis 1979), *Songs for the Sleepless* (improvisations on lines from the works of Elizabeth Smart, Pig Press 1982), and *Gut Reaction* (selected prose pieces 1977-87, North and South 1987).

MICHÈLE ROBERTS was born a twin, of a French mother and English father in Bushey, Herts in 1949. M A in English (Oxon), writer-in-residence in the boroughs of Lambeth and Bromley, and at Essex University. Lives and works in London. Involved in Women's Liberation movement since 1970 and looks on it as "the place that encouraged me to write . . . Writing doesn't change the world in an obvious way, but it demonstrates that a person has taken the power to name the world her way – and that's political: language becomes the place where power struggles are going on." Long terms followed as poetry editor of the feminist magazine *Spare Rib*, and then of *City Limits*.

Her sensuous, lyrical fiction has received critical acclaim and also some notoriety: *A Piece of the Night* (Women's Press 1978), *The Visitation* (W P, 1983), and *The Wild Girl* (Methuen 1984) which claimed to be the Fifth Gospel – a claim hotly disputed, and denounced as blasphemous, by lawyers and MPs. Michèle is a self-confessed lapsed Catholic: "I gave it up when I was 21, became an intellectual atheist . . . But I'm haunted, quite painfully, by Catholic images in my subconscious. I have to fish them up, look at them; I'm interested in that numinous level of experience. I think it's allied to poetry."

The Book of Mrs Noah (Methuen 1947) continued the radical reworking of biblical imagery. *In the Red Kitchen* (Methuen 1990) was inspired by the true story of a 19th-century medium, Florence Cook. Michèle is also co-author of two anthologies: *Tales I tell my Mother* (Journeyman Press 1978), and *More Tales I tell my Mother* (Journeyman 1988). She's published her poetry in four collections, the most recent being *The Mirror of the Mother: Selected Poems 1975-85* (Methuen 1986), and *Psyche and the Hurricane: Poems 1986-1990* (Methuen 1991).

"Writing a poem fills me with happiness. I can't make myself write a poem; can't force it to happen. So the inspiration, when it comes, is a gift to me from something outside myself. Feels a bit like coming; that sudden certainty of bliss. Doesn't happen that often! Sometimes I'll write six poems in one year; once I wrote none; last year I wrote a dozen. There's a tug on my earlobe. A connection made between the inner world and the outer one via the words and phrases I've scribbled in my notebook, usually visual images of the world beyond myself. I sit at my desk, or in bed, and scribble on sheets of paper. A poem takes at least a day of writing, usually, to become more or less finished. It advances slowly, word by word, phrase by phrase. I keep going back to the beginning and starting it again. Perhaps fourteen drafts.

A lot of mess and scribble. Pare it down as much as possible. When I was a child I believed in the magical power of words; words were what they denoted; a poem was a gift from God. I still think words are powerful and mysterious even though I've learned to separate the signifier from the signified. I still believe in the power of signs. Word-signs point to what is not there: a beloved body, a landscape, food; synonyms for God. The poems of mine printed in this book were all written over twelve years ago; I'm glad they're seeing the light again."   (MR, 1991)

MARIA SOOKIAS was born to an English mother and Armenian father in 1964 in Croydon, where she spent most of her first 20 years. She started writing poetry at 16, on commencing a course at Westminster Catering College: ". . . My two years there were deeply disillusioning. The classes were full of yuppies, Sloanes, wallies and wind-up artists – in fact, the place was a factory for mindless morons. On discovering I belonged to the Labour Party, one of them said 'Oh no, not a socialist, haw haw haw: there just *aren't* any socialists in catering.' I resented this but, after I was kicked out, began to realise why. Catering has no effective trade union, and so constitutes one of the most exploitative, bigoted, sexist, racist and oppressive atmospheres to work in.

"After three years of jobs in this slave trade I jacked in chefing and became a vegetarian, also a lesbian, and got to work with the homeless, in youth clubs, and in a women's refuge. This is a great standpoint from which to see the world and women's positions in it. Much of what I do now stems from experiences in Women's Aid.

"Straight poetry assumes that everyone can read English – can read at all. Visual representations surmount educational barriers, and their communication is more immediately and universally understandable. Since 1988 I've  been mainly concerned with creating visual art that's particularly accessible to women; with cutting down the élitism that still restricts or throttles so much art and literature; and with drawing attention to the inequalities of today's corrupt and rotten society.

"I've been inspired by strong women in my family – mother, sister, grandmother. Also by some lyrics in punk and new wave music (notably Paul Weller's), and by Orwell, Wilfred Owen, Dali and (longer ago) Enid Blyton."

The Conjugal Rights of a Pig (page 304), Maria's first and still almost her only poetry in print, was awarded the customary English accolade of censorship instantly following publication. When the poem appeared in the Croydon Youth Council's freebie magazine *Transmission*, she was dubbed "the porno poet" by local and national newsprint, the issue was banned, and its funding withdrawn. The Royal Jubilee Trust director responsible for this action "found the article very distasteful." He stopped short, however, of commenting on the distasteful realities *Conjugal Rights* so lucidly depicts, or answering Sookias's defence of its strong language: "It's no good writing about life to make it seem different from what it is. This is the way people talk and behave nowadays."

CHRIS SPARKES was born in Birmingham in 1951, moved in '55 to rivery South Downs valley backwood. Grandpa Sparkes was a lyric Cotswold water-colourist, and father a scribe. At 18 Chris "repined and read all of Keats, then Welsh caravan isolation hedged me in" to continuing addiction to poetry. Started reading and chanting with guitars and fellow poets, minstrels, musos, mimers and dancers, in folk clubs, theatres, pubs, churches, festivals – and busking in London, Amsterdam and France.

Worked in DHSS, a bank in Lambeth, tyre fitting, storekeeping, parks and gardens, porter, industrial management, assembly line, building site, book-shop, farming hops and apples, postman, typing, dishwasher – and now, after 5 years as lawyer, at college studying the Scriptures "and untraining my proud heart to be a full-time preacher and evangelist."

Poetry and prose published in *Strait, The Cut, Viaduct, Stride, Tirana Thrash, Buzz, Words International* and *Verbal Mutation* anthology. First book *Kissing Through Glass* – selected poems, prose, songs, music, drawings and photos (Mighty Conqueror Productions, Petersfield, 1986).

NEIL SPARKES was born in Crayford, Kent in 1967 to a mother who taught English, textiles and sports, and a painter-lecturer-teacher father. He developed an early interest in writing, music and the visual arts. A gaggle of ex-army grammar school teachers, who engaged former Falklands War padrés to take assemblies, helped provoke a beatnik-style rebellion in Neil, who gradually spent more time away from school than at it.

He got his first double-bass in 1983, by which time he'd also started to play percussion. He gigged with a variety of jazz groups and garage bands, touring Holland in 1987 as a drummer with Kill Ugly Pop, and West Germany in '89 with Wreckless Eric, playing a drum-set that included a barbecue stand and a motley of domestic utensils.

Sparkes studied painting at Maidstone College of Art and then (1986-89) the BA Fine Art course at Goldsmiths' College, London. The first one-man show of his art work was at the East London Half Moon Theatre. From 1987-1989 he worked as a performance artist and musician in London with cabaret groups, and organised two venues – the Krokodil Club and Karloff Kabaret.

His passion for jazz and blues also found expression in stints as a DJ at the Shack Club in Soho, among others.

Poetry books so far – *All Metal and Other Men's Wives* (Hangman Books, Rochester 1989) and *Rumba Rumba (Jazz from Hell)*, also from Hangman in 1990. Neil's early poetry was much encouraged by Hangman's creative driving-force Billy Childish, and by other of the Medway poets such as Bill Lewis and Sexton Ming. Responses to his poems worth quoting include those of the painter Patrick Hughes ("They give dazzling colour to many greys, and always hit that blue note"), Jeff Nuttall ("Matched by the poet's sharp drawings, the verse is about urban squalor, vivid and ironic"), Michael Baldwin (". . . a raw edge of truth and bittersweet wit"), and John Williams (". . . laconic evocations of lost love and a Bud Powell-at-four-in-the-morning state of mind").

As well as the nine illustrations to his own poems on pages 322-331, Neil's visual gifts embellish other parts of this book in the form of the drawings on pages 37 and 185, and the woodcut on p55. His long-term preoccupation with synthesizing his multi-medic talents, in concert with like-minded peers, has achieved a promising degree of fulfilment in his experiments with three jazz-&-poetry troupes – *Rhythm-A-Ning* (including alto sax-poet Imogen Rodgers and US troubadour Chris Brown); *Jazz Poetry SuperJam* (with Jeff Nuttall and Michael Horovitz); and *Rhythm-N-Ink* (with reed virtuoso Dick Heckstall-Smith, District Six drummer Brian Abrahams, and congalera Ramona Metcalfe). His contributions as a spontaneous lyricist were a palpable hit during the Real World Recording Week at Peter Gabriel's Real World Studios in the summer of 1991.

'Fire and Skill' was the legend daubed on **PAUL WELLER**'s guitar amplifier back in the early days of The Jam, and over the years it's proved an enduring credo for an artist never content to rest on past glories.

Weller seemed to fall to earth as an already perfectly formed pop star, an instant teenage guitar hero, rock poet and fashion plate. He came, in fact, from planet Woking, where he was born in 1958 and where he spent his formative years nurturing an obsession with '60s modernism; by 14 he was fronting his own Who-style group, by 18 he was to take London by storm.

With their neat suburban haircuts, matching suits and white shoes, The Jam were a gauche oddity among the spiky cuts and bondage strides of punk London, in which the three likely lads from Woking quickly found themselves embroiled. They were altogether too '60s-retro for a movement dedicated to Now. But Weller could sneer with punk's worst, and quickly proved he could pen three minute pop anthems with the best, as well as pogo higher while busting better power chords.

The Jam's early records – *In The City* and *This is the Modern World* (both '77) – had punk's noise and anger, its self-consciously English identity, its tower-block imagery, while owing much to the R&B-based sound of the '60s beat boom. The group became the focal point of the late '70s mod revival, but soon evolved into something more challenging. *All Mod Cons* (1978) produced the chilling 'Down In The Tube Station At Midnight,' a precursor of songs like 'Eton Rifles' and 'Strange Town' on the next year's *Setting Sons,* which showed Weller shrugging off his home counties sensibility (he famously plumped for the Tories at the '78 election) for an altogether grittier look at contemporary Britain than the previous youth anthems.

From 1979 until the group's dissolution in 1982, The Jam were rarely out of the singles or album charts, producing an effortless string of crisp pop classsics ('Going Underground', 'Funeral Pyre', 'Town Called Malice', 'Beat Surrender') and showing an increasing sophistication with studio technology. Weller's taste for the '60s continued – he plundered the Beatles for 'Start' and rediscovered Colin MacInnes's novels several years before the rest of the '80s on 'Absolute Beginners' – but his songs were mostly about the here and now, and increasingly articulated dismay at the UK's social dislocation.

Weller was also drawn to books and poetry. In 1980 he set up an imprint, *Riot Stories*, which published a book of poems by his old schoolfriend Dave Waller, and later a couple of issues of the arts-and-poetry fanzine *December's Child.* In 1981 Weller contributed a solo set of his quietly glittering poetry with backing tapes to the second London *Poetry Olympics* at the Young Vic Theatre, and three of his poems were published in the following year's issue of *New Departures* (No. 14).

The Jam's next LP *Sound Affects* (1980) quoted Shelley on its cover and showed Arthurian and Blakean interests creeping in, though its most celebrated track, 'That's Entertainment', was a stark dissection of the UK's new brutalism. In 1982 Weller decided to disband The Jam before atrophy set in. His new group, The Style Council, rapidly went beyond previous confines, with a sound oriented around soul and jazz, more mature material, and a line-up which cut across gender and racial barriers and included keyboardist Mick Talbot and singer D C Lee. The group's greatest hits were such classics of blue-eyed soul as 'Long Hot Summer' ('83), and 'You're the Best Thing ('84), but LPs *Cafe Bleu* ('84) and *Our Favourite Shop* ('85) and singles *Soul Deep* ('84 – a benefit for the striking miners), and *Walls Come Tumbling Down* ('85) were reminders that the old anger was still there, and more purposefully directed. In fact, Weller's political edge had never cut so deep as on *Favourite Shop* tracks like 'The Lodgers' and 'Home-breakers'. In 1987 Weller was to campaign with Billy Bragg, Junior Giscombe, The Communards and others as part of Red Wedge, an attempt to raise the political awareness of the young and radicalise Labour policies.

The Cost of Loving (1987) continued to mix funk and social comment with tracks like 'Life at a Top People's Health Farm', and included a contribution from soul star Curtis Mayfield. 1987 also saw the release of the short film *Jerusalem*, a romantic attempt to place the group amid wider ideas about England.

After a Style Council greatest hits package, Weller disbanded the group and returned to basics with The Paul Weller Movement, whose first single, *Into Tomorrow* (1991), echoed the optimism of early Jam, though from a perspective largely alien to his former self. The Fire and Skill, however, remain intact. (Neil Spencer, 1991)

IFIGENIJA ZAGORICNIK-SIMONIVIC writes: "I was born in 1953 of working-class parents in Ljublana, Yugoslavia. My mother became a single parent after my father decided to marry a woman who was pregnant at the same time. This made me an unwanted child. I have a brother and a sister at my father's, whom I don't know, and two brothers at my mother's, whom I quite like. The games I remember most are pretending to be mummy to my little brothers, planning to run away, acting as though I was dying, and imagining being a small invisible creature.

"I left home at 20 when I was at the University of Ljublana (1972-77), studying Comparative Literature and Slavonic Linguistics. From '72-76 I edited the literary pages of the student newspaper *Tribuna*, the cultural review *Problemi*, and the youth magazine *Mladina*. I took a degree with many difficulties and little enthusiasm (I've never felt myself to be acad-emically minded). Whilst a student I earned my living as a babysitter. I then did lots of proof-reading for various publishers, wrote book reviews and theatre criticism, and spent a lot of time hanging around in cafés, 'admiring' my contemporaries, mainly artists and writers. It wasn't as bohemian as I would have liked because I kept myself very much at the fringes, fighting internal fears that I'm stupid and ugly. I still have such fears, but don't mind it that much any more.

"Since puberty, writing has been my one private (rather than professional) indulgence. I once started comparing it with masturbation, but the idea didn't go down well with my colleagues. My pieces were published pretty consistently since I was 13, but in most cases I hoped no-one had read them or would read them. After coming to live in London in 1978 I did all sorts of jobs. I also studied studio pottery at Harrow College of Art and Design from 1983-85, and since then have ben a full-time potter. I teach at Epping Forest College, and sell my pottery every Wednesday and Thursday in Covent Garden Apple Market (10am - 7pm).

"As a writer I was dug out of the closet by Anthony Rudolf and Michael Horovitz. Anthony co-translated my poems and published them in his Menard Press publications, Michael in *New Departures* (No.14, 1982) and at *Poetry Olympics* festivals. They keep reminding me not to forget. I continue (co)translating from my writings in Slovene, and also more recently writing straight into English. There have been eight volumes of my verse in Slovene, and other publications in Hungarian, French, Italian, Serb, Croat and Macedonian, and – years ago – in English in a special issue of *Modern Poetry in Translation.*"

Poet, playwright, performer, musician, political activist, teacher . . . **BENJAMIN ZEPHANIAH**'s many parts add up to more than their total. He emerged from the murky depths of Handsworth, Birmingham as the '80s were raising their rapacious claws, and during the decade's long haul his work came to be one of the zippiest antidotes to the prevailing mood of callous self-interest.

Born in Birmingham in 1958, Benjamin, like many first generation black Britons, had a childhood split between Jamaica and the UK. Wayward from an early age, he spent time in approved school and jail. It was while serving a prison sentence for burglary that his spiritual and literary epiphany arrived. He left prison a Rasta and writer, his name taken from the tribes of the Old Testament, and was soon performing his verses, comic and angry by turns, to audiences from the Afro-Caribbean community and from the emergent new cabaret scene. His first record *Dub Ranting*, an EP issued on the tiny Radical Wallpaper label, extended his reach into the rock scene.

Soundly built on metre and rhyme, his scores of innocence and experience flow in streams unsullied by campus-based literary currents, though the apparent orthodoxy of their structure has endeared him to a public that doggedly holds out against free verse. Like a lot of contemporary West Indian poetry, his wordplay is bi-lingual, slipping between Jamaican patois and English, and uses the cadences of street-talk from both ends of the UK-Caribbean axis to articulate its concerns. Social and racial injustice have always been at the heart of Zephaniah's writings, but he has developed a more ironic detachment over the years, while sharp humour and Rasta spirituality have always been present.

Pen Rhythm (Page One Books 1981) was his first printed collection, and *The Dread Affair* (Arena 1985) gathered much of the work that made him

successful, including the celebrated 'Dis Policeman Keeps on Kicking me to Death'. Benjamin has been one of the most regular and extraordinarily inventive galvanisers of the *Poetry Olympics* movement from the outset, giving a particularly memorable performance in a spontaneous word-jam he improvised with the late lamented Mikey Smith (it was the first time they'd met) in the Young Vic series of 1982. Four of his poems were published in *New Departures 15* (1983).

As the '80s progressed, Zephaniah's gap-toothed grin, hurtling dreadlocks and pungent poems became increasingly ubiquitous, popping up everywhere from breakfast TV to agit-prop concerts. He achieved folk-devil status when shortlisted to become Professor of Poetry at Oxford, a valediction of his challenge to the Eng Lit establishment.

Theatre and music have provided two other avenues for his work. His plays, some in verse, include *Playing The Right Time, Job Rocking, Hurricane Dub* (winner of BBC Radio's Young Playwright's award, 1988), *Streetwise* and *Delirium.* He has made several expeditions into music: aside from *Dub Ranting* there have been *Big Boys Don't Make Girls Cry, Free South Africa,* (recorded with the Wailers Band) and *Rasta.* His most recent album, *Us and Dem,* (Antilles 1990), took his blend of music and verse into more sophisticated areas. The CD version features the seminal and salutary 'Green' (see pages 352-355) which no-one else could have written.

Benjamin has maintained an intense commitment to community and education projects, working long hours in schools, prisons, writers' work-shops and the like, while his political activism has brought him together with groups from Pakistan, Palestine, Ethiopia, Chile, Guyana and Kurdistan, among others. A year as writer-in-residence in Liverpool with the Africa Arts Collective produced the collection *Inna Liverpool* (A A C 1990), and his exploration of Palestine and Israel catalysed *Rasta Time in Palestine* (available for £2.95 from Shakti, POB 37, Liverpool L15 5DF). He continues to be an abiding presence on all manner of media, even unto playing Moses in the Ethiopian film *Farendg* (1990). Tireless and prolific, comet Zephaniah continues to flame through the cultural firmament.   (Neil Spencer, 1991)

Acknowledgements

Michael Horovitz and *New Departures* thank each of the contributors for texts or pictures published here for the first time. For permission to recycle other copyright material, we gratefully acknowledge the following: –

Laughter is an Egg (Viking 1990) for 'I know you wouldn't think I'm serious'; *Mangoes & Bullets* (Pluto 1985/Serpent's Tail 1990) for *Palm Tree King, Listen Mr Oxford Don, Finders Keepers, One Question from a Bullet, Web of Sound,* and *Rainbow; Lovelines for a Goat-born Lady* (Serpent's Tail 1990) for *The Lover;* by permission of **John Agard** c/o Caroline Sheldon Literary Agency;

Brunizem (Carcanet Press 1988) for the poems by **Sujata Bhatt**, excepting *Angels' Wings*, which appears in *Monkey Shadows* (Carcanet 1991); *Touch Mi, Tell Mi* (Bogle l'Ouverture (1983 and 1990) for *Yuh Hear 'Bout . . . ?* by **Valerie Bloom**; Sincere Management and **Billy Bragg** for *Tender Comrade, Island of No Return, Between the Wars, Strange Things Happen* and *The Busy Girl Buys Beauty,* (C) Chappell Music, used by permission – and for *Trust* and *Tank Park Salute* (C) B.M.G. Music, used by permission;

Riddym Ravings and Other Poems (Race Today Publications 1988) for *Burning, We Speak Through the Silence of Our Stares* and *Repatriation* by **Jean Binta Breeze**; *Because the Dawn Breaks* (Karia Press 1985) for *Fear* and *The Search* by **Merle Collins**, and also *Watchers and Seekers* (edited by Rhonda Cobham and Merle Collins, The Women's Press 1987) for Merle's *No Dialects Please*;

Standing Female Nude (Anvil Press Poetry 1985) for *Head of English, Comprehensive, A Provincial Party 1956, You Jane, Liverpool Echo, War Photographer* and *Debt* by **Carol Ann Duffy**; *Selling Manhattan* (Anvil 1987) for *Deportation;* and *The Other Country* (Anvil 1990) for Carol Ann's poems *A Shilling for the Sea, River, Originally, In Your Mind, Ape, Poet for Our Times, Making Money, Losers, The Literature Act, Dream of a Lost Friend,* and *Mrs Skinner, North Street*;

Hit and Run Music Publishing for *Mother of Violence* (C) 1978 by **Jill and Peter Gabriel**; *The Family and the Fishing Net* (C) 1982 Peter Gabriel; *Family Snapshot* (C) 1980 Peter Gabriel; *Wallflower* (C) 1982 Peter Gabriel; *Here Comes the Flood* (C) 1977 Peter Gabriel; *Waiting for the Big One* (C) 1977 Peter Gabriel; *Rhythm of the Heat* (C) 1982 Peter Gabriel;

Silence Inside a Gun's Mouth (Kala Press 1984) for *Silence, Swamped, Immigrant, The Alien Star, Sitar Player* and *Against Clichés* by **Mahmood Jamal**; *Rage Without Anger* (Laserwolf/Hangman 1988) for *Desire, Epilepsy, Café Poem, Therapy Room, Conflict Observed* and *Ants* by **Bill Lewis**;

One Atom to Another (Polygon 1987) for all **Brian McCabe's** set, excepting *'Thousand forced to flee disputed region'; Now It Can Be Told* (Carcanet Press 1983) and *Selected Poems* (Carcanet 1987) for *The Meaning of Life, Barge Journey, Call Me Irresponsible, The Red Indian Rugby Team . . . ,* and *Life on Earth* by **Ian McMillan**; *Unselected Poems* (Wide Skirt Press '88) for *June Evening*; and *A Chin?* (Wide Skirt Press '91) for *'Dad, the donkey's on fire – ', Stone I Presume,* and *Kake Yourself Comfortable* also by Ian; *Walks in a Daisy Chain* (Magenta 1991) for *The Policeman* and *The Mathematician*; *La Quinta del Sordo* (Writers' Forum 1980) for *'lunar masque . . . ';* *Quaquaversals* (Writers' Forum 1990) for *'WHAT . . . Recipes for the hungry', Molecular Power Progressives* and *Reductio ad Absurdum;* and *Animal Crackers* (Writers' Forum 1984) for *Glass Snake Electric Eel, Earth Pig Sun Spider* and *Rainbow Butcher Bird,* all by **Geraldine Monk**;

410

I is a long memoried woman (Karnac House 1983) for the excerpts from **Grace Nichols's** cycle of that name, on pages 232 – 237; *Lazy Thoughts of a Lazy Woman* (Virago 1989) for *Tapestry, Always Potential, 'Who was it . . .?', With Apologies to Hamlet, Wherever I Hang . . .*, *'Dead ya fuh tan'* and *Out of Africa*, also by Grace; *The Fat Black Woman's Poems* (Virago 1984) for *'Beauty is a fat black woman . . .'*, and *Looking at Miss World; No Hickory No Dickory no Dock* (Viking 1991) for Grace's *Baby-K Rap Rhyme*; and *Come on into my Tropical Garden* (A & C Black 1988) for her *Crab Dance.*

Threats and Promises (Iron Press 1991) for *Houseboat, War Games, Home, Saline, Love Poem*, and *After* by **Rosemary Norman;** her *"iron gate"* poem appeared in *You're Sweet, You're Speedy* (Fox Hall Press 1984), type-set by Jenny Vuglar; *An African Elegy* (Cape 1992) for **Ben Okri's** set; *Andy P. says 1985 – Don't! Relax* (DIY Publications 1985) for *Gary and Gail – True* by **Andrew Pearmain**, and *Thatcherism, Social Democracy & various other things* (DIY) for *Works Outing* by Andy; *Private Parts* (Chatto & Windus 1987/Abacus 1990) for *Private Parts* by **Fiona Pitt-Kethley**, and *Sky Ray Lolly* (Chatto 1987/Abacus '91) for *Girlie Mags, Sky Ray Lolly, Penis-Envy, Night London*, and *Apples*, (C) Fiona Pitt-Kethley, by permission of Sheil Land Associates; *Beyond All Other* (Pig Press 1986) for *Dusting, Watching Women with Children*, the first six of the seven *Scenes from the Sauna*, and *Case Note* by **Elaine Randell;** and *Gut Reaction: prose pieces* (North & South 1987) for all seven *from the Sauna;*

The Mirror of the Mother: Selected Poems (1986) for **Michèle Roberts's** set, reprinted by permission of Methuen London; *All Metal and Other Men's Wives* (Hangman 1989) for *Tunnel Vision* and *Knowing People* by **Neil Sparkes;** and *Rumba Rumba – Jazz from Hell (1990)* for Neil's *Night Train* and *On the Train;*

EMI Music for **Paul Weller's** *The Story of Someone's Shoe* (C) 1988; *Ghosts of Dachau* (1984); *Bloodsports* (C) 1985; *The Whole Point of No Return* (C) 1984; and Son Music/EMI for *Saturday's Kids* (C) 1979; *Private Hell* (C) 1979; *Eton Rifles* (C) 1979; *Little Boy Soldiers* (C) 1979, and *Down in the Tube Station at Midnight* (C) 1978; *Inna Liverpool* (Africa Arts Collective 1990) for *What yu Eat* by **Benjamin Zephaniah;** and *Rasta Time in Palestine* (Shakti 1990) for *My God! your God!* by Benjamin.

Picture Credits

Cartoon on p20 by **Mike Williams;** illustrations on pages 28 and 32-33 by **Tim Emlyn Jones,** 1991; drawing on page 37 from Punch and Judy series by **Neil Sparkes,** 1988; illustration for *Death in Bromley* p.40 by **Philip Jupitus;** drawings on pages 42 and 43 from *The Passion* series by **Timothy Emlyn Jones,** 1984;

Photograph of Sujata Bhatt on p47 and spine by **Jutta Golda;** *Iris* drawing on p52 by **Jane Percival;** woodcut on page 55 by **Neil Sparkes;** illustrations to Valerie Bloom's children's poems on pages 61 to 65 by **Michael Charlton;** comic strip version of Billy Bragg's *Strange things Happen* p.76 by **Porky Jupitus;** *'Blake was right'* 77 – anon; Collage for Zoë Brooks's poems p85 by **Hannah Kodicek;** oil painting on p89, *Counterpane*, by **Rita Donagh** 1987/88; illustrations to *Pyscle Sluts* and *Salome Maloney* on pp92 and 97 by **Steve Maguire;** photo of John Cooper Clarke p95 by **David Rose;** *Track Suit* drawing (C) **David Hockney** 1982; photomontages on pages 101 and 102 by **Michael Bennett;**

Drawing of John Cooper Clarke as *The Pest* (hanging from the ceiling) by **Jeff Nuttall;** drawings on pages 117-119 by **Pat Condell;** photo of Carol Ann Duffy by **Neil Mayell;**

photograph from outside Bradford Comprehensive School by **Sally and Richard Greenhill**; drawings on pages 124, 125, 127, 128, 135 and 140 from the sketchbooks and fax productions of **David Hockney** 1989-91; photo-collage *i.m. John Lennon* p.126 by **Peter Blake**, 1981; photo of Peter Gabriel p143 by the **Douglas Brothers**; drawings on pp152 and 156 (C) **David Hockney** 1990;

Drawing of clay figures on p158 by **Susan Hedley**; oil pastel drawing p159 by **Adam Horovitz**; picture poem sequence *Man as a Window* by **Timothy Emlyn Jones**, 1974; *Menorah*, Star of David, and *Disco Luv* (picture-poems on pages 179, 181 and 186)by **Bill Lewis**; oil painting of Bill Lewis p182 by **Billy Childish**; drawing from *Punch and Judy* p185 by **Neil Sparkes** 1988; photo of Ian McMillan on a good gig, with students at Winsford High School, Cheshire 1988, p205, courtesy Chester Chronicle;

Drawing for *Page Three Girl* p207 by **Alexis Hunter** 1990; photograph on p211 of the ill-fated Ronan Point, Canning Town, Newham by **Pam Isherwood** (Format Photographers); detail from 'The Kidnapping Horse' *(El Caballo Raptor)* from Goya's print series *The Disparates (Los Proverbios)*; drawings on pages 222, 224, 227 (*The Dreamer*), 229 and 231 by **Nik Morgan** 1985-86; photo of Grace Nichols on the beach at Brighton on p241 by **John Agard**, 1987;

Photo of Rosemary Norman p247 by **John Norman**; photo facing *Between Legs* on p.248 by **Sheri Laizer**; photomontage parts of *Page 3* spread 254-255 by **Michael Bennett**; photograph of Pip (*– not* a Page 3 model . . .) by **Nic Tucker**; photo of Ben Okri p.262 by **Douglas Brown**; sketch of Fiona P-K p.271 by **Michael Horovitz**, 1989; chalk drawing p.276 of *Woman Planting* by **Vincent Van Gogh**, 1885; chalk drawings p.277, *Peasant Woman Digging Potatoes* by **Van Gogh**, 1885;

Painting of *Wheatfield with Crows* p.278 by **Van Gogh**, 1890; drawings on pages 296-297 and 301 by **Michèle Roberts**; illustrations to *Conjugal Rights of a Pig* pages 304-305 by **Alexis Hunter**, 1990; illustrations to *London – City of Night* pp306-307, and collage for *Remedial Class* p.310, by **Maria Sookias**; drawings of Chaucer, Milton, Wordsworth and Keats as baseball hit-men on pages 312-317 by **Chris Sparkes**; also the penitentially crouching self-portrait on p320;

Brush drawing *SE11 Totems* p322 by **Neil Sparkes** 1988; drawings on pp323-331 also by Neil; photo on p338 of 'A pile of human bones and skulls at Maidanek extermination camp' by **Novosti**; photo of Arsenal tube station by **Sally & Richard Greenhill**; photograph of Ifigenija Zagoricnik-Simonivic on p349 by **Ifgenija**, as are the sketch on p350 and print on 352; drawing of Benjamin Zephaniah handcuffed p.354, and of *Beat Drummers* p.359, by **Ahmet Ahmet**; collages and drawings illustrating other Zephaniah poems on pages 360-367 by **Andrew Wood**;

Photograph of Attila the Stockbroker p370 by **Tony Mottram**; photo of Pat Condell on p380 by **Susan Premru**; photo of Michael and Adam Horovitz on p384 by **Caroline Forbes**; photo of Tim Emlyn Jones in front of his charcoal drawing *What the Eye Likes, 1990,* on p.388 by **Richard Demarco**; photo of John Cooper Clarke and Linton Kwesi Johnson on p387 by **Chris Moyse**; photo of Brian McCabe in Stromness, Orkney, by **Gunnie Moberg**; photo of Tony Marchant on p394 by **Nigel Coke**; photo of Fiona Pitt-Kethley on p399 by **John Williams**; photo of Neil Sparkes on p405 by **Peter Williams**; Photomontage of 'the Downing Street Kids' on p413 by **Michael Bennett**; drawing of ' *the innermost nave of the abbey of trees –* ' from Michael Horovitz's *Midsummer Morning Jog Log* on p.416 by **Peter Blake**.

To each of these, and to all the other artists, photographers, writers and friends who helped in so many ways to bring this book into being – multitudinous thanks. May you be rewarded on earth as in Elysium.

412

Personal acknowledgement is due to many more than there's space to list here. But among those without whose unstinting support the production would probably still be in labour are: AdCo, Apples & Snakes, Cecilia Boggis, Mark Borkowski, Léonie Brittain, the staff of Dillon's Arts Bookshop in Long Acre, Alan Fletcher, Mette Heinz, Inge Elsa Laird, Phil Lloyd, Annie Maclean, Quentin Newark, Pentagram, Private Eye, Julian Rothenstein, David Russell, the Science Photo Library, the Small Press Group, Neil Spencer and Ruth Vaughn   – not forgetting

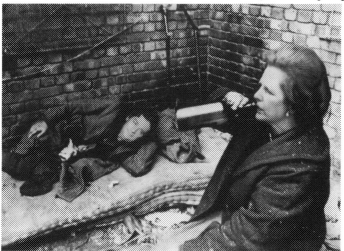

– Nige and Maggie . . . who helped turn so much of the period covered by this collection into such a swell party for the less comfortably situated members of the population. But soft – eheu, how low are the mighty fallen: the market expects every yuppie straight back on its bike and peddle, ya bums.

Afterword

Ever since the *Children of Albion* anthology I edited for Penguin was published in 1969 I've had various sequels in mind. That collection was subtitled *Poetry of the Underground in Britain*, and although the 'alternative society' has long since come up and out all over the globe – to the extent that even high Tories and rednecks are going green – the hard spadework of resistance to authoritarianism, profiteering, racism, sexism, war, philistinism and other pollutions, feels just as urgently needed in the '90s as it did then.

When *Children of Albion* came out, Ted Hughes wrote that "for me it is full of surprises, real new beginnings," and it's my hope that you're finding the same applies to this gathering from the next generation, born between 1947 and 1971.

A *Times Literary Supplement* leader about early 'Live New Departures' gigs noted in 1960 the emergence of:

". . . a nucleus of poets who are starting to treat the writing and delivery of a poem as two stages in a single process, and this in turn leads to a new view of the popular media. The presence of an audience, provided it is alert and responsive, forces the poet-reader to

take greater care about the meaning of his words, while a reasonably strong formal pattern is almost essential in any poem that is going to be read aloud. There's also a growing realisation that poetry can be entertaining. Logue, Horovitz, Mitchell and others have done something most valuable in luring jazz-conscious audiences to listen to genuine poetry and find that they can get the same kind of fun, and even the same kind of kick out of it, as they can get from music. The next decade could see a real break-through here."

– As it did, and as the following two decades continued to do – as witness pages 21 to 367 of this book.

In 1966 Adrian Mitchell wrote:

"... It's no surprise 6,000 plus came to the Albert Hall feast. It wasn't the beginning of anything; it was public proof that something had been accelerating for years. Within another ten years I hope that plenty of advertising posters (& neon signs) will be replaced by poems (& neon poems), that poets will chant from the TV screen and poems leap among the stories in daily papers. I want poetry to bust down the walls of its museum/tomb and learn to survive in the corrosive real world. The walls are thick but a hundred Joshuas are on the job."

– By now there must be more like a thousand worthy the name Joshua hard at it across the planet.

And it seems to me, all the more after putting this collection together, that this is a particularly golden age for poetry on these islands, worthy the 'new Elizabethan' tag. The strongest younger voices are mercifully contemptuous of the parochial game reserves of élitist backscratching or academic back-reference that have arrested the development of so many previous periods. Much as music and the visual arts have opened up of late to the uninhibited interpenetrations of pluralistic and worldwide concerns, so are these last days of the British in Britain given good ground for new growth by the cross-fertilisation of unlimited linguistic, cultural, stylistic, (a)political and experimental roots and branches.

I started *Poetry Olympics* in 1980 in order to help restore adventure, enjoyment, answerability and internationalism to a climate of poetry readings which was then by and large in the little-Englandist doldrums. It was inspiring to discover so many brilliantly inventive younger writer-performers whose talents and impulses overlapped so directly with those of the original Children of Albion. And it came naturally to represent in this book a quorum of the most energetic diversity of black, Asian, female and feminist, regional, urban and rural, communal, ecological and heterodox extremes based in Britain (though not much given to waving the Union Jack around).

The muse is palpably alive and kicking, most healthfully kicking a number of manifestly outworn habits. The displays of unquestioned white male supremacy, emptily formalistic pedantry, syllable-counting and scansion still encouraged by a few misguided but influential, fame-and-hierarchy-fixated authorities, risk getting hooted off stage in the living community of poets and auditors that has grown up of late as of yore, giving and getting its essence in performance before print.

Most UK events I get to hear about feature as many non-white and female as Caucasian and male troubadours. Most citizens of the English-speaking world now dwell in a richly multicultural climate, though blimps and fascists in Cheltenham or South Africa seek to throttle its expression. So I was amazed to discover on the last page of *The '30s and the '90s* (Carcanet 1990) that Julian Symons believes "... although it is natural to sympathise with those who suffer because they have a different skin colour, nobody will benefit by the pretence that their literature and art should replace those of the white societies in which they live."

Such 'thinking' suggests its author's mind got fossilised circa 1935. Julian Symons and his ilk would surely benefit from a crash course in recent and current

414

spoken, sung and multifariously performed poetry. Life as lived today in the Americas and the Caribbean and British Isles is no longer definable as that of exclusively white societies. If Julian Symons wants to return from his Thirties to the lands of the living, he could do a lot worse than study this anthology at 6th Form or University level. Poems such as John Agard's *'Listen Mr Oxford Don'* (pages 26-27), or Merle Collins's *'No Dialects Please . . .'* (pp.112-113) could have been composed expressly as pitying, ironic retorts to Symons's arrogantly unscholastic assumptions.

It's now ten years since the infamously narrow, insular and careerist Penguin Book of *Contemporary British Poetry* appeared, perpetuating among other things the grotesquely uncontemporary definition of British as meaning all-white's alright. The time for a full-blooded colloquium of multiracial poetry to expose, counter and replace this pseudo-literary confidence trick of a book's attempted take-over and carve-up of the field, is long overdue.

I've assembled the present volume as only the first of a series, and plan – should I live so long – further anthologies, on the themes of *Children of Albion Revisited* (to project the much matured output of most of the 64 contributors whose first frenzies and juvenilia peopled the 1969 *Children),* and of *Other Voices and Visions of Albion* (to bring together both older and younger poets worth encouraging, who aren't in the other volumes). There's more on all this in *New Departures 21,* a special supplement to this book (including the mysteriously displaced first sixteen pages).   Trusting that these issues afford you some pleasure and enlightenment,

Yours sincerely,

Back Issues

This is the first *New Departures* for eight years, the last (number 16) being *A Celebration of & for Frances Horovitz.* Very few copies remain of this issue, or of its predecessors, so the price at which these can be supplied will be going up in relation to the scarcity of copies left. The prices listed here will only apply while current stocks last.

New Departures 1 to 12 and *14* - completely out of stock, except a handful of limited multi-signed editions.

New Departures 13, UK issue including Arden, Blake, JCC, Coxhill, Cutler, Harwood, A Henri, Horovitzes A, F & M, F Landesman, Logue, McGough, McGrath, Mitchell, Nuttall, Patten, T Raworth, S Tracey, H Williams, R Williamson + Joolz, R Fisher, L Houston & *(i.m.)* John Lennon, *inter alios* – £5.

New Departures 15 – third *Poetry Olympics* issue including K Acker, E Boland, P Blake, Burroughs, Cutler, Condell, Coyne, Gascoyne, G Grass, *(i.m.)* H Fainlight, Hockney, A & M Horovitz, LKJ, R Jobson, Jandl, T Hughes, Kazantzis, I E Laird, J Micheline, Jill Neville, Patten, Rothenberg, Mikey Smith, Snyder, Attila, Steadman, Topolski, M Wandor, H Williams, Ifigenija, Zephaniah *et al* – £5.

New Departures 16 – *A Celebration of & for Frances Horovitz* (1938-83): with 30 of her best poems including some uncollected elsewhere, and many reproduced in her own beautiful handwriting, and an evergreen wreath of photographs and drawings of and by her, along with tributes and poems by Kathleen Raine, Inge Laird, Valerie Sinason, D S Houédard, Adam and Michael Horovitz *et al* – £15.

Water Over Stone – Frances Horovitz's third book of poetry originally published by Enitharmon Press – a few left of both paper and corrected hardback editions: price negotiable.

Midsummer Morning Jog Log – Michael Horovitz's rural rhapsody illustrated by Peter Blake, and published by Five Seasons Press of Hereford –@ £3.50, £8.95 and £150 (see overleaf).

For further details, lists, updates etc, write enclosing return postage to *New Departures, Piedmont, Bisley, Stroud, Glos GL6 7BU.*

MIDSUMMER MORNING JOG LOG

A poem by Michael Horovitz with drawings by Peter Blake

Poetry Book Society Recommendation

"Horovitz's very own Song of Innocence, dedicated to the memory of his wife Frances, discovering a universe in the observations on a morning run . . . its 670 lines are full of wonder and sunlight." (John Gill in Time Out)

"Horovitz's characteristic exuberance gains new levels of linguistic exactness in this long poem . . . The work succeeds in evoking that other England which exists beneath the pallor of monetarism; the Albion in which each particular partakes of a springing dream. Horovitz charts his discoveries with wit, energy and – finally – philosophical seriousness. . . Some of the images are fleshed out in illustrations by Peter Blake: 'inviolate globes of dew beam silver' or 'the innermost nave of the abbey of trees'. Blake has entered fully into the experience described; his drawings are detailed and gloriously resonant." (Gavin Selerie in City Limits)

"Off goes the poet, puffing and bumping along the lanes; off goes the language with him in an exuberant virtuoso performance in which the rhythms run unflaggingly down page after page, veering to right and left of the typographical centre, sometimes leaping from hummock to hummock as the jogger might leap to avoid spring water or cowpats. As it goes it spins its fabric out of the passing detail; dewdrops, flowers, beasts, light, the pastoral currency of the tradition which Horovitz knows better than anyone . . ." (Jeff Nuttall in Resurgence)

Published in three editions at £8.95 clothbound, £3.50 paper, and a special deluxe boxed and signed limited edition at £150, whilst copies remain available. Brochure on request from the publishers, Five Seasons Press, Madley, Hereford HR2 ONZ